D1518862

The Haynes
Automotive
Tools
Manual

by Eric Godfrey
and John H Haynes
Member of the Guild of Motoring Writers

The Haynes Manual for buying
and using automotive tools

(5X1 - 2107)

ABCDE
FGHIJ
KLMNO
PQRS

AUTOMOTIVE
PARTS &
ACCESSORIES
ASSOCIATION   MEMBER

Haynes Publishing Group
Sparkford Nr Yeovil
Somerset BA22 7JJ England

Haynes North America, Inc
861 Lawrence Drive
Newbury Park
California 91320 USA

Acknowledgements

We are grateful for the help and cooperation of all the tool manufacturing companies that contributed photographs and information on the products shown in this manual. We also wish to thank Actron Manufacturing Company, K-D Tools, Lisle Corporation, R and B/Motormite, SK Hand Tool Corporation and Thorsen Tool Company for providing many of the photographs seen in this manual. Photo of tool set shown on rear cover courtesy of K-D Tools. Contributing to this project were Technical Author Robert Maddox, Senior Technical Editor Bob Henderson and Editor Andrew Krim.

© **Haynes North America, Inc. 1994**

With permission from J.H. Haynes & Co. Ltd.

A book in the Haynes Automotive Repair Manual Series

Printed in the U.S.A.

ISBN 1 56392 107 3

Library of Congress Catalog Card Number 94-78661

While every attempt is made to ensure that the information in this manual is correct, no liability can be accepted by the authors or publishers for loss, damage or injury caused by any errors in, or omissions from, the information given.

94-192

Contents

Chapter 6 Diagnostic tools and equipment

Chapter 7 Engine rebuilding tools and equipment

Chapter 8 Body and paint tools; working facilities

Glossary

Manufacturers listing

Index

Introduction

A Selection of good tools is a basic requirement for anyone who plans to maintain and repair his or her own vehicle. For the home mechanic who has few tools, the initial investment might seem high, but, when compared to the spiraling costs of professional auto maintenance and repair, it is a wise one.

To help the home mechanic decide which tools are needed to perform repairs and maintenance on today's automobiles, the following tool lists are offered to aid the reader in acquiring a well rounded set of tools, tailored to his or hers personal needs: *General purpose tool set, Master mechanic tool set, and Major repair and overhaul tool set.*

The newcomer to practical mechanics should start off with a general purpose tool set, which is adequate for the simpler tasks performed on a vehicle. Then as confidence and experience grow, the home mechanic can tackle more difficult jobs, buying additional tools as they become necessary. Eventually the general purpose set will be expanded into the master set. Over a period of time, the experienced do-it-yourselfer will assemble a tool set complete enough for most repair procedures and will add tools from the major repair and overhaul category when it is felt that the expense is justified by the need.

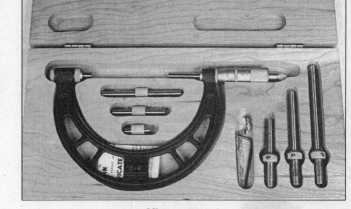

Micrometer set

General purpose tool set

The tools in this list should be considered the minimum required for performance of routine maintenance, servicing, and minor repair work:

3/8 inch drive socket set (3/8 inch to 3/4 inch and/or 10mm to 19mm);
    including a reversible ratchet handle, 3 inch and 6 inch extensions
    and a universal joint
5/8 inch and/or 13/16 inch spark plug socket (with rubber insert)
Combination end wrench set (1/4 inch to 1 inch and/or 6mm to 19mm)
8 inch slip-joint pliers
10 inch groove-joint pliers
8 inch long nose pliers
7 inch diagonal cutting pliers
No. 2 x 4 inch Phillips screwdriver
No. 1 x 2 inch Phillips screwdriver

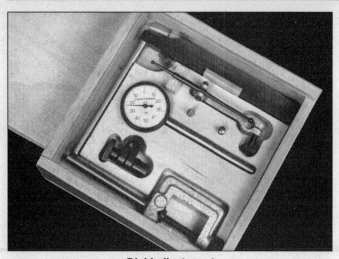

Dial indicator set

1/4 inch x 6 inch flat blade screwdriver
1/4 inch x 4 inch flat blade screwdriver
1/8 inch x 2 inch flat blade screwdriver
8 inch adjustable wrench
16 oz. ball-peen hammer
Spark plug gap adjusting tool
Tire pressure gauge
Battery post and cable cleaning tool
Battery cable clamp puller
Oil filter wrench
18 inch pry bar
Utility knife
Tool box of appropriate size
Funnel
Drain pan
Grease gun
Oil can
Safety goggles
Jack stands

Master tool set

The tools included in the master set are essential for anyone who plans to perform major repair work and are in addition to those included in the general purpose tool set. Included in the master set is a comprehensive set of sockets which, are invaluable because of their versatility, especially when the various extensions, universal joints, and other accessories are utilized:

1/2 inch drive socket set (1/2 inch to 1 1/2 inch); including a ratchet handle, 3 inch, 6 inch and 10 inch extensions, and a universal joint
1/2 inch drive flex handle
1/4 inch drive socket set (5/32 inch to 1/2 inch): including a ratchet handle, 3 inch and 6 inch extensions, universal joint, and a spinner handle
3/8 inch deep sockets (same sizes as standard sockets)
1/2 inch drive deep sockets (most common sizes as needed)
1/4 inch deep sockets (most common sizes as needed)
3/8 inch drive hex bits (5/32 inch to 3/8 inch and/or 4mm to 10mm)
3/8 inch drive Torx bits (T-30 to T-55)

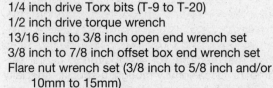

1/4 inch drive Torx bits (T-9 to T-20)
1/2 inch drive torque wrench
13/16 inch to 3/8 inch open end wrench set
3/8 inch to 7/8 inch offset box end wrench set
Flare nut wrench set (3/8 inch to 5/8 inch and/or 10mm to 15mm)
Crow foot wrench set (3/8 inch to 1 inch and/or 10mm to 19mm)
8 inch locking pliers
6 inch long nose locking pliers
8 inch linesman pliers
No. 3 x 6 inch Phillips screwdriver
3/8 inch x 8 inch flat blade screwdriver
3/8 inch x 12 inch flat blade screwdriver
1/4 inch x 1 1/2 inch stubby flat blade screwdriver
No. 2 x 1 1/2 inch stubby Phillips screwdriver
10 inch adjustable wrench
12 inch adjustable wrench
12 oz. soft face hammer
32 oz. ball-peen hammer
Rubber mallet

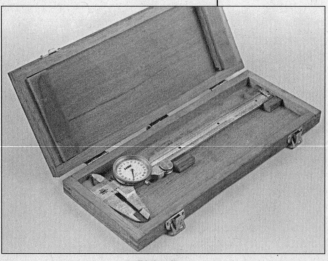

Dial caliper

Hacksaw
Wire brush
1 1/4 inch scraper
1/2 inch x 6 inch cold chisel
3/4 inch x 7 inch cold chisel
Pin punches (1/8 inch to 5/16 inch)
Drift punch
Center punch
Scratch awl
File
Straight cutting snips
Steel rule/straight edge
Electrical circuit/continuity tester
Wire stripper and crimping pliers
Stroboscopic timing light
Multimeter
Compression gauge
Remote starter switch
Hand operated vacuum/pressure pump
Vacuum/pressure gauge
Spark plug boot pliers
Brake spring removal and installation tools
Drum brake adjusting tool
Brake cylinder hone
Impact driver set
Balljoint separator
Electric drill and bits
Tool box of appropriate size
Jackstands (second set)
Floor jack and/or hydraulic bottle jack

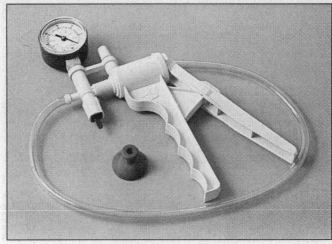

Hand-operated vacuum pump

Major repair and overhaul tool set

The tools in this list include those which are not used regularly, but are those that are necessary to perform major overhaul tasks to engines and other drivetrain components. This list contains those tools and instruments widely available to the public and not those specialty tools produced by the vehicle manufacturer for distribution to dealer service departments. Occasionally though, a specific specialty tool may be absolutely necessary to complete a job, and the home mechanic will be forced to obtain the tool:

Feeler gauge set
Internal snap ring pliers
External snap ring pliers
Hex wrench set (1/16 inch to 3/8 inch)
1/4 inch drive torque wrench
Puller set
Valve spring compressor
Piston ring compressor
Piston ring groove cleaning tool
Piston ring installation tool
Cylinder ridge reamer
Cylinder surfacing hone
Cylinder bore gauge

Timing light

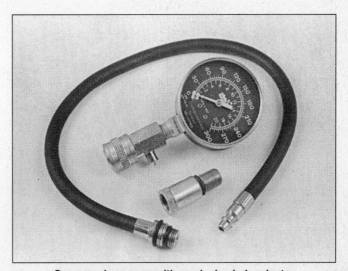

Compression gauge with spark plug hole adapter

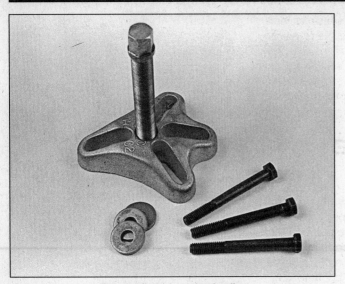

Damper/steering wheel puller

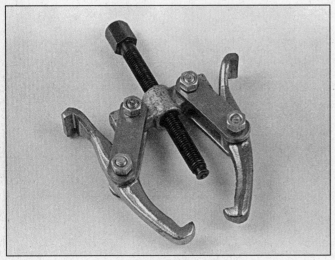

General purpose puller

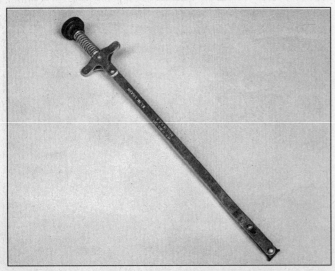

Hydraulic lifter removal tool

Micrometer set
Dial calipers
Dial indicator set
Hydraulic lifter removal tool
Clutch alignment tool
Screw extractor set
Seal and bearing remover and installer set
Tool storage cabinet
Engine lifting device
Engine stand
Workbench
Vise (at least 4 inch jaw opening, mounted securely to the workbench)

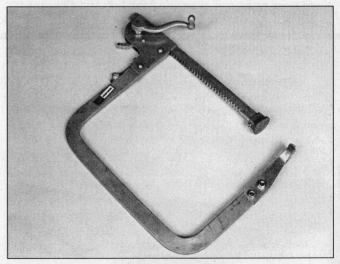

Valve spring compressor

Buying tools

For the do-it-yourselfer who is just staring to get involved in vehicle maintenance and repair, there are a number of options available when purchasing tools. If maintenance and minor repair is the extent of the work to be done, the purchase of a limited number of individual tools is satisfactory. If, on the other hand, extensive work is planned, it would be wise to purchase a modest tool set to start. A set can usually be bought at a substantial savings over the individual tool prices, and a tool chest is often included. As additional tools are needed and subsequently purchased, add-on sets, individual tools, and a larger tool chest or cabinet can be purchased to expand the tool selection. Building a tool set gradually allows the cost of the tools to be spread over a longer period of time and gives the home mechanic the freedom to choose only those tools that will actually be needed and used.

Most of the tools listed here can be purchased at major department, hardware, and auto parts stores. The exception is the major repair and overhaul tools and the specialty tools. Major repair and overhaul tools can be found at major auto parts stores, tool specialty stores and mail order. While dealership service departments and tool specialty stores or mail order are often the only source of some of the specialty tools that may be needed to complete a job. Regardless of where the tools are purchased, try to avoid tools of inferior quality. Especially when buying high use items like screwdrivers, pliers, wrenches, and sockets. Inferior quality tools will not last very long under hard use, and the expense involved in replacing inferior tools will eventually be greater than the initial cost of good quality tools.

Care and maintenance of tools

Good tools are expensive, so it makes sense to treat them with respect. Keep them clean and in usable condition and store them properly when not in use. Always wipe off any dirt, grease, or metal chips before putting them away. Never leave tools lying around in the work area. Upon completion of a job , always check closely under the vehicle, under the hood, and inside the vehicle for tools that may have been left behind so they won't become lost.

Some tools, such as screwdrivers, pliers, and wrenches can be hung on a panel or pegboard mounted on the garage or workshop wall, while others should be kept in a tool chest, cabinet or tray. Measuring instruments, gauges, meters, etc. must be carefully stored where they cannot be damaged by weather or impact from other tools.

Ridge reamer

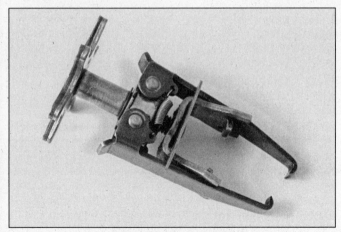

Valve spring compressor

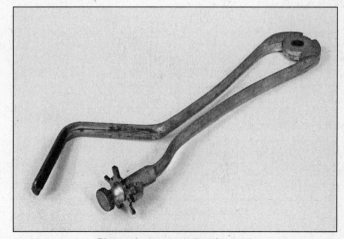

Piston ring groove cleaning tool

When tools are used with care and stored properly, they will last a long time. Even with the best of care, though, certain tools may wear out under extreme use. When a tool is damaged or worn out, replace it immediately. subsequent jobs will be safer and more enjoyable if you do.

Working facilities

Not to be overlooked when discussing tools is the workshop. If anything more than routine maintenance is to be carried out, some sort of suitable work area is essential.

It is understood, and appreciated, that many home mechanics do not have a good workshop or garage available, and end up removing an engine or doing major repairs outside. It is recommended, however, that a major repair or overhaul be completed under the cover of a roof.

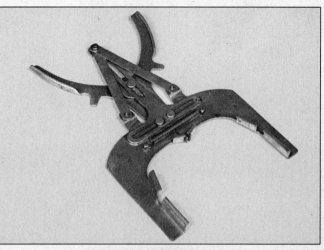

Ring removal/installation tool

Ring compressor

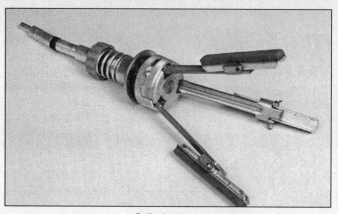

Cylinder hone

A clean, flat workbench or table of comfortable working height is an absolute necessity. The workbench should be equipped with a vise that has a jaw opening of at least four inches.

As mentioned previously, clean, dry storage space is also required for tools, as well as the lubricants, fluids, cleaning solvents, etc. which will soon become necessary.

Sometimes waste oil and fluids, drained from the engine, transmission, or cooling system during normal maintenance or repairs, present a disposal problem. Under any circumstances do not pour them on the ground or into a sewage system. Pour the used fluids into appropriate containers, seal them with caps and dispose of them properly at an authorized disposal site or recycling center. Plastic bottles, such as old antifreeze containers, are ideal for transporting used automotive fluids.

Always keep a supply of clean rags available. Old newspaper or towels are excellent for mopping up spills. Many home mechanics use rolls of paper towels for most purposes because they are readily available and disposable. To help keep the area under the vehicle clean, a large cardboard box can be cut open, flattened and laid on the floor to protect the garage or shop floor from spills.

Whenever working over the painted surface of the vehicle, such as when leaning over the fender to service something under the hood, always protect the surface with a fender protector. Vinyl covered pads, made especially for this purpose, are available at auto parts stores.

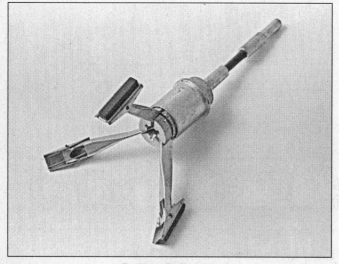

Brake cylinder hone

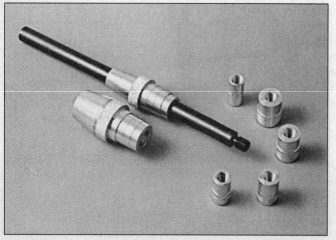

Clutch plate alignment tool

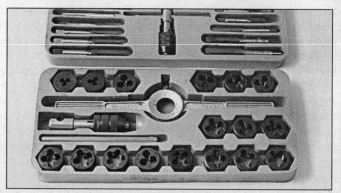

Tap and die set

1 The Workshop

Before considering which tools to collect, or how to use them, a suitable workplace should be located. It doesn't have to be particularly large, but it should be clean, safe, well-lit, organized and adequately equipped for the job. True, without a good workshop or garage you can still service and repair your vehicle, even if you have to work outside. But major repair and overhaul work should be carried out in a sheltered area with a roof.

The size, shape and location of a shop building is usually dictated by circumstance rather than personal choice. Every do-it-yourselfer dreams of having a spacious, clean well-lit building specially designed and equipped for working on everything from small engines on lawn mowers and garden equipment, to automobiles, light trucks and other vehicles. In reality, however, most of us must content ourselves with a garage, basement or shed in the backyard.

Spend some time considering the potential, and drawbacks, of your current facility. Even a well established workshop can benefit from intelligent design. Lack of space is the most common problem, but you can significantly increase usable space by carefully planning the locations of work and storage areas. One strategy is to observe how others have done it. Visit a local repair shop, one that has a reputation of producing high quality work, and take a look around. Note how they've arranged their work areas, storage and lighting, then scale down their solutions to fit your own shop space, finances and needs.

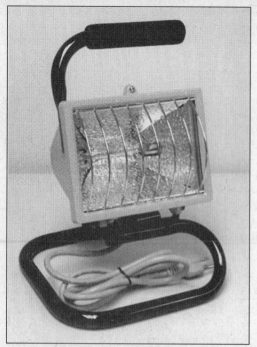

1.1 A work light like this Designers Edge 500 watt halogen utility light is excellent for lighting up a large area.

1 General workshop requirements

A solid concrete floor is the best surface for a shop area. The floor should be level, smooth and dry. A coat of paint or sealant formulated for concrete surfaces will make oil spills and dirt easier to remove and help cut down on dust which is always a problem with concrete.

The walls and ceiling should be painted white for maximum reflection. Use a gloss or semi-gloss enamel, that is washable and reflective. If your shop or garage has windows, situate workbenches under them to take advantage of their natural light. If it's feasible to install a skylight, do so, you can't have too much natural light.

Make certain the building is adequately ventilated. This is critical during the winter months in wet climates to prevent condensation. It's also a vital safety consideration where solvents, gasoline and other volatile liquids are being used or stored.

Electricity and lights

Of all the useful shop facilities, electricity is by far the most essential. It's relatively easy to arrange if the workshop is near to, or part of, a house, but it can be difficult and expensive to install if it isn't. It must be stressed that safety is the number one consideration when dealing with electricity; unless you have a very good working knowledge of electrical installations, any work required to provide power and/or lights in the shop should be left to a professional electrician.

Consider the total electrical requirements of the shop, making allowances for possible later additions of lights and equipment. Don't substitute extension cords for legal and safe permanent wiring. If the wiring isn't adequate, or is substandard, have it upgraded.

Careful consideration should be given to the amount of lighting fixtures installed in the workshop. A pair of 150 watt incandescent bulbs, or two 48 inch long 40 watt fluorescent tubes, suspended approximately 48 inches above the workbench or work area are about the minimum requirements for a typical 20 x 20 foot workshop. Generally, fluorescent lights are the best choice for installation. Their light is bright, evenly distributed, shadow free and more economical to operate than incandescent lighting. For the ones that don't care for the bluish tinge fluorescent lighting casts, a compromise would be a mix of fluorescent and incandescent fixtures.

Location of the light fixtures is also an important consideration. Don't place a fixture directly above the area you're most likely to work under. Lighting directly overhead, even fluorescent lighting, will cast shadows on your work. Locate the light fixtures slightly to the rear, or to each side, of the workbench or work area to provide shadow free lighting. Don't use fluorescent lighting above machine tools (like a drill press). The flicker produced by alternating current is especially pronounced with this type of light and can make a rotating chuck appear stationary at certain speeds, producing a very dangerous situation.

Portable work lights are also very useful when overhead lighting is inadequate or when working under a hood or underneath a vehicle **(see illustrations)**. They are commonly available in fluorescent, incandescent and powerful halogen quartz models, powered by either household current or 12 volt direct current. Cigar lighter socket adapters are provided on the 12 volt models, allowing them to be powered by the vehicle battery when household current is unavailable. Last but not least, another invaluable light source for use in automotive work is an ordinary flashlight. Flash-

1.2 Designers Edge "Mighty Mite" is a 100 watt halogen 12 volt work light with a hang hook and a clamp; it has a 12 foot cord that plugs into either the lighter socket or clips to the car battery

lights, commonly found around the home, can provide a readily available beam of light quickly and easily. Always keep a supply of fresh batteries handy; there is nothing more frustrating than picking up your flashlight only to find the batteries weak or dead.

Workbenches

A workbench is an essential part of any garage or workshop. It provides a place to lay out tools and disassembled parts during a maintenance or repair procedure and is a lot more comfortable than working on the floor or driveway **(see illustration)**. The workbench should be as large, strong, and sturdy as space and finances allow. Many types of benches are commercially available and include; benches made of all wood, a wood frame with a metal top, a metal frame with a wood top, and all metal benches **(see illustration)**. They're also available in various lengths, so you can buy the exact size you need to fill the space along a wall. Unassembled kits of all types can also be found at most major building and hardware retail outlets, allowing you to complete the assembly process for a savings.

The industrial steel benches are generally the most desirable. They are heavy and strong, are able to support the weight of an engine and their metal top surface can withstand years of hard use. They are available with accessories such as, drawers, shelves, drain pans and rubber wheels or casters that allow them to be moved around the workshop **(see illustrations)**. Regardless of type of bench you choose, be certain the top is level and at a comfortable working height.

One of the most useful pieces of equipment, and one that's usually associated with a workbench, is a vise **(see illus-**

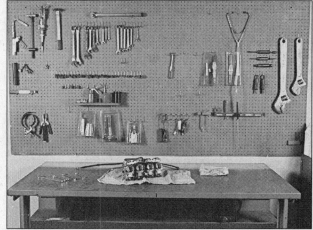

1.3 A sturdy metal workbench is an essential part of any workshop - pegboard, hanging on the wall behind the workbench, is a convenient place to store tools when they're not in use

1.4 Excellent quality metal workbenches are manufactured by Shure Mfg. Corp. - this model has a hardwood top and all models have locking drawers and/or cabinets

1.5 Shure's "Big Red" is a portable teardown bench - equipped with heavy-duty casters and a top that is designed to allow fluids to drain into the drain pan, this bench is excellent for tearing down transmissions

1.6 A Black and Decker Workmate comes in handy for holding large parts, such as this lawnmower engine, while working on them - the quick release clamping feature makes it easy to change positions quickly

1.7 A bench vise is one of the most useful pieces of equipment you can have in the shop - larger ones are usually more desirable, you'll need a vise with jaw opening width of at least four inches

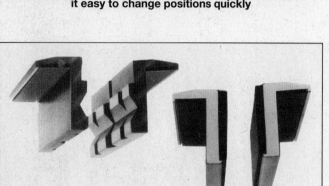

1.8 Sometimes, the work you'll need to clamp in the vise is delicate, or made of a soft material - to avoid damaging the item a set of jaw pads should be installed on the vise

1.9 Another indispensable piece of equipment is the bench grinder - attach a wire wheel to one arbor and make sure it's securely bolted down to the workbench

tration). It's a versatile tool that will be used often and should be given careful consideration before purchasing a new one. Generally a vise with a jaw opening of at least four inches is the minimum required for most automotive work. The bigger the better, but size isn't necessarily the most important factor to consider when shopping for a vise; the quality of materials and workmanship is. Inferior quality vises will not stand up to hard use and their jaws may actually bend under extreme clamping force. Mount your vise securely to your bench with the largest fasteners possible. An un-mounted or insecurely mounted vise is a dangerous safety hazard and could cause serious bodily injury if used. A set of soft jaw inserts will also be necessary if you will be performing any major repair or overhaul work. They are available in aluminum, brass (the most desirable), fiberglass, plastic and rubber (see illustration). They fit over the vise jaws and are used to grip components that could be damaged by the hardened steel vise jaws.

A bench mounted grinder is also a very versatile tool associated with a workbench (see illustration). With a wire wheel mounted on one arbor and a grinding wheel on the other, it's great for cleaning fasteners, sharpening tools and removing gaskets, rust or corrosion. Make certain the bench grinder is mounted securely to the workbench and always wear eye protection when operating a bench grinder (see illustration). Never grind aluminum parts on the grinding wheel, the aluminum fills the porous cavities of the grinding wheel, rendering it useless.

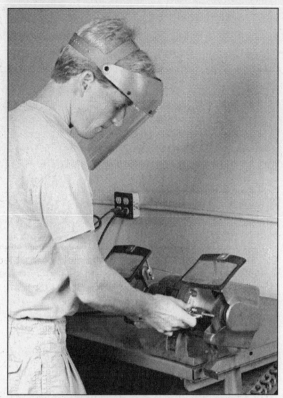

1.10 Never use a bench grinder with the tool rests or eye shields removed

Storage and shelves

Storage space for hardware, lubricants, solvents, rags, tools and equipment will be required, at some point, in the workshop **(see illustration)**. An organized storage area consisting of shelving, bins, and possibly a cabinet will keep your workshop free of clutter, making it a safe, comfortable place to work. Metal shelving units are available at most major building supply and hardware stores. They can be installed along a wall to make the best use of available space. Their shelf heights are adjustable, allowing you to arrange them widely spaced near the bottom for storage of large and heavy items.

Small parts and hardware can be stored in small plastic drawer cabinets and larger hardware, such as nuts and bolts, stores nicely in stackable plastic bins. They to, are available at your local hardware store.

Actually, all types of containers are useful in the workshop. When removing parts from your vehicle, keep like components and fasteners together in the same container, it will make reassembly much more efficient. Plastic containers are available in a variety of sizes and colors for easy identification. Muffin tins also make very good storage containers for small parts.

1.11 Metal shelving units, available at most building discount stores, are very handy for storing oil, anti-freeze, aerosol products and small parts - the shelves are adjustable too!

2 Shop equipment

There are several pieces of equipment you will need in the workshop, to make working on your vehicle a safer and more enjoyable experience. If you are going to be working under the vehicle a suitable means for lifting and supporting

1.12 A small 2 1/4 or 2 1/2 ton floor jack and a set of jack stands are perfect for the home mechanic who does his/her own maintenance - this Pro-Lift model is very compact and lightweight; the 2 1/4 ton model weighs just about 30 lbs., while the 2 1/2 ton model weighs about 75 lbs.

the vehicle will be necessary. The jack that the manufacturer provides with a vehicle is only designed to raise the vehicle for changing a tire and should not be used for automotive maintenance or repair work. For those purposes, you'll need a scissors jack, a hydraulic bottle jack rated for at least 2-tons, or better yet, a good hydraulic floor jack. A floor jack rolls easily over the garage floor and under the vehicle. It raises the vehicle with the least amount of effort. The small 2 ton to 2 1/2 ton models are very light weight and affordable **(see illustration)**. They can even be placed in the trunk of the car and transported. Larger models are available for heavy duty use **(see illustration)**. Their longer chassis and handle allows them to reach farther under a vehicle and, of course, they are capable of lifting more weight.

Once the vehicle is raised, a means of support is absolutely necessary. <u>Never</u> under any circumstances, crawl under a vehicle supported only by a jack. Once raised high enough, lower the vehicle onto a strong set of jackstands.

1.13 For heavier lifting chores this Pro-Lift extended reach floor jack is available in 4, 5 and 10 ton models

1.14 Ramps are one of the most convenient methods of attaining the extra clearance needed to safely work underneath a vehicle - the Tru-Cut Automotive "Ultra-Ramp" is a heavy duty ramp with several built in safety features, such as; traction-gripping pods, a higher front wheel stop, deep side rails and extra width

Another method of raising a vehicle to a working height is to drive it onto a set of ramps specially made for this purpose **(see illustration)**. Ramps are very convenient to use and less expensive than a floor jack, but careful attention must be given to driving the vehicle onto the ramps. Regardless of which method is used, once the front (or rear) end of the vehicle is raised and supported, chock the opposite-end tires with a suitable set of wheel chocks.

1.15 Everything you need to safely work underneath the vehicle is shown here: Tru-Cut ramps, jack, jack stands, creeper, roller seat and wheel chocks

To make working underneath your vehicle a safer, more enjoyable experience (if you have to crawl under there, you might as well be comfortable), consider using one of the many high quality mechanics "creepers" available today **(see illustration)**. They allow you to slide in and out from under the vehicle with a minimum amount of effort and are invaluable in making a fast exit in case an emergency arises. Work stools are also available which, when used, save wear and tear on your back when performing brake jobs and other outside-the-vehicle type work.

Of course, you'll also want to protect the paint finish of your valuable vehicle. Use fender protectors, when working under the hood, to lay across the vehicle's fender **(see illustration)**. Fender protectors shield the paint surface from chips and scratches that could arise from leaning across the fender or laying tools on it. They're padded for extra protection, and some types have built in magnets to hold them in place.

For the truly well equipped shop, there are portable lifts available that offer all the convenience of a professional shop **(see illustration)**. They are portable, they fold up for compact storage and the motor uses household current. Of course, not everyone can use such a device, but, for those who work on their vehicles often, there is nothing more convenient than raising the complete vehicle off the ground for service.

1.16 For the serious automotive enthusiast, Rotary Lift introduces a portable, low-rise lift for working on vehicles in the garage, shop or driveway - the lift features spring-loaded wheels and a pull handle which allows for easy movement. Five locking height positions will support up to 6,000 lbs. The power unit operates from 115 volt outlet, and, when the lift is not in use, it's small enough to park over it.

1.17 A fender protector is necessary to keep from scratching or denting the fender while working under the hood - some, like this one from MTS, are magnetic to keep them from slipping off

1.18 Always have a fire extinguisher handy in the workshop - make sure it's rated for trash-wood-paper, flammable liquids-grease, and electrical equipment fires (A,B,C) - and KNOW HOW TO USE IT

3 Safety items that should be in every shop

Fire extinguishers

Have at least one fire extinguisher handy before beginning any maintenance or repair procedure **(see illustration)**. Be certain it's rated for trash-wood-paper, flammable liquids-grease and electrical equipment fires (A,B,C). Familiarize yourself with its use as soon as you obtain it, not waiting until you actually need to use it in an emergency to figure out how. Have your fire extinguisher checked and recharged at regular intervals, at least once a year. Refer to the safety tips at the end of this Chapter for more information about the hazards of gasoline and other flammable liquids.

Gloves

If your handling hot components on your engine, or metal parts with sharp edges such as sheet metal, wear a pair of industrial work gloves to protect your hands from burns or cuts **(see illustration)**. Use a pair of heavy duty rubber gloves to protect your hands when washing parts in solvent. Also, surgical gloves should be worn for protection when there's the possibility of getting gasoline or used motor oil (which is carcinogenic) on your skin.

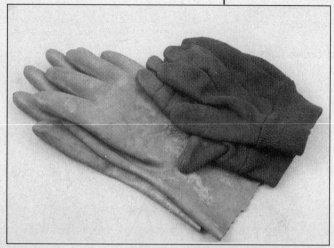

1.19 Use a pair of heavy work gloves for handling hot or sharp-edged objects and a pair of rubber gloves for washing parts with solvent

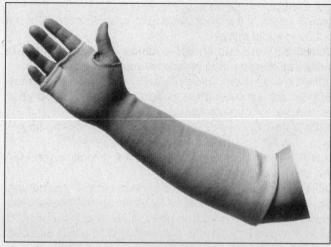

1.20 Lisle's "Hot sleeve" protects your arm from being burned while working around a hot engine

Safety glasses or goggles

<u>Never</u> use a bench grinder or wire wheel without eye protection **(see illustration)**. What ever you are doing is not worth the risk of getting a metal sliver in your eye. Eye protection, such as a face shield or goggles, should also be worn whenever you are striking an object with a hammer. Its also a good idea to use goggles or safety glasses whenever your washing parts in solvent or using an aerosol cleaner. Solvents and cleaners can damage your eyes or skin if splashed in your face. Also wear your goggles or safety glasses when working under the vehicle, particles of dirt or grease could fall into your face or eyes, causing permanent damage. You are only given one set of eyes - protect them.

Think safety first!

Regardless of how enthusiastic you may be about getting on with the job at hand, take the time to ensure that your safety is not being jeopardized. A moment's lack of attention can result in an accident, as can failure to observe certain simple safety precautions. The possibility of an accident will always exist, and the following points should not be considered a comprehensive list of all the dangers. Rather, they are intended to make you aware of the risks and to encourage a safety conscious approach to all work you carry out on your vehicle.

Essential DOs and DON'Ts

DON'T rely on a jack when working under a vehicle. Always use approved jackstands to support the weight of the vehicle and place them at the recommended lift or support points.

DON'T attempt to loosen extremely tight fasteners (i.e. wheel lug nuts) while the vehicle is on a jack - it may fall.

DON'T start the engine without first making sure that the transmission is in Neutral (manual transmission) or Park (automatic transmission) and the parking brake is securely applied.

DON'T remove the radiator cap from a hot cooling system - let it cool down, cover it with a rag and release the pressure gradually.

DON'T attempt to drain the engine oil until you are sure it has cooled to the point that it will not burn you.

DON'T touch any part of the engine or exhaust system until it has cooled sufficiently to avoid burns.

DON'T siphon toxic liquids such as gasoline, antifreeze and brake fluid by mouth, or allow them to remain on your skin.

DON'T inhale brake lining or clutch disc dust - they may contain asbestos which is potentially hazardous to your health (see Asbestos below).

DON'T allow spilled oil or grease to remain on the floor - wipe it up before someone slips on it.

DON'T use loose fitting wrenches or other tools which may slip and cause injury.

DON'T push on wrenches when loosening or tightening fasteners **(see illustration)**. Always try to pull the wrench toward you. If the situation calls for pushing the wrench away from you, push with a open hand to avoid scraped knuckles if the wrench should slip.

DON'T attempt to lift a heavy component alone - get someone to help you.

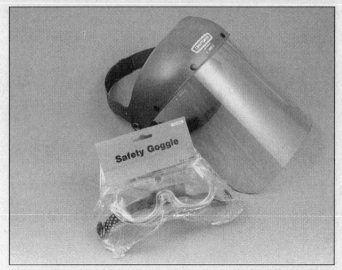

1.21 One of the most important items you'll need in the shop is a face shield or safety goggles, especially when you're using a hammer, washing parts in solvent or using the bench grinder

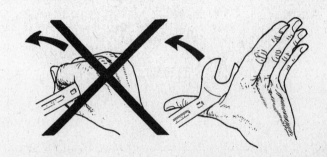

1.22 Always pull on a wrench when loosening a fastener - if you can't pull on it, push with your hand open as shown here

DON'T rush or take unsafe shortcuts to finish a job.

DON'T allow children or pets in or around the vehicle while you are working on it.

DO wear eye protection when using power tools such as a drill, sander, bench grinder, etc. and when working under a vehicle.

DO keep loose clothing and long hair well out of the way of moving parts.

DO make sure that any hoist, lift or jack used has a safe working load rating adequate for the job.

DO get someone to check on you periodically when working on a vehicle alone.

DO carry out work in a logical sequence and make sure that everything is correctly assembled and properly tightened.

DO keep chemicals and fluids tightly capped and out of the reach of children and pets.

DO remember that your vehicle's safety affects that of yourself and others. If in doubt on any point of your vehicles safety, seek professional help.

Asbestos

Certain friction, insulating, sealing and other products such as; brake linings, brake bands, clutch linings, torque converters, gaskets, etc., may contain asbestos. Asbestos is a known carcinogenic. Extreme care must be taken to avoid inhalation of dust from any products known to, or suspected of, containing asbestos.

Batteries

Batteries can give off a certain amount of hydrogen gas (especially when charging), which is extremely explosive. If you are charging the battery from an external source (i.e. battery charger), monitor the battery periodically, and do not allow it to become overheated or overcharged. Never create a spark, or allow a bare light bulb near a battery.

Take care when adding water to a conventional type battery. The electrolyte, which is hydrochloric acid, is very corrosive and should not be allowed to contact your skin or clothing.

Always wear eye protection when cleaning a battery to prevent the caustic deposits from entering your eyes.

Always disconnect the cable at the negative battery terminal before working on the fuel or electrical system of your vehicle.

Fire

It is strongly recommended that a fire extinguisher suitable for use on wood, gasoline and electrical fires be kept handy in the garage or workshop at all times. Never try to extinguish a fuel or electrical fire with water. Post the phone number of the fire department in a conspicuous location near the phone.

Fumes

Certain fumes are highly toxic and can quickly cause unconsciousness and even death if inhaled to any extent. Gasoline vapor falls into this category, as do the vapors from some cleaning solvents. Any draining or pouring of such volatile fluids should be done in a well ventilated area.

When using cleaning fluids and solvents, read the instructions on the container carefully. Never use materials from unmarked containers.

Never run the engine in an enclosed space, such as a garage. Exhaust fumes contain carbon monoxide, which is extremely poisonous. If you need to run the engine, always do so in the open air, or at least have the rear of the vehicle outside the work area.

Gasoline

Remember at all times that gasoline is highly flammable, never smoke or allow any type of open flame nearby when working on a vehicle. The risk does not end there. A spark caused by an electrical short circuit, steel striking steel or, under certain conditions, static electricity built up in your hands or body can ignite gasoline vapors, which in a confined space are highly explosive.

Do not under any circumstances, use gasoline for cleaning parts. Use an approved safety solvent. Also, do not store gasoline in a glass container, use an approved metal or plastic container only **(see illustration)**!

Always disconnect the cable from the negative battery terminal before working on any part of the fuel or electrical system. Never risk spilling fuel on a hot engine or exhaust component.

Household current

When using an electrical power tool, inspection light, etc., which operates on household current, always make sure that the tool is correctly connected to its receptacle and that it is properly grounded **(see illustration)**. Do not use electrical power tools in damp conditions such as a wet floor. Do not create a spark or apply excessive heat in the vicinity of fuel or fuel vapor.

Make certain the electrical wiring in the garage or workshop is up to code, and that all outlets and switches are covered and no bare wire is exposed.

Never use an unshielded light bulb in the shop, a broken light bulb can be an extreme safety hazard **(see illustration)**. Not only is the broken glass dangerous, but the spark caused by a light bulb breaking could ignite gasoline vapors.

1.23 Transport and store gasoline in an approved container ONLY - never use a glass jar or bottle

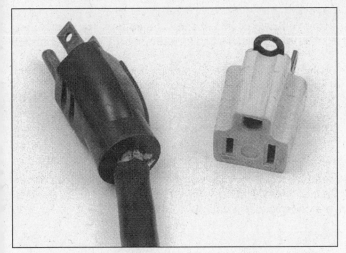

1.24 Check the plugs on power tools and extension cords to make sure they're securely attached, with no burned or frayed wires, and use an adapter to ground the plug at the outlet if necessary

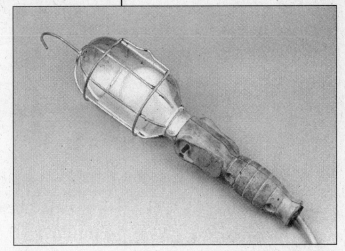

1.25 Never use an unshielded light bulb in the shop - the wire cage on a work light is designed to prevent broken bulbs and the accompanying safety hazards

Secondary ignition system voltage

A severe electrical shock can result from touching certain parts of the ignition system (such as the spark plug wires) when the engine is running or being rotated by the starter, particularly if the components are damp or the insulation is defective. In the case of an electronic ignition system, the secondary system voltage is much higher (up to 40,000 volts) and could prove fatal.

Cleanliness

Get in the habit of taking a regular look around the work area to check for potential dangers. Keep the area neat and clean. Mop up spills, sweep up debris and dispose of it as soon as possible. Don't leave tools or parts lying around on the floor.

Be very careful with storage of used oily rags. Spontaneous combustion can occur if they're left in a pile or bucket. Dispose of oily rags properly in an approved covered metal container.

Periodically check all equipment and tools for security and safety hazards. Frayed cords and damaged plugs on electrical tools, or a shelf unit that is about to collapse should be repaired immediately.

Accidents and emergencies

Shop accidents range from minor cuts and skinned knuckles to serious injuries requiring immediate medical attention. The former are inevitable, while the latter are, hopefully, avoidable or at least uncommon. Think about what you would do in the event of an accident. Have a good complete first-aid kit within easy reach and know how to use it.

If possible, never work alone just in case something goes wrong. Think about what you would do if you were alone and badly hurt or incapacitated. Would someone be nearby who could be summoned quickly? If you had to cope with someone else's accident, would you know what to do? Dealing with accidents is a large and complex subject. It's easy to make matters worse if you have no idea how to respond. Rather than attempt to deal with this subject in a superficial manner, buy a good first-aid book and read it carefully. Better yet, take a course in first-aid at a local junior college or adult education center.

Environmental safety

Several state and federal regulations govern the storage and disposal of oil, lubricants, gasoline, solvents, antifreeze, thinners, paint, etc. Contact the appropriate government agency or your local auto parts store for the latest information. Be absolutely certain that all materials are properly stored, handled and disposed of. Never pour used or leftover oil, solvents, antifreeze or paint down the drain or dump them on the ground. Don't allow volatile liquids to evaporate, keep them in sealed containers. Air-conditioning refrigerant must never be expelled into the atmosphere. If necessary to discharge your air- conditioning system, have the refrigerant recovered and recycled by a properly equipped and licensed air-conditioning technician.

2 Mechanics' hand tools and equipment

For some home mechanics, the idea of using the correct tool is completely foreign. They'll cheerfully tackle the most complex repair procedures with only a set of inferior quality open-end wrenches (of the wrong type), a single screwdriver (with a worn tip), a large hammer and a worn-out adjustable wrench. Though they often get away with it, this cavalier approach is foolish and could be dangerous. It can result in relatively minor annoyances like stripped fasteners, or it can cause catastrophic consequences such as damaged engines. It can also result in serious injury.

A complete assortment of good tools is essential for anyone who plans to repair automobiles. If you don't already have most of the tools listed below, the initial investment may seem high, but compared to the spiraling costs of routine maintenance and repairs it's a deal. Besides, you can use a lot of the tools around the house for other types of mechanical repairs.

1 Using and buying mechanics' hand tools

There are two ways to buy tools. The easiest and quickest way is to simply buy an entire set **(see illustration)**. Tool sets are often priced substantially below the cost of the same individually priced tools - and sometimes they even come with a tool box. When purchasing such sets, you often wind up with some tools you don't need or want. But if low price and convenience are your concerns, this might be the way to go. Keep in mind that you're going to keep a quality set of tools a long time (maybe the rest of your life), so check the tools carefully; don't skimp too much on price, either. Buying tools individually is usually a more expensive and time-consuming way to go, but you're more likely to wind up with the tools you need and want. You can also select each tool on its relative merits for the way you use it.

You can get most of the hand tools shown from the tool department of any large department store, hardware store, or automotive parts store that sells hand tools. Until you're a good judge of the quality levels of tools, avoid buying tools of questionable quality. Especially when you're purchasing high-use items like screwdrivers, wrenches and sockets. Inferior quality tools may wear-out prematurely, bend or break. Their initial cost plus the additional expense of replacing them will exceed the initial cost of better-quality tools. All of the tools shown in this manual are high quality tools.

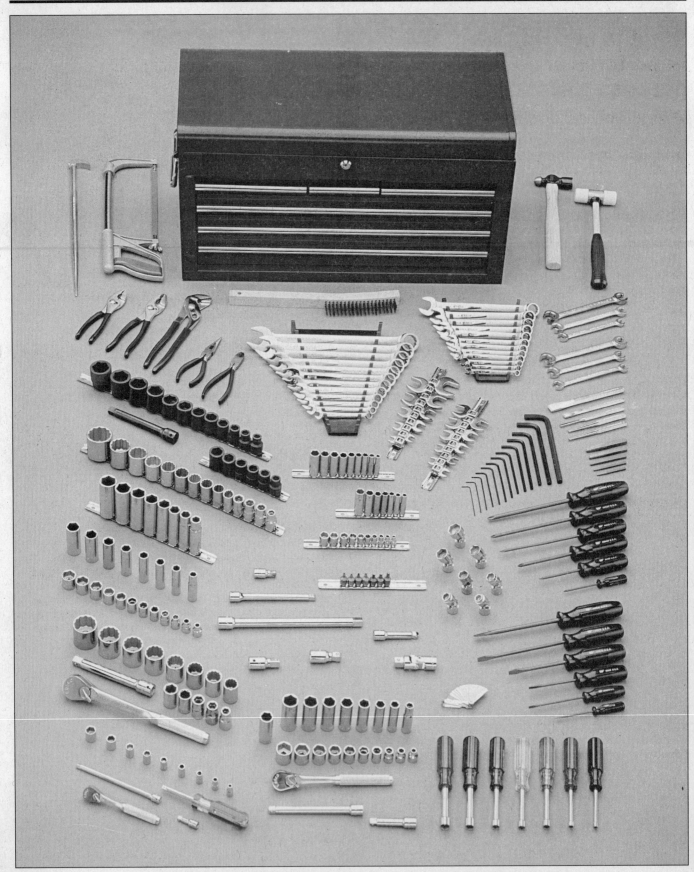

2.1 Purchasing a complete tool set is an excellent way to start your tool collection

What to look for when buying hand tools and general purpose tools

Wrenches and sockets

Wrenches vary widely in quality (see illustration). One indication of their quality is their cost: The more they cost, the better they are. Buy the best wrenches you can afford. You'll use them a lot.

Start with a set containing wrenches from 1/4 to 1-inch in size. The size, stamped on the wrench, indicates the distance across the nut or bolt head, or the distance between the wrench jaws - not the diameter of the threads on the fastener - in inches (see illustration). For example, a 1/4-inch bolt usually has a 7/16-inch hex head - the size of the wrench required to loosen or tighten it. However, the relationship between thread diameter and hex size doesn't always hold true. In some instances, an unusually small hex may be used to discourage over-tightening or because space around the fastener head is limited. Conversely, some fasteners have a disproportionately large hex-head.

Wrenches are similar in appearance, so their quality level can be difficult to judge just by looking at them. There are bargains to be had, just as there are overpriced tools with well-known brand names. On the other hand, you may buy what looks like a reasonable value set of wrenches only to find they fit badly or are made from poor-quality steel.

With a little experience, it's possible to judge the quality of a tool by looking at it. Often, you may have come across the brand name before and have a good idea of the quality. Close examination of the tool can often reveal some hints as to its quality. Prestige tools are usually polished and chrome-plated over their entire surface, with the working faces ground to size. The polished finish is largely cosmetic, but it does make them easy to keep clean. Ground jaws normally indicate the tool will fit well on fasteners.

A side-by-side comparison of a high-quality wrench with a inferior equivalent is an eye opener. The better tool will be made from a good-quality material, often a forged/chrome-vanadium steel alloy. This, together with careful design, allows the tool to be kept as small and compact as possible. If, by comparison, the inferior tool is thicker and heavier, especially around the jaws, it's usually because the extra material is needed to compensate for its lower quality. If the tool fits properly, this isn't necessarily bad, but in situations where it's necessary to work in a confined area, the inferior tool may be too bulky to fit.

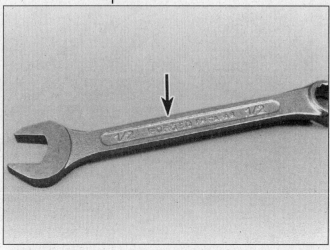

2.2 One quick way to determine whether you're looking at a quality wrench is to read the information printed on the handle - if it says "chrome vanadium" or "forged", it's made out of the right material

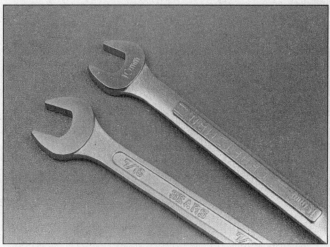

2.3 The size stamped on a wrench indicates the distance across the nut or bolt head (or the distance between the wrench jaws) in inches, not the diameter of the threads on the fastener

Open-end wrenches

Because of its versatility, the open-end wrench is the most common type of wrench. It has a jaw on either end, connected by a flat handle section. The jaws either vary by a size, or overlap sizes between consecutive wrenches in a set. This allows one wrench to be used to hold a bolt head while a similar-size nut is removed. A typical fractional size wrench set might have the following jaw sizes: 1/4 x 5/16, 3/8 x 7/16, 1/2 x 9/16, 9/16 x 5/8 and so on.

Typically, the jaw end is set at an angle to the handle, a feature which makes them very useful in confined spaces **(see illustration)**; by turning the nut or bolt as far as the obstruction allows, then turning the wrench over so the jaw faces in the other direction, it's possible to move the fastener a fraction of a turn at a time. The handle length is generally determined by the size of the jaw and is calculated to allow a nut or bolt to be tightened sufficiently by hand with minimal risk of breakage or thread damage (though this doesn't apply to soft materials like brass or aluminum).

Common open-end wrenches are usually sold in sets **(see illustration)** and it's rarely worth buying them individually, unless it's to replace a lost or broken tool from a set. Single tools invariably cost more, so check the sizes you're most likely to need regularly and buy the best set of wrenches you can afford in that range of sizes. If money is limited, remember that you'll use open-end wrenches more than any other type - it's a good idea to buy a good set and cut corners elsewhere.

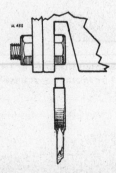

2.4 Open-end wrenches can do several things other wrenches can't - for example, they can be used on bolt heads with limited clearance (above) and they can be used in tight spots where there's little room to turn a wrench by flipping the offset jaw over every few degrees of rotation

Box-end wrenches

Box-end wrenches have ring-shaped ends with a 6-point (hex) **(see illustration)** or 12-point (double hex) **(see illustration)** opening . This allows the tool to fit on the fastener hex at 15 (12-point) or 30-degree (6-point) intervals. Normally, each tool has two ends of different sizes, allowing an overlapping range of sizes in a set, as described for open-end wrenches.

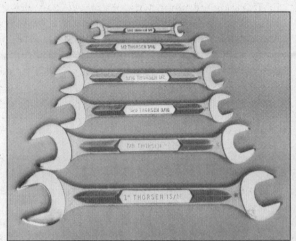

2.5 Here's a Thorsen 6-piece SAE open-end wrench set - note that each wrench can remove two different size fasteners. This set ranges from 1/4 inch to 1-inch.

Although available as flat tools, the handle is usually offset at each end to allow it to clear obstructions near the fastener, which is normally an advantage. In addition to normal length wrenches, it's also possible to buy long handle types to

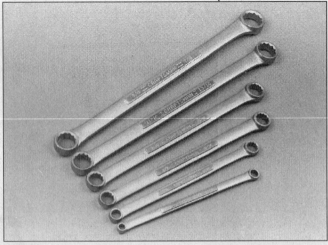

2.6 Box-end wrenches have a ring-shaped "box" at each end - when space permits, they offer the best combination of "grip" and strength

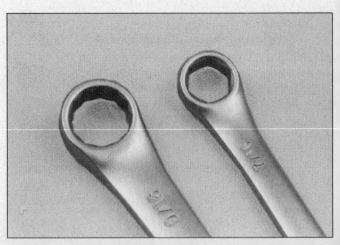

2.7 Box-end wrenches are available in 12 (left) and 6-point (right) openings; the 12-point design offers twice as many wrench positions, but the 6-point is less likely to strip off the corners of a nut or bolt head

allow more leverage (very useful when trying to loosen rusted or seized nuts). It is, however, easy to shear off fasteners if not careful, and sometimes the extra length impairs access.

As with open-end wrenches, box-ends are available in varying quality, again often indicated by finish and the amount of metal around the ring ends. While the same criteria should be applied when selecting a set of box-end wrenches, if your budget is limited, go for better-quality open-end wrenches and a slightly inferior set of box-ends.

Combination wrenches

The most common type of combination wrench combines a box-end and open-end of the same size in one tool. Offering the many advantages of both types, it is the most widely used type of end wrench. Like the others, they're widely available in sets and as such, are probably a better choice than box-ends only **(see illustration)**. They're generally compact, short-handled tools and are well suited for tight spaces where access is limited. They're also available in long handled models to use where extra leverage is needed **(see illustration)**.

Another type of combination wrench combines an open end and a socket **(see illustration)**. The socket swivels 180 degrees making it very convenient to use and its extra gripping ability is another advantage.

There are also ratcheting end-wrenches available **(see illustration)**. In situations where you must use an end-wrench, the ratcheting box-end allows you to remove the fastener a lot faster.

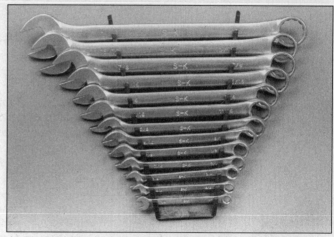

2.8 A set of combination wrenches from 1/4 to 1-inch is probably the most versatile set of wrenches you will have in your tool box

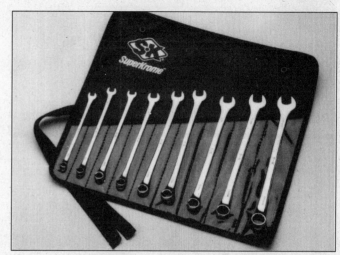

2.9 SK Tools long pattern combination wrench set - the extra length of a long handle wrench offers added leverage for removing fasteners

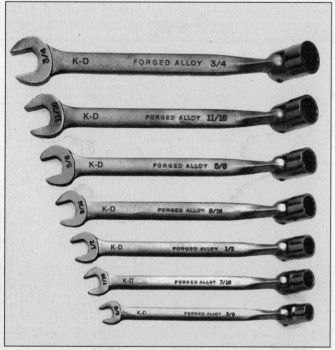

2.10 The combination open-end-socket wrench offers the added versatility of a socket in an end wrench

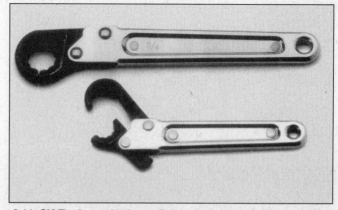

2.11 SK Tools ratcheting split box-end wrench - these handy wrenches offer convenient ratcheting action whenever an open-end flare-nut wrench is your only choice. The jaw "splits" open to surround the fastener, then closes to provide box wrench gripping power

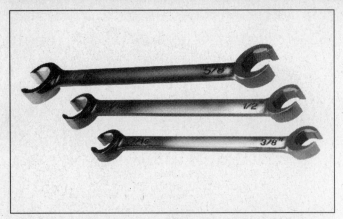

2.12 You will need a set of flare-nut wrenches; they are available in standard SAE and metric sizes

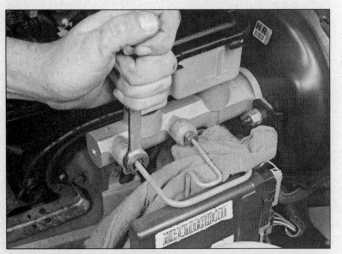

2.13 Flare-nut wrenches are used to remove flared tubing fittings found on brake, fuel and power steering lines. They are necessary to prevent rounding of the nut

Flare-nut wrench

A flare-nut wrench **(see illustration)** is used to remove flared tubing fittings. It is sort of a box-end wrench with a section cut away. The cut-out allows you to slip the wrench over the tubing, then on to the nut. The box end is necessary to keep from damaging the soft flare-nut fitting, which would surely be rounded-off by an open-end wrench.

You'll use your flare-nut wrenches often. They're used to remove brake line fittings **(see illustration),** fuel line fittings and power steering line fittings, just to name a few.

Adjustable wrenches

Adjustable wrenches come in several sizes **(see illustration)**. Each size can handle a broad range of fastener sizes. Adjustable wrenches aren't as effective as one-size tools and it's easy to damage fasteners with them. However, they can be an invaluable addition to any tool kit - if they're used with discretion. **Note:** *If you attach the wrench to the fastener with the movable jaw pointing in the direction of wrench rotation , an adjustable wrench will be less likely to slip and damage the fastener head* **(see illustration)**.

The most common adjustable wrench is the open-end type with a set of parallel jaws that can be set to fit the head of a fastener. Most are controlled by a threaded spindle, though there are various cam and spring-loaded versions available. Don't buy large tools of this type for automotive work; you'll rarely be able to find enough clearance to use them.

Ratchet and socket sets

Ratcheting socket wrench sets are highly versatile tools. Besides the sockets themselves, many other interchangeable accessories - extensions, universal joints, step-down adapters, screwdriver bits, hex bits, etc. - are avail-

2.14 Adjustable wrenches can handle a wide range of fastener sizes - they're not as good as single-size wrenches but they're handy for loosening and tightening those odd-sized fasteners

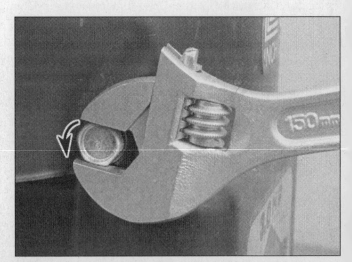

2.15 When you use an adjustable wrench, make sure the movable jaw points in the direction the wrench is being turned (arrow) so the wrench doesn't distort and slip off the fastener head

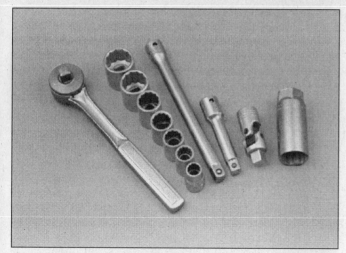

2.16 A typical ratchet and socket set includes a ratchet, a set of sockets, a long and a short extension, a universal joint and a spark plug socket

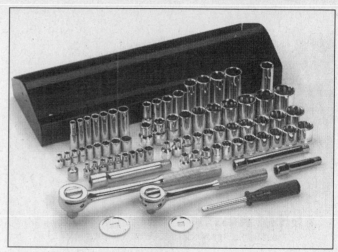

2.17 Sockets sets are available as complete sets, such as this Thorsen 75-piece SAE/metric 1/4, 3/8, and 1/2-inch drive set . . .

able to use with them **(see illustration)**. If possible, buy six-point sockets - they're less likely to slip and strip the corners off bolts and nuts. Don't buy sockets with extra-thick walls - they might be stronger but they can be hard to use on recessed fasteners or fasteners in tight quarters.

The most economical way to buy sockets is in a set **(see illustrations)**. Socket sets are available in 1/4, 3/8, 1/2, 3/4 and 1-inch drive sizes. You'll need a 3/8-inch drive set for most automotive type work. It's the most common type and the one you'll use most of the time. A 1/2-inch drive set is very useful also. Although the larger drive is bulky and more expensive, it

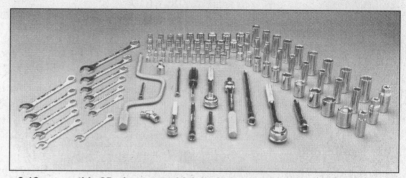

2.18 . . . or this 95-piece set which includes combination end-wrenches and other accessories

has the capacity of accepting a very wide range of larger sockets. You may also want to consider a 1/4-inch drive set. It is very useful for small fasteners or where space is very confined. Some of the sets you find may combine drive sizes **(see illustration)**; they're well worth having and you can often find a nice set at a good price. The 3/4 and 1-inch drive sets accept very large sockets and are used, most commonly, on heavy-duty trucks and industrial applications.

A socket set consists of a ratchet handle and the interchangeable sockets which fit it. The socket itself is made of a forged-steel alloy cylinder with a hex (6-point) or double-hex (12-point) formed inside one end. The other end is formed into the square drive recess that engages over the corresponding square end of the ratchet or other socket drive tool. The ratchet handles are all reversible, with some having finer teeth in the ratchet head or plastic handles that are easier to use **(see illustration)**. They are also available with flex-heads and long handles **(see illustration)**.

Additionally, you'll need at least one extension, a spark plug socket and maybe a T-han-

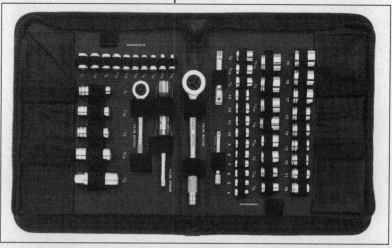

2.19 This Blackhawk 3/8 and 1/4-inch drive socket set comes in a nylon soft-sided carrying case

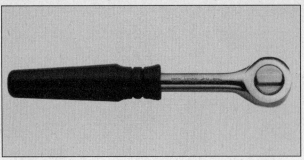

2.20 SK's "ergonomic" handle ratchet is specially designed to fit the contours of the users hand, a definite plus when pulling hard to break or tighten a fastener

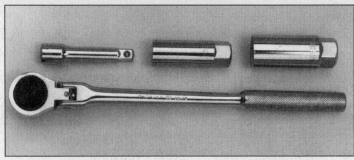

2.21 Flex handle ratchets are also available; this Thorsen 3/8-inch drive tune-up set makes removing spark plugs easier

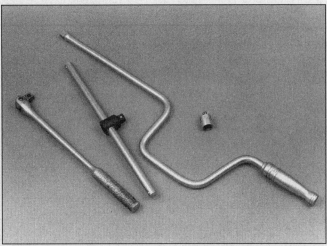

2.22 Lots of other accessories are available for ratchets; From left to right, a breaker bar, a sliding T-handle, a speed handle and a 3/8-to-1/4-inch adapter

dle or breaker bar **(see illustration)**. Other desirable, though less essential items, are a speed handle, a universal-joint, extensions of various lengths and adapters that allow you to adapt one drive size to another. Most socket sets include a special deep socket for 14 millimeter spark plugs. They have rubber inserts to protect the spark plug porcelain insulator and hold the plug in the socket to avoid burned fingers.

One of the best things about a socket set is the built-in facility for expansion. Once you have a basic set, you can purchase extra sockets when necessary and replace worn or damaged tools. There are special deep sockets **(see illustration)** available for reaching recessed fasteners or to allow the socket to fit over a projecting bolt or stud. You can also buy screwdriver, hex and Torx bits to fit various drive tools (they can be absolutely necessary in some applications **(see illustrations)**. Many other accessories are available to make a socket sets even more versatile **(see illustration)**.

As always, quality will govern the cost of the tools. Once again, the "buy the best" approach is usually advised when selecting socket sets. Apart from well-known and respected brand names, you'll have to take a chance on the quality of the set you buy. If you know someone who has a set that has held up well, try to find the same brand, if possible. Take a pocketful of nuts and bolts with you and check the fit in some of the sockets. Check the operation of the ratchet. Good ones operate smoothly and crisply in small steps; inferior ones are coarse and stiff - a good basis for guessing the quality of the rest of the pieces.

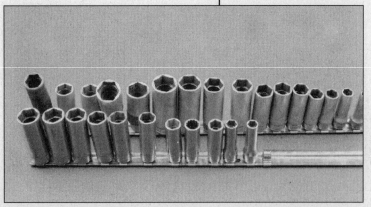

2.23 Deep sockets enable you to loosen or tighten an elongated fastener, or to get at a nut with a long bolt or stud protruding from it

2.24 Standard and Phillips bits, Hex-head and Torx drivers will expand the versatility of your ratchet and extensions even further

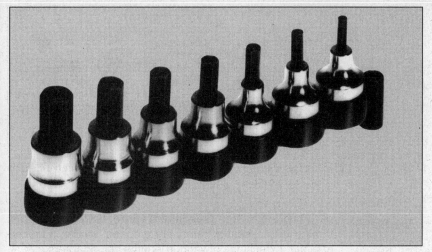

2.25 Lisle 3/8-inch drive hex bit set - for use on hex-head fasteners

2.26 Ball hex bits are used in hard-to-reach places. The access does not need to be directly above the fastener - they can be used at an angle of up to 25 degrees

2.27 The Torx head fastener is becoming more popular with the automobile manufacturers . . .

2.28 . . . so you'll need a set of Torx bits

2.29 Torx sockets may also be necessary for a few special applications

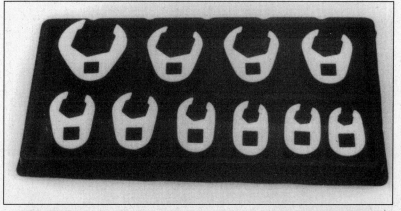

2.30 SK Tools flare-nut crowfoot wrench set - the flare-nut crowfoot enables the user to reach around obstructions and into tight places, while the flare-nut design provides a secure grip on the fastener

Automotive Tools Manual

2.31 SK Tools 1/4-inch drive flex-socket set - flex sockets allow you to get into very tight places

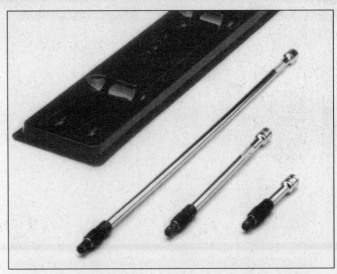

2.32 SK Tools 1/4-inch drive locking extensions - locking extensions have a permanent lock mounted on the extension which holds the socket to the extension until it is released

2.33 Locking adapters are also available in 1/4 and 3/8-inch drive allowing for the easy conversion of any extension into a locking extension. The adapter can also be used with universal joints, speeder handles, spinner handles and flex bars

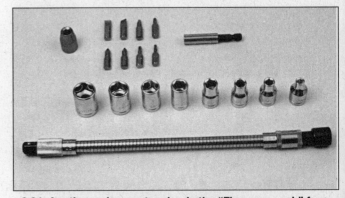

2.34 Another unique extension is the "Flex-a-wrench" from Easypower - This flexible extension allows you to get to fasteners usually unreachable with a ratchet. Available in sets along with sockets and bits as shown, or individually. A version is also available for use with electric and cordless power tools

Torque wrenches

Torque wrenches are essential for tightening critical fasteners like rod bolts, main bearing cap bolts, head bolts, etc. **(see illustration)**. Attempting a major engine repair or overhaul without a torque wrench is an invitation to oil leaks, distortion of the cylinder head, damaged or stripped threads or worse.

The two most common types of torque wrenches are the beam type, which indicates torque loads by deflecting a flexible shaft, and the micrometer type, which allows you to dial the specific torque value in on the handle and emits an audible click when the torque resistance reaches the specified torque value set **(see illustrations)**.

Torque wrenches are available in a variety of drive sizes and torque ranges for particular applications. A 1/2-inch drive torque wrench with a range of 30 to 250 ft-lbs should be adequate for most major repairs and engine rebuilding, while a 3/8-inch drive with a range of 10 to 80 ft-lbs is

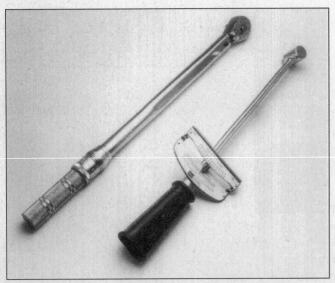

2.35 Torque wrenches (micrometer-type on left, beam-type on right) are the only way to accurately tighten critical fasteners like connecting rod bolts, cylinder head bolts, etc.

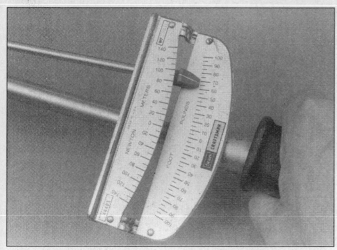

2.36 The deflecting beam-type torque wrench is inexpensive and simple to use - just tighten the fastener until the pointer points to the specified torque setting

2.37 Micrometer type torque wrenches emit a definite feel and sound when the pre-set torque is reached, which makes them very accurate and easy to use

needed for the smaller jobs **(see illustration)**. Keep in mind that micrometer types are usually more accurate (and more expensive).

Using wrenches and sockets

Before you start tearing an engine apart, figure out the best tool for the job; in this instance the best wrench for a hex-head fastener. Sit down with a few nuts and bolts and look at how various tools fit the bolt heads.

A golden rule is to choose a tool that contacts the largest area of the hex-head. This distributes the load as evenly as possible and lessens the risk of damage. The shape most closely resembling the bolt head or nut is another hex, so a 6-point socket or box-end wrench is usually the best choice **(see illustration)**. Many sockets and box-end wrenches have double hex (12-point) openings **(see illustration)**. If you slip a 12-point box-end wrench over a

2.38 Torque wrenches are necessary in applications other than cylinder heads and crankshaft bearing tightening. Here a throttle body unit is tightened to the proper torque value.

nut, look at how and where the two are in contact. The corners of the nut engage in every other point of the wrench. When the wrench is turned, pressure is applied evenly on each of the six corners. This is fine unless the fastener head was previously rounded off. If so, the corners will be damaged and the wrench will slip. If you encounter a damaged bolt head or nut, always use a 6-point wrench or

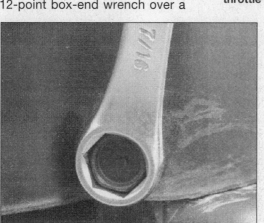

2.39 Try to use a six-point box wrench (or socket) whenever possible - it's shape matches that of the fastener, which means maximum grip and minimum slip

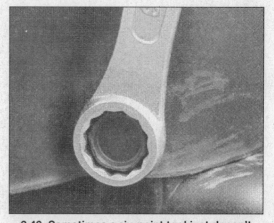

2.40 Sometimes a six-point tool just doesn't offer you any grip when you get the wrench at the angle it needs to be in to loosen or tighten a fastener - when this happens, use the 12-point socket or wrench - but remember; they're much more likely to strip the corners off a fastener

2.41 Open-end wrenches contact only two sides of the fastener and the jaws tend to open up when you put some muscle on the wrench handle - that's why they should only be used as a last resort

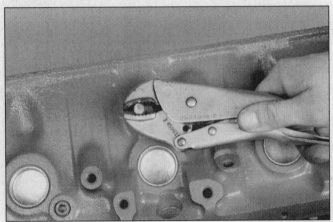

2.42 Locking-pliers can be used to remove fasteners with rounded off heads

socket if possible. If you don't have one of the right size, choose a wrench that fits securely and proceed with care.

If you slip an open-end wrench over a hex-head fastener, you'll see the tool is in contact on two faces only **(see illustration)**. This is acceptable provided the tool and fastener are both in good condition. The need for a snug fit between the wrench and nut or bolt explains the recommendation to buy good-quality open-end wrenches. If the wrench jaws, the bolt head or both are damaged, the wrench will probably slip, rounding off and distorting the head. In some applications, an open-end wrench is the only possible choice due to limited access, but always check the fit of the wrench on the fastener before attempting to loosen it; if it's hard to get at with a wrench, think how hard it will be to remove after the head is damaged.

The last choice is an adjustable wrench or self-locking pliers. Use these tools only when all else has failed **(see illustration)**. In some cases, self-locking pliers may be able to grip a damaged head that no wrench could deal with, but be careful not to make matters worse by damaging it further.

Bearing in mind the remarks about the correct choice of tool in the first place, there are several things worth noting about the actual use of the tool. First, make sure the wrench head is clean and undamaged. If the fastener is rusted or coated with paint, the wrench won't fit correctly. Clean off the head and, if it's rusted, apply some penetrating oil. Leave it to soak in for a while before attempting removal.

It may seem obvious, but take a close look at the fastener to be removed before using a wrench. On many mass-produced machines, one end of a fastener may be fixed or captive, which speeds up initial assembly and usually makes removal easier. If a nut is installed on a stud or a bolt threads into a captive nut or tapped hole, you may have only one fastener to deal with. If, on the other hand, you have a separate nut and bolt, you must hold the bolt head while the nut is removed. In some areas this can be difficult. In this type of situation you may need an assistant to hold the bolt head with a wrench while you remove the nut from the other side. If this isn't possible, you'll have to try to position a box-end wrench so it wedges against some other component to prevent it from turning.

Be on the lookout for left-hand threads. They aren't common but are sometimes used on the ends of rotating shafts to make sure the nut doesn't come loose during engine operation. If you can see the shaft end, the thread type can be checked visually. If you're unsure, place your thumbnail in the threads and see which way you have to turn your hand so your nail "unscrews" from the shaft. If you have to turn your hand counterclockwise, it's a conventional right-hand thread.

Beware of the upside-down fastener syndrome. If you're loosening a fastener from the under side of a something, it's easy to get confused about which way to turn it. What seems like counterclockwise to you can easily be clockwise (from the fastener's point of view). Even after years of experience, this can still catch you once in a while.

In most cases, a fastener can be removed simply by placing the wrench on the nut or bolt head and turning it. Occasionally, though, the condition or location of the fastener may make things more difficult. Make sure the wrench is square on the head. You may need to reposition the tool or try another type to obtain a snug fit. Make sure the engine you're working on is secure and can't move when you turn the wrench. If necessary, get someone to help steady it for you. Position yourself so you can get maximum leverage on the wrench.

If possible, locate the wrench so you can pull the end towards you. If you have to push on the tool, remember that it may slip, or the fastener may move suddenly. For this reason, don't curl your fingers around the handle or you may crush or bruise them when the fastener moves; keep your hand flat, pushing on the wrench with the heel of your thumb. If the tool digs into your hand, place a rag between it and your hand or wear a heavy glove.

If the fastener doesn't move with normal hand pressure, stop and try to figure out why before the fastener or wrench is damaged or you hurt yourself. Stuck fasteners may require penetrating oil, heat or an impact driver or air tool.

Using sockets to remove hex-head fasteners is less likely to result in damage than if a wrench is used. Make sure the socket fits snugly over the fastener head; then attach an extension, if needed, and the ratchet or breaker bar. Theoretically, a ratchet shouldn't be used for loosening a fastener or for final tightening because the ratchet mechanism may be overloaded and could slip. In some instances, the location of the fastener may mean you have no choice but to use a ratchet, in which case you'll have to be extra careful.

Never use extensions where they aren't needed. Whether or not an extension is used, always support the drive end of the breaker bar with one hand while turning it with the other. Once the fastener is loose, the ratchet can be used to speed up removal.

Pliers

Some tool manufacturers make 25 or 30 different types of pliers. You need only a fraction of this selection **(see illustration)**. Obtain a good pair of slip-joint pliers for general use and a pair of long-nose pliers is handy for reaching into hard-to-get-at places. A set of diagonal wire cutters is essential for electrical work and pulling out cotter pins. Locking pliers are adjustable. Locking pliers that grip a fastener firmly and won't let go when locked into place are invaluable. Parallel-jaw, adjustable pliers have angled jaws that remain parallel at any degree of opening, and they're terrific for gripping a big fastener with a lot of force.

Slip-joint pliers have two open positions; a figure eight-shaped, elongated slot in one handle slips back-and-forth on a pivot pin on the other handle to change positions **(see illustration)**. Good quality pliers have jaws made of tempered steel and there's usually a wire-cutter at the base of the jaws. The primary uses of slip-joint pliers are for holding objects, bending and cutting throttle wires and crimping and bending metal parts, not loosening nuts and bolts.

Groove-joint pliers have parallel jaws you can open to various widths by engaging different tongues and grooves near the pivot pin **(see illustration)**. Since the tool expands to fit many size objects, it has countless uses for engine and equipment maintenance **(see illustration)**. Groove-joint pliers come in various sizes. The medium size is adequate for general work; small and large sizes are nice to have as your budget permits **(see illustration)**. You'll use all three sizes frequently.

As the name suggests, long-nose pliers have long, thin

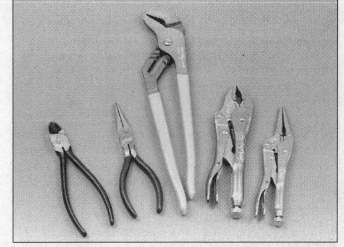

2.43 A typical assortment of the types of pliers you need to have in your box - from the left; diagonal cutters, long-nose pliers, groove-joint pliers, locking pliers, long-nose locking pliers

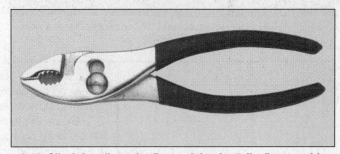

2.44 Slip-joint pliers; the figure eight slot "slips" to provide two different opening widths

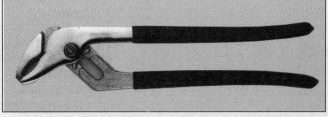

2.45 Groove joint pliers: the "grooves" provide several opening widths and they're available in different jaw configurations

2.46 The extra-wide opening capability of groove-joint pliers makes them very versatile tools

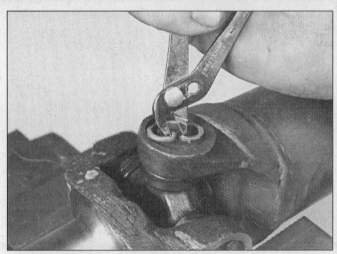

2.47 Groove-joint pliers come in many sizes; here a small set of groove-joint pliers is used to remove a retaining ring

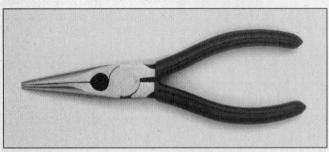

2.48 Long-nose pliers: so-named because of their long jaws, often have a wire cutter included

2.49 The long narrow tip of long-nose pliers allows them to grab small items

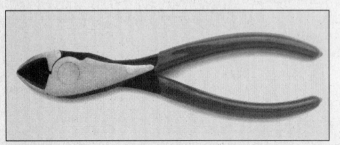

2.50 Diagonal cutting pliers: used to cut small diameter wire or light metal

jaws designed for reaching into holes and other restricted areas **(see illustrations)**. Most long-nose, or needle-nose as their sometimes called, pliers also have wire cutters at the base of the jaws and are available with curved jaws.

Diagonal cutting pliers have hardened cutting edges and are designed to cut small diameter wire and light steel **(see illustration)**. They can also be used to remove cotter pins and other types of fasteners **(see illustration)**.

Another type of pliers useful in automotive work is the lineman's pliers **(see illustration)**. Their strong side cutting jaws can be used to cut battery cable and other large diam-

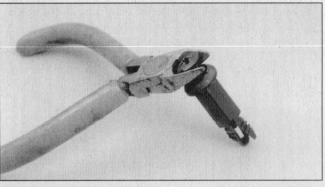

2.51 Diagonal pliers are also a very versatile tool; they can be used to remove cotter pins and other types of retainers

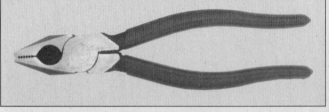

2.52 Linesman pliers are also a handy tool for your tool box. They are used to cut larger-diameter wire and cable. Their milled jaws are very strong.

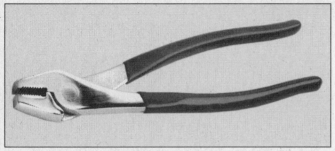

2.53 Battery nut pliers are used to remove the often-corroded battery cable terminal fasteners when an end-wrench won't do

eter wire or cable.

Battery-nut pliers are used to remove corroded battery cable fasteners **(see illustration)**. They are usually made of stainless-steel or some other corrosion resistant material which is resilient to battery acid.

Locking pliers come in various sizes; the medium size with curved jaws is best for all-around work **(see illustration)**. However, buy a large and small one if possible, since they're often used in pairs. Although this tool falls somewhere between an adjustable wrench, a pair of pliers and a portable vise, it can be invaluable for loosening and tightening fasteners - it's the only pliers that should be used for this purpose.

The jaw opening is set by turning a knurled knob at the end of one handle **(see illustration)**. The jaws are placed over the head of the fastener and the handles are squeezed together, locking the tool onto the fastener. The design of the tool allows extreme pressure to be applied at the jaws and a variety of jaw designs enable the tool to grip firmly even on damaged heads. Locking pliers are great for removing fasteners that have been rounded off by poorly fitting wrenches **(see illustration)**.

Look for these qualities when buying any type of pliers: Smooth operating handles and jaws, jaws that match up and grip evenly when the handles are closed, a nice finish and the word "forged" somewhere on the tool.

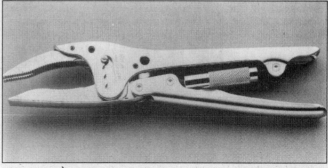

2.54 Locking pliers are available in a wide variety of sizes and jaw configurations as shown by these SK Tool locking pliers

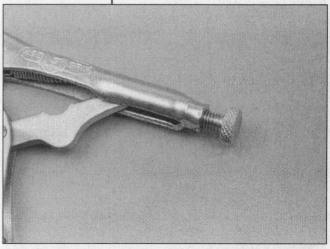

2.55 To adjust the jaws on a pair of locking pliers, grasp the part you want to hold with the jaws, tighten them down by turning the knurled knob on the end of one handle and snap the handles together - if you tightened the knob all the way down, you'll probably have to open it up (back it off) a little before you can close the handles

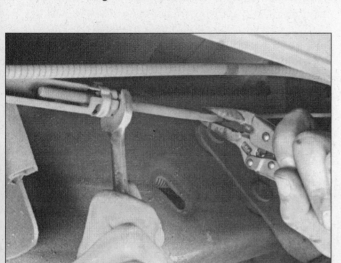

2.56 A pair of locking-pliers with long-nose jaws are a very versatile tool

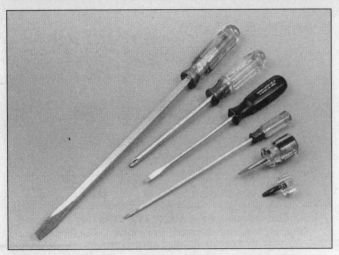

2.57 Screwdrivers come in multitude lengths, sizes and styles

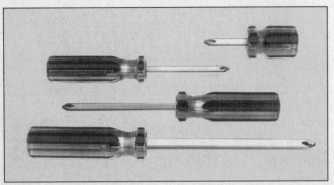

2.59 . . . or sets that contain screwdrivers of different sizes

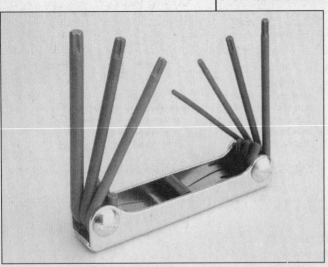

2.60 Another handy tool is this fold-up Torx key set from Eklind They are also available in a hex key set

Screwdrivers

Screwdrivers are available in a wide variety of sizes and price ranges **(see illustrations)**. Be very cautious with buying a large screwdriver set for what may seem like a "deal" at a discount tool store or swap meet. Even if they look exactly like more expensive brands, the metal tips and shafts are made with inferior alloys and aren't properly heat treated. They usually bend or break the first time you apply some serious torque and their tips and are certain to wear out prematurely.

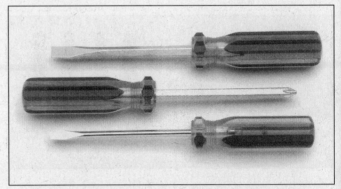

2.58 Screwdrivers can be purchased in sets containing standard and Phillips screwdrivers . . .

A screwdriver consists of a steel blade or shank with a drive tip formed at one end. The most common tips are standard (also called straight slot and flat-blade) and Phillips. The other end has a handle attached to it. Traditionally, handles were made from wood and secured to the shank, which had raised tangs to prevent it from turning in the handle. Most screwdrivers now come with plastic handles, which are generally more durable than wood.

The design and size of handles and blades vary considerably. Some handles are "ergonomically" shaped to fit the human hand and provide a better grip. The shank may be either round or square and some have a hex-shaped bolster under the handle to accept a wrench to provide more leverage when trying to turn a stubborn screw. The shank diameter, tip size and overall length may vary too. As a general rule, it's a good idea to use the longest screwdriver possible, which allows the greatest possible leverage.

If access is restricted, a number of special screwdrivers are designed to fit into confined spaces. The "stubby" screwdriver has a specially shortened handle and blade. There are also offset screwdrivers, folding screwdrivers and driver handles that except 1/4-inch drive sockets or have reversible shafts and extra bits that store in the handle **(see illustrations)**.

Magnetic tip screwdrivers are fast becoming popular. The magnetic bits are available in standard, Phillips and Torx configurations **(see illustrations)**. One driver handle with many interchangeable bits saves much needed space in the toolbox.

The important thing to remember when buying screwdrivers is that they really do come in sizes designed to fit different size fasteners. The slot in any screw has definite

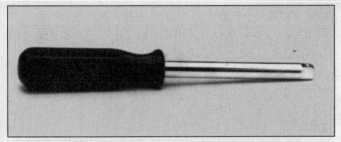

2.61 A spinner handle can be used with 1/4-inch drive sockets to drive small screws with hex heads

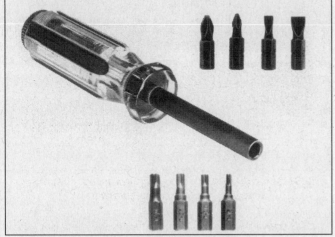

2.63 This Lisle magnetic screwdriver set has eight different magnetic bits that fit one handle

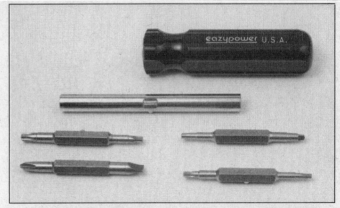

2.62 Screwdrivers are available with reversing shafts and bits, such as this one from Easypower, which has the advantage of carrying several different bits in one handle

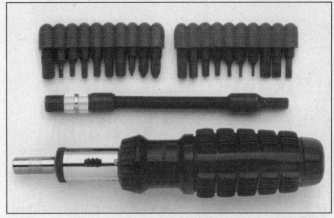

2.64 A very compact and useful tool, this Thorsen 22-piece ratcheting screwdriver set has magnetic bits, a flexible extension and a reversible ratcheting handle

dimensions - length, width and depth. Like a bolt head or a nut, the screw slot must be driven by a tool that uses all of the available bearing surface and doesn't slip. Don't use a big wide blade on a small screw and don't try to turn a large screw slot with a tiny, narrow blade. The same principles applies to Hex heads, Phillips heads, Torx heads, etc. Don't even think of using a slotted screwdriver on one of these heads! And don't use your screwdrivers as levers, chisels or punches! This kind of abuse turns them into bad screwdrivers very quickly.

Standard screwdrivers

These are used to remove and install conventional slotted screws and are available in a wide range of sizes denoting the width of the tip and the length of the shank (for example: a 3/8 x 10-inch screwdriver is 3/8-inch wide at the tip and the shank is 10-inches long). You should have a variety of screwdrivers so screws of various sizes can be dealt with without damaging them. The blade end must be the same width and thickness as the screw slot to work properly, without slipping **(see illustration)**. When selecting standard screwdrivers, choose good-quality tools, preferably with chrome moly, forged steel shanks. The tip of the shank should be ground to a parallel, flat profile (hollow ground) and not to a taper or wedge shape, which will tend to twist out of the slot when pressure is applied.

All screwdrivers wear with use, but standard types can be reground to shape

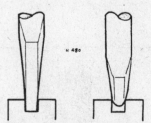

Misuse of a screwdriver – the blade shown is both too narrow and too thin and will probably slip or break off

The left-hand example shows a snug-fitting tip. The right-hand drawing shows a damaged tip which will twist out of the slot when pressure is applied

2.65 Standard screwdrivers - wrong size (left), correct fit in screw slot (center) and worn tip (right)

a number of times. When reshaping a tip, start by grinding the very end flat at right angles to the shank. Make sure the tip fits snugly in the slot of a screw of the appropriate size and keep the sides of the tip parallel. Remove only a small amount of metal at a time to avoid overheating the tip and destroying the temper of the steel.

Phillips screwdrivers

Phillips screws are sometimes installed during initial assembly with air tools and are next to impossible to remove later without ruining the heads, particularly if the wrong size screwdriver is used. Don't use other types of cross-head screwdrivers (Torx, Posi-drive, etc.) on Phillips screws - you'll end up damaging the screw head or the driver.

The only way to ensure the screwdrivers you buy will fit properly, is to take a couple of screws with you when shopping to make sure the fit between the screwdriver and fastener is snug. If the fit is good, you should be able to angle the blade down almost vertically without the screw slipping off the tip. Use only the proper screwdriver for the type of fastener involved - anything else is guaranteed to damage the screw head instantly.

The idea behind all cross-head screw designs is to make the screw and screwdriver blade self-aligning. Provided you aim the blade at the center of the screw head, it will engage correctly, unlike conventional slotted screws, which need careful alignment. This makes the screws suitable for machine installation on an assembly line (which explains why they're sometimes so tight and difficult to remove). The drawback with these screws is the driving tangs on the screwdriver tip are very small and must fit very precisely in the screw head. If this isn't the case, the huge loads imposed on small flats of the screw slot simply tear the metal away, at which point the screw ceases to be removable by normal methods. The problem is made worse by the normally soft material chosen for screws.

To deal with these screws on a regular basis, you'll need high-quality screwdrivers with various size tips so you'll be sure to have the right one when you need it. Phillips screwdrivers are sized by the tip number and length of the shank (for example: a number 2 x 6-inch Phillips screwdriver has a number 2 tip - to fit screws of only that size recess - and the shank is 6-inches long). Tip sizes 1, 2 and 3 should be adequate for most automotive repair work **(see illustration)**. If the tips get worn or damaged, buy new screwdrivers so the tools don't destroy the screws they're used on **(see illustration)**.

Here's a tip that may come in handy when using Phillips screwdrivers - if the screw is extremely tight and the tip tends to back out of the recess rather than turn the screw, apply a small amount of valve lapping compound to the screwdriver tip so it will grip the screw better.

Impact drivers

An impact driver is used to free very stubborn fasteners. It works by converting a hammer blow on the end of its handle into a sharp twisting movement **(see illustration)**. A set usually consists of the driver, several standard and

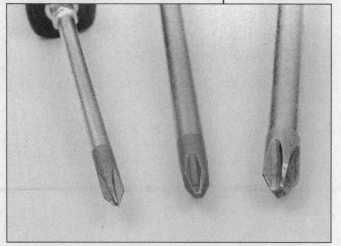

2.66 The tip size on a Phillips screwdriver is indicated by a number from 1 to 4, with 1 the smallest (left - No. 1: center - No. 2; right - No. 3)

2.67 New (left) and worn (right) Phillips screwdriver tips

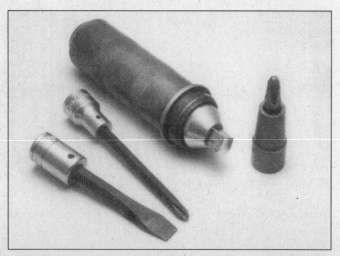

2.68 The impact driver converts a sharp blow into a twisting motion - this is a handy addition to your socket arsenal for those fasteners that won't let go - you can use it with any bit that fits a 3/8-inch drive ratchet

Phillips bits of different sizes, a bit holder and a storage box **(see illustration)**. Impact drivers normally are 3/8-inch square drive so sockets can be used also. While this is a great way to jar a seized fastener loose, the loads imposed on the socket are excessive. Use sockets that are designed for use with impact drivers or expect to replace damaged sockets on occasion.

Hammers

You'll need a hammer or two in your tool box **(see illustration)**. They're used for driving seals, bearing races, chisels, punches, etc. or for simply installing a hub cap **(see illustration)**. Resorting to a hammer to loosen a fastener, though, should always be the last resort. When nothing else will do the job, a medium-to-large size ball peen hammer is often the only way to loosen or install a part.

A ball-peen hammer has a head with a conventional cylindrical face at one end and a rounded ball end at the other and is a general-purpose tool found in almost any type of shop. It has a shorter neck than a claw hammer and the face is tempered for striking punches and chisels. A fairly large hammer is preferable to a small one. Although it's possible to find small ones, you won't need them very often and it's much easier to control the blows from a heavier head. As a general rule, a single 12 or 16-ounce hammer will work for most jobs, though occasionally larger or smaller ones may be useful **(see illustration)**.

A soft-face hammer is used where a steel hammer could cause damage to the component or other tools being used **(see illustration)**. A steel hammer head might crack an aluminum part, but a rubber or plastic hammer can be used with more confidence. Soft-face hammers are available with interchangeable heads (usually one made of rubber and another made of relatively hard plastic). When the heads are worn out, new ones can be installed. If finances are really limited, you can get by without a soft-face hammer by placing a small hardwood block between the component and a steel hammer head to prevent damage.

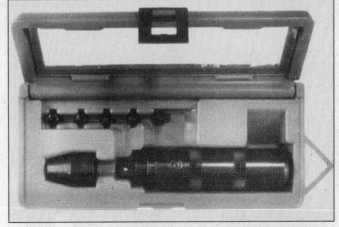

2.69 Lisle's hand impact tool comes in a hard plastic carrying case

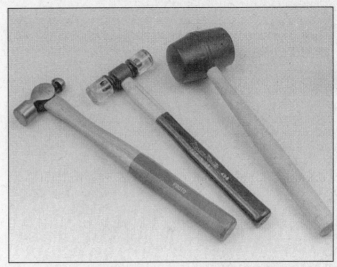

2.70 A ball-peen hammer, a soft-face hammer and a rubber mallet (left-to-right) will be needed for various tasks

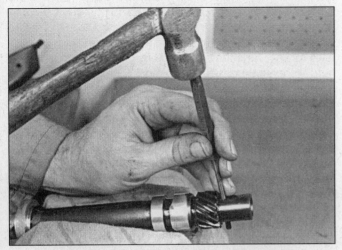

2.71 A ball-peen hammer is used to drive out pins or strike a chisel

2.72 A soft-face hammer is used to strike an object (such as this seal) that would be damaged by the hard head of a ball peen hammer

Automotive Tools Manual

2.73 Dead blow hammers reduce hammer recoil when an object is struck, allowing a more precise blow to be delivered. These one and two pound models from SK Tools are available with either a steel or a plastic face, while a unique two pound model is available with a steel face on one side and a plastic face on the other

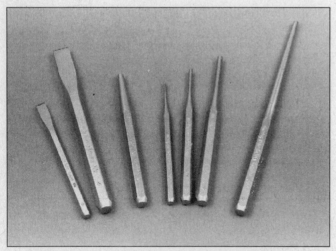

2.74 Cold chisels, center-punches, pin punches and alignment punches (left-to-right) will be needed sooner or later for many jobs

Hammers should be used with common sense; the head should strike the desired object squarely and with the right amount of force. For many jobs, little effort is needed - simply allow the weight of the head to do the work, using the length of the swing to control the amount of force applied. With practice, a hammer can be used with surprising finesse, but it'll take a while to achieve. Initial mistakes include striking the object at an angle, in which case the hammer head may glance off to one side, or hitting the edge of the object. Either one can result in damage to the part, or to your thumb, if it gets in the way, so be careful. Hold the hammer handle near the end, not near the head, and grip it firmly but not too tightly.

Check the condition of your hammers on a regular basis. The danger of a loose head coming off is self-evident, but check the head for chips and cracks too. If damage is noted, buy a new hammer - the head may chip in use and the resulting fragments can be extremely dangerous. It goes without saying that eye protection is essential whenever a hammer is used.

Punches and chisels

Punches and chisels are used along with a hammer for various purposes in the shop **(see illustration)**. Drift punches are often simply a length of round steel bar used to drive a component out of a bore. A typical use would be for removing or installing a bearing or bushing. A drift of the same diameter as the bearing outer race is placed against the bearing and tapped with a hammer to knock it in or out of the bore. Most manufacturers offer special drifts for the various bearings in a particular engine. While they're useful to a busy dealer service department, they are prohibitively expensive for the do-it-your-selfer who may only need to use them once. In such cases, it's better to improvise.

Smaller diameter drift punches can be purchased or fabricated from steel bar stock. In some cases, you'll need to drive out items like corroded engine mounting bolts. Here, it's essential to avoid damaging the threaded end of the bolt, so the drift must be a softer material than the bolt. Brass or copper is the usual choice for such jobs; the drift may be damaged in use, but the thread will be protected.

Punches are available in various shapes and sizes and a set of assorted types will be very useful **(see illustration)**. One of the most basic is the center punch, a small cylindrical punch with the end ground to a point. It'll be needed whenever a hole is drilled. The center of the hole is located first and the punch is used to make a small indentation at the intended point. The indentation acts as a guide for the drill bit so the hole ends up in the right place. Without a punch mark the drill bit will wander and you'll find it impossible to drill with any real accuracy. You can also buy automatic center punches. They're spring loaded and are pressed against the surface to be marked, without the need to use a hammer.

Pin punches are intended for removing items like roll pins (semi-hard, hollow pins that fit tightly in their holes). Pin punches have other uses, however. You may occasionally have to remove rivets or bolts by cutting off the heads and driving out the shanks with a pin punch. They're also very handy for aligning holes in components while bolts or screws are inserted.

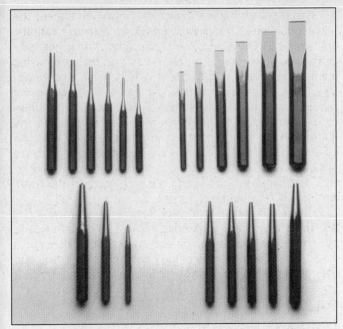

2.75 A complete set of punches and chisels from SK Tools

Of the various sizes and types of metal-cutting chisels available, a simple cold chisel is essential in any mechanic's workshop. One about 6-inches long with a 1/2-inch wide blade should be adequate. The cutting edge is ground to about 80-degrees , while the rest of the tip is ground to a shallower angle away from the edge. The primary use of the cold chisel is rough metal cutting - this can be anything from sheet metal work to cutting off the heads of seized or rusted bolts or splitting nuts. A cold chisel is also useful for turning out screws or bolts with damaged heads.

All of the tools described in this section should be good quality items. They're not particularly expensive, so it's not really worth trying to save money on them. More significantly, there's a risk that with inferior tools, fragments may break off in use - a potentially dangerous situation.

Even with good-quality tools, the heads and working ends will inevitably get worn or damaged, so it's a good idea to maintain all such tools on a regular basis **(see illustration)**. Using a file or bench grinder, remove all burrs and mushroomed edges from around the head. This is an important task because the build-up of material around the head can fly off when it's struck with a hammer and is potentially dangerous. Make sure the tool retains its original profile at the working end, again, filing or grinding off all burrs. In the case of cold chisels, the cutting edge will usually have to be reground quite often because the material in the tool isn't usually much harder than materials typically being cut. Make sure the edge is reasonably sharp, but don't make the tip angle greater than it was originally; it'll just wear down faster if you do.

The techniques for using these tools vary according to the job to be done and are best learned by experience. The one common denominator is the fact they're all normally struck with a hammer. It follows that eye protection should be worn. Always make sure the working end of the tool is in contact with the part being punched or cut. If it isn't, the tool will bounce off the surface and damage may result.

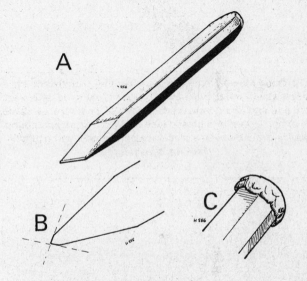

2.76 A typical general purpose cold chisel - note the angle of the cutting edge (A), which should be checked and resharpened on a regular basis; the mushroomed head (B) is dangerous and should be filed to restore it to its original shape

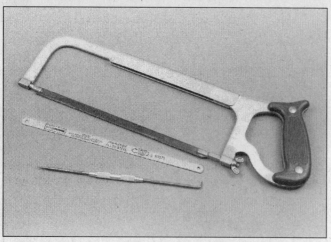

2.77 Hacksaws are handy for small cutting jobs like sheet metal and rusted fasteners

Hacksaws

A hacksaw consists of a handle and frame supporting a flexible steel blade under tension (**see illustration**). Blades are available in various lengths and most hacksaws can be adjusted to accommodate the different sizes. The most common blade length is 10-inches.

Most hacksaw frames are adequate. There's little difference between brands. Pick one that's rigid and allows easy blade changing and repositioning.

The type of blade to use, indicated by the number of teeth per inch, (TPI) , is determined by the material being cut (**see illustration**). The rule of thumb is to make sure at least three teeth are in contact with the metal being cut at any one time. In practice, this means a fine blade for cutting thin sheet materials, while a coarser blade can be used for faster cutting through thicker items such as bolts or bar stock. When cutting thin materials, angle the saw so the blade cuts at a shallow angle. More teeth are in contact and there's less chance of the blade binding and breaking, or teeth breaking (**see illustration**).

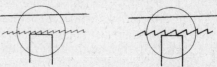

When cutting thin materials, check that at least three teeth are in contact with the workpiece at any time. Too coarse a blade will result in a poor cut and may break the blade. If you do not have the correct blade, cut at a shallow angle to the material

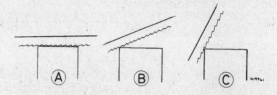

2.79 Correct procedure for use of a hacksaw

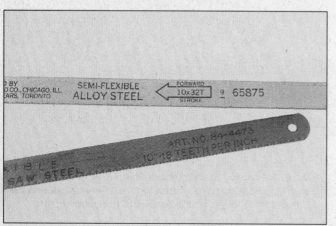

2.78 Hacksaw blades are marked with the number of teeth per inch (TPI - use a relatively course blade for aluminum and thicker items such as bolts or bar stock; use a finer blade for materials like thin sheet steel

When you buy blades, choose a reputable brand. Inferior, unbounded blades may seem perfectly acceptable, but you can't tell by looking at them. Poor quality blades will be insufficiently hardened on the teeth edge and will dull quickly. Most reputable brands will be marked -Flexible High Speed Steel" or a similar term, to indicate the type of material used. It is possible to buy "unbreakable" blades (only the teeth are hardened, leaving the rest of the blade less brittle) (**see illustration**).

Sometimes, a full-size hacksaw is too big to allow access to a frozen nut or bolt. On most saws, you can overcome this problem by turning the blade 90-degrees. Occasionally you may have to position the saw around an obstacle and then install the blade on the other side of it. Where space is really restricted, you may have to use a handle that clamps onto a saw blade at one end. This allows access when a hacksaw frame would not work at all and has another advantage in that you can make use of broken off hacksaw blades instead of throwing them away. Note that because only one end of the blade is supported, and it's not held under tension, it's difficult to control and less efficient when cutting.

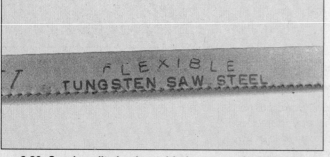

2.80 Good quality hacksaw blades are marked like this

Before using a hacksaw, make sure the blade is suitable for the material being cut and installed correctly in the frame **(see illustration)**. Whatever it is you're cutting must be securely supported so it can't move around. The saw cuts on the forward stroke, so the teeth must point away from the handle. This might seem obvious, but it's easy to install the blade backwards by mistake and ruin the teeth on the first few strokes. Make sure the blade is tensioned adequately or it'll distort and chatter in the cut and may break. Wear safety glasses and be careful not to cut yourself on the saw blade or the sharp edge of the cut.

Files

Files come in a wide variety of sizes and types for specific jobs, but all of them are used for the same basic function of removing small amounts of metal in a controlled fashion **(see illustration)**. Files are used by mechanics mainly for deburring, marking parts, removing rust, filing the heads off rivets, restoring threads and fabricating small parts.

File shapes commonly available include flat, half-round, round, square and triangular. Each shape comes in a range of sizes (lengths) and cuts ranging from rough to smooth. The file face is covered with rows of diagonal ridges which form the cutting teeth. They may be aligned in one direction only (single cut) or in two directions to form a diamond-shaped pattern (double-cut) **(see illustration)**. The spacing of the teeth determines the file coarseness, again, ranging from rough to smooth in five basic grades: Rough, coarse, bastard, second-cut and smooth.

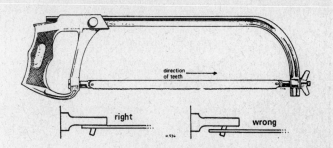

2.81 Correct installation of a hacksaw blade - the teeth must point away from the handle and butt against the locating lugs

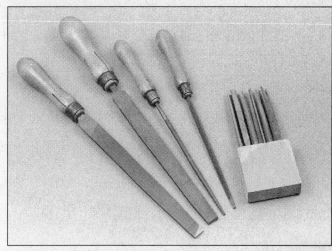

2.82 Get a good assortment of files - they're handy for deburring, marking parts, removing rust, filing the heads off rivets, restoring threads and fabricating small parts

2.83 Files are either single-cut (left) or double-cut (right) - generally speaking, use a single-cut file to produce a very smooth surface; use a double-cut file to remove large amounts of material quickly

You'll want to build up a set of files by purchasing tools of the required shape and cut as they're needed. A good starting point would be flat, half-round, round and triangular files (at least one each - bastard or second-cut types). In addition, you'll have to buy one or more file handles (files are usually sold without handles, which are purchased separately and pushed over the tapered tang of the file when in use). You may need to buy more than one size handle to fit the various files in your tool box, but don't attempt to get by without them. A file tang is fairly sharp and you almost certainly will end up stabbing yourself in the palm of the hand if you use a file without a handle and it catches in the workpiece during use **(see illustration)**. Adjustable handles are

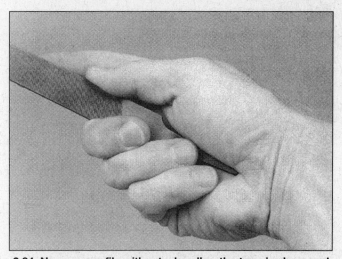

2.84 Never use a file without a handle - the tang is sharp and could puncture your hand

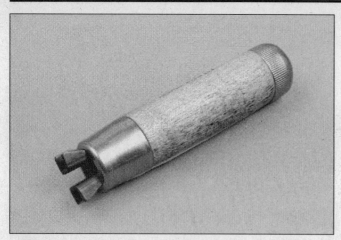

2.85 Adjustable handles that will work with many different size files are also available

also available for use with files of various sizes, eliminating the need for several handles **(see illustration)**.

Exceptions to the need for a handle are fine Swiss pattern files, which have a rounded handle instead of a tang. These small files are usually sold in sets with a number of different shapes. Originally intended for very fine work, they can be very useful for use in inaccessible areas.

The correct procedure for using files is fairly easy to master. As with a hacksaw, the work should be clamped securely in a vise, if needed, to prevent it from moving around while being worked on. Hold the file by the handle, using your free hand at the file end to guide it and keep it flat in relation to the surface being filed. Use smooth cutting strokes and be careful not to rock the file as it passes over the surface. Also, don't slide it diagonally across the surface or the teeth will make grooves in the workpiece. Don't drag a file back across the workpiece at the end of the stroke - lift it slightly and pull it back to prevent damage to the teeth.

Files don't require maintenance in the usual sense, but they should be kept clean and free of metal filings. Steel is a reasonably easy material to work with, but softer metals like aluminum tend to clog the file teeth very quickly, which will result in scratches in the workpiece. This can be avoided by rubbing the file face with chalk before using it. General cleaning is carried out with a file card or a fine wire brush. If kept clean, files will last a long time - when they do eventually dull, they must be replaced; there is no satisfactory way of sharpening a worn file.

Tap and die sets

Taps

Tap and die sets are available in inch and metric sizes. Taps are used to cut internal threads and clean or restore damaged threads. A tap consists of a fluted shank with a drive square at one end. It's threaded along part of its length - the cutting edges are formed where the flutes intersect the threads. Taps are made from hardened steel so they will cut threads in materials softer than what they're made of.

Taps come in three different types: Taper, plug and bottoming **(see illustration)**. The only real difference is the length of the chamfer on the cutting end of the tap. Taper taps are chamfered for the first 6 or 8 threads, which makes them easy to start but prevents them from cutting threads close to the bottom of a hole. Plug taps are chamfered up about 3 to 5 threads, which makes them a good all around tap because they're relatively easy to start and will cut nearly to the bottom of a hole. Bottoming taps, as the name implies, have a very short chamfer (1-1/2 to 3 threads) and will cut as close to the bottom of a blind hole as practical. However, to do this, the threads should be started with a plug or taper tap.

Taps are normally used by hand (they can be used in machine tools, but not when doing engine repairs). The square drive end of the tap is held in a tap wrench (an adjustable T-handle) **(see illustration)**. For smaller sizes, a T-handled chuck can be used. The tapping process starts by drilling a hole of the correct diameter. For each tap size, there's a corresponding twist drill that will produce a hole of the correct size **(see illustration)**. Note how the tapered section progressively decreases across the ridge. Plug taps are normally needed for finishing tapped holes in blind bores.

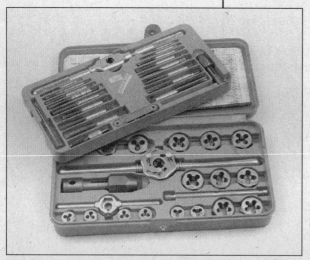

2.86 Tap and dies sets are available in inch and metric sizes - taps are used for cutting internal threads and cleaning and restoring damaged threads; dies are used for cutting, cleaning and restoring external threads

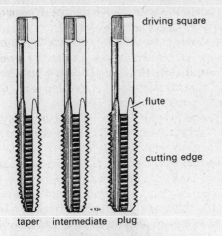

2.87 Taper, plug and bottoming taps (left-to-right)

driving square

flute

cutting edge

taper   intermediate   plug

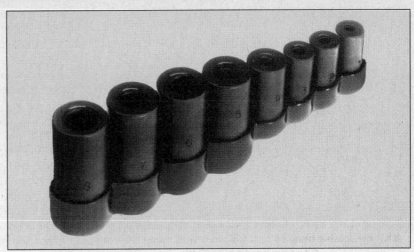

2.88 This tap socket set from Lisle allows the tap to be driven by a ratchet handle

This is important; too large a hole will leave the finished thread with the tops missing, producing a weak and unreliable grip. Conversely, too small a hole will place excessive loads on the hard and brittle shank of the tap, which can break it off in the hole. Removing a broken off tap from a hole is no fun! The correct tap drill size is normally marked on the tap itself or the container it comes in .

Dies

Dies are used to cut, clean or restore external threads **(see illustrations)**. Most dies are made from a hex-shaped or cylindrical piece of hardened steel with a threaded hole in the center. The threaded hole is overlapped by three or four cutouts, which equate to the flutes on taps and allow metal waste to escape during the threading process. Dies are held in a T-handled holder (called a die stock) . Some dies are split at one point, allowing them to be adjusted slightly (opened and closed) for fine control of thread clearances.

Dies aren't needed as often as taps, for the simple reason it's normally easier to install a new bolt than to salvage one. However, it's often helpful to be able to extend the threads of a bolt or clean up damaged threads with a die. Hex-shaped dies are particularly useful for mechanic's work, since they can be turned with a wrench and are usually less expensive than adjustable ones **(see illustration)**.

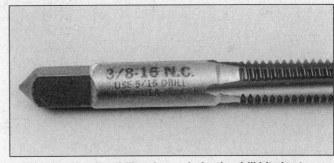

2.89 If you need to drill and tap a hole, the drill bit size to use for a given bolt (tap) size is marked on the tap

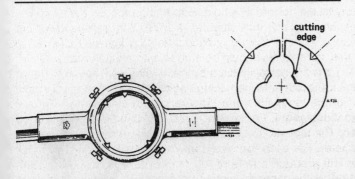

cutting edge

2.90 A die (right) is used for cutting external threads (this one is a split-type/adjustable die) and is held in a tool called a die stock (left)

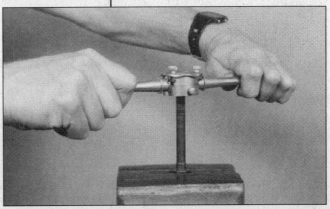

2.91 A die is very useful in cleaning sealant and corrosion from head bolts prior to installation

2.92 Hex-shaped dies are especially handy for mechanic's work because they can be turned with a wrench

The procedure for cutting threads with a die is broadly similar to that described above for taps. When using an adjustable die, the initial cut is made with the die fully opened, the adjustment screw being used to reduce the diameter of successive cuts until the finished size is reached. As with taps, a cutting lubricant should be used, and the die must be backed off every few turns to clear swarf from the cutouts.

Pullers

You'll need at least one general-purpose puller for most automotive repair jobs or engine repair work. Pullers can removed seized or corroded parts, bad bushings or bearings, steering wheels and harmonic balancers **(see illustrations)**. Universal two- and three-legged pullers are widely available in numerous designs and sizes **(see illustrations)**.

The typical puller consists of a central boss with two or three pivoting arms attached. The outer ends of the arms are hooked jaws which grab the part you want to pull off **(see illustrations)**. You can reverse the arms on most pullers to use the puller on internal openings when necessary. The central boss is threaded to accept a puller bolt, which does the work. You can also get hydraulic versions of these tools which are capable of more pressure, but they're expensive.

You can adapt pullers by purchasing, or fabricating, special jaws for specific jobs. If you decide to make your own jaws, keep in mind that the pulling force should be concentrated as close to the center of the component as possible to avoid damaging it.

Before you use a puller, assemble it and check it to make sure it doesn't snag on anything and the loads on the part to be removed are distributed evenly. If you're dealing with a part held on the shaft by a nut, loosen the nut but don't remove it. Leaving the nut on helps prevent distortion of the shaft end under pressure from the puller bolt and stops the part from flying off the shaft when it comes loose.

Tighten a puller gradually until the assembly is under moderate pressure, then try to jar the

2.93 Lisle harmonic balancer puller is designed to ease the operation of pulling the balancer

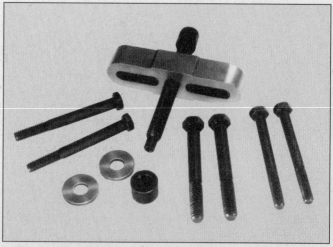

2.95 Lisle steering wheel puller is universal and fits most makes and models

2.94 The balancer puller must bolt directly to the balancer hub, a jaw type puller will damage the outer ring of the balancer

2.96 The puller must bolt to the steering wheel hub; pulling from anywhere else will damage the steering wheel

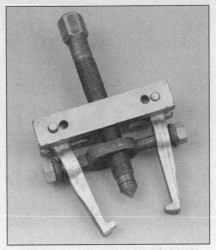

2.97 A two or three-jaw puller will come in handy for many tasks in the shop and can also be used for working on other types of equipment

2.98 The Posi Lock line of quality gear and bearing pullers are quick, convenient and easy to use. The cage design provides superior locking power. The T-handle and cage control the jaws at all times, meaning that opening, closing, locking and aligning the jaws is all done automatically by simply turning the T-handle.

component loose by striking the puller bolt a few times with a hammer. If this doesn't work, tighten the bolt a little further and repeat the process. If this approach doesn't work, stop and reconsider. At some point you must make a decision whether to continue applying pressure in this manner. Sometimes, you can apply penetrating oil around the joint and leave it overnight, with the puller in place and tightened securely. By the next day, the taper has separated and the problem has resolved itself.

If nothing else works, try heating the area surrounding the troublesome part with a propane or gas welding torch (We don't, however, recommend using welding equipment if you're not already experienced in its use). Apply the heat to the hub area of the component you wish to remove. Keep the flame moving to avoid uneven heating and the risk of distortion. Keep pressure applied with the puller and make sure that you're able to deal with the resulting hot component and the puller jaws if it does come free. Be very careful to keep the flame away from aluminum parts.

If all reasonable attempts to remove a part fail, don't be afraid to give up. It's smarter to quit while your ahead than to repair a badly damaged engine or component. Either buy, rent or borrow the correct tool, or take the engine to a professional and ask him to remove the part for you.

2.99 A two jaw puller works well for pulling the hub from a front wheel drive axle . . .

2.100 . . . or for separating a tie-rod end from the steering knuckle

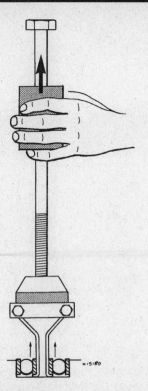

2.101 Details of how an internal slide hammer puller can be used for removing bearings and bushings from blind holes

Internal slide hammer pullers

Bushings or bearings installed in "blind holes" often require special pullers **(see illustrations)**. Some bearings can be removed without a puller if you can heat the component evenly in an oven and tap it face down on a clean wooden surface to dislodge the bearing. Wear heavy gloves to protect yourself when handling the heated components. If you need a puller to do the job, use a slide-hammer with interchangeable tips. Slide hammers range from universal two or three-jaw puller arrangements to special bearing pullers. Bearing pullers are hardened steel tubes with a flange around the bottom edge. The tube is split at several places, which allows a wedge to expand the tool once it's in place. The tool fits inside the bearing inner race and is tightened so the flange or lip is locked under the edge of the race. The slide-hammer consists of a steel shaft with a stop at its upper end. The shaft carries a sliding weight which slides along the shaft until it strikes the stop. This allows the tool holding the bearing to drive it out of the bore.

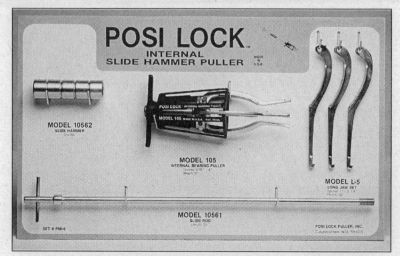

2.102 Ideal for many internal pulling jobs such as crankshaft pilot bearings, bearing cups, needle bearings, bushings, seals and grease retainers, the Posi Lock internal slide hammer puller set includes the tool board and accessories

Tightening sequences and procedures

Most threaded fasteners should be tightened to a specific torque value **(see charts below)**. Torque is the twisting force applied to a threaded component such as a nut or bolt. Over tightening the fastener can weaken it and cause it to break, while under tightening can cause it to eventually come loose. Bolts, screws and studs, depending on the material they are made of and their thread diameters, have specific torque values. Be sure to follow the manufacturer's torque recommendations closely. For fasteners not assigned a specific torque, a general torque value chart is presented here as a guide. These torque values are for dry (unlubricated) fasteners threaded into steel or cast iron (not aluminum). As was previously mentioned, the size and grade of a fastener determine the amount of torque that can safely be applied to it. The figures listed here are approximate for Grade 2 and Grade 3 fasteners. Higher grades can tolerate higher torque values.

If fasteners are laid out in a pattern – such as cylinder head bolts, oil pan bolts, differential cover bolts, etc. – loosen and tighten them in sequence to avoid warping the component. Where it matters, we'll show you this sequence. If a specific pattern isn't that important, the following rule–of thumb guide will prevent warping.

Metric thread sizes	Ft-lbs	Nm
M-6	6 to 9	9 to 12
M-8	14 to 21	19 to 28
M-10	28 to 40	38 to 54
M-12	50 to 71	68 to 96
M-14	80 to 140	109 to 154

Pipe thread sizes		
1/8	5 to 8	7 to 10
1/4	12 to 18	17 to 24
3/8	22 to 33	30 to 44
1/2	25 to 35	34 to 47

U.S. thread sizes		
1/4 – 20	6 to 9	9 to 12
5/16 – 18	12 to 18	17 to 24
5/16 – 24	14 to 20	19 to 27
3/8 – 16	22 to 32	30 to 43
3/8 – 24	27 to 38	37 to 51
7/16 – 14	40 to 55	55 to 74
7/16 – 20	40 to 60	55 to 81
1/2 – 13	55 to 80	75 to 108

First, install the bolts or nuts finger–tight. Then tighten them one full turn each, in a criss-cross or diagonal pattern. Then return to the first one and, following the same pattern, tighten them all one–half turn. Finally, tighten each of them one–quarter turn at a time until each fastener has been tightened to the proper torque. To loosen and remove the fasteners, reverse this procedure.

2 How to remove broken fasteners

Sooner or later, you're going to break off a bolt inside its threaded hole. There are several ways to remove it, but before you drill it and use an extractor set, try some of the following methods first (see illustration).

First, regardless of which of the following methods you use, be sure to use penetrating oil. Penetrating oil is a special light oil with excellent penetrating power for freeing dirty and rusty fasteners. But it also works well on tightly torqued broken fasteners.

If enough of the fastener protrudes from its hole and if it isn't torqued down too tightly – you can often remove it with locking pliers or a small pipe wrench. If that doesn't work, or if the fastener doesn't provide sufficient purchase for pliers or a wrench, try filing it down to take a wrench, or cut a

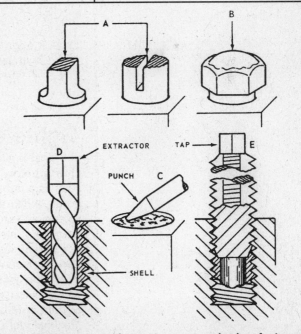

2.103 There are several ways to remove a broken fastener

A   File it flat or slot it
B   Weld on a nut
C   Use a punch to unscrew it
D   Use a screw extractor
E   Use a tap to remove the shell

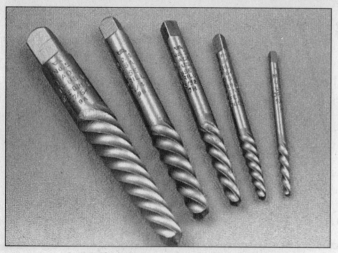

2.104 Typical assortment of extractors

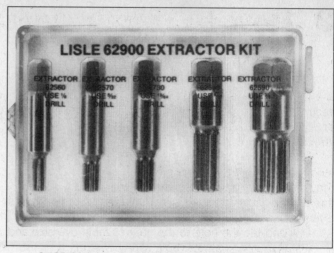

2.105 Lisle's extractor kit works on both right and left hand threads

slot in it to accept a screwdriver. If you still can't get it off – and you know how to weld and have access to a welder – try welding a flat piece of steel, or a nut, to the top of the broken fastener. If the fastener is broken off flush with, or below, the top of its hole, try tapping it out with a small, sharp punch. If that doesn't work, try drilling out the broken fastener with a bit only slightly smaller than the inside diameter of the hole. For example, if the hole is 1/2–inch in diameter, use a 15/32–inch drill bit. This leaves a shell which you can pick out with a sharp chisel.

If THAT doesn't work, you'll have to resort to some form of screw extractor **(see illustrations)**. Screw extractors are sold in sets which can remove anything from 1/4–inch to 1–inch bolts or studs. Most extractors are fluted and tapered high-grade steel. To use a screw extractor, drill a hole slightly smaller than the O.D. of the extractor you're going to use (Extractor sets include the manufacturer's recommendations for what size drill bit to use with each extractor size). Then screw in the extractor and back it – and the broken fastener – out **(see illustration)**. Extractors are reverse–threaded, so they won't unscrew when you back them out.

A word to the wise: Even though an extractor will usually save your bacon, it can cause even more grief if you're careless or sloppy. Drilling the hole for the extractor off–center, or using too small, or too big, a bit for the size of the fastener you're removing will only make things worse. So be careful!

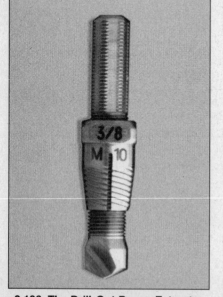

2.106 The Drill-Out Power Extractor from Alden combines a left hand drill bit and the extractor all-in-one tool, making broken bolt removal an easy time saving operation

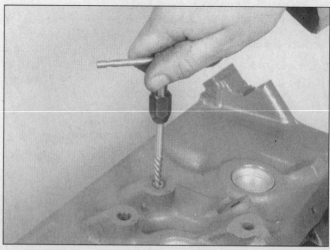

2.107 When screwing in the extractor, make sure it's centered properly

3 How to repair damaged threads

Sometimes, the internal threads of a nut or bolt hole can become stripped, usually from over tightening. Stripping threads is an all too common occurrence, especially when working with aluminum parts because aluminum is so soft that it easily strips out. Over tightened spark plugs are another common cause of stripped threads.

Usually, external or internal threads are only partially stripped. After they've been cleaned up with a tap or die, they'll still work **(see illustration)**. Sometimes, however, threads are badly damaged. When this happens, you've got three choices:

1 Drill and tap the hole to the next suitable oversize and install a larger diameter bolt, screw or stud.
2 Drill and tap the hole to accept a threaded plug, then drill and tap the plug to the original screw size. You can also buy a plug already threaded to the original size. Then you simply drill a hole to the specified size, then run the threaded plug into the hole with a bolt and jam nut. Once the plug is fully seated, remove the jam nut and bolt.
3 The third method uses a patented thread repair kit like Heli-Coil **(see illustration)**. These easy–to–use kits are designed to repair damaged threads in spark plug holes, straight–through holes and blind holes. Both are available as kits which can handle a variety of sizes and thread patterns. Drill the hole, then tap it with the special included tap. Install the Heli–Coil and the hole is back to its original diameter and thread pitch.

Regardless of which method you use, be sure to proceed calmly and carefully. A little impatience or carelessness during one of these relatively simple procedures can ruin your whole day's work and cost you a bundle if you wreck an expensive head or block.

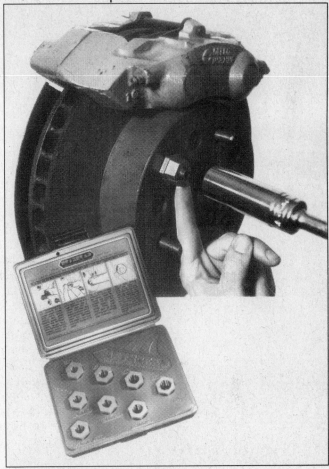

2.108 ESCO makes a wheel stud repair kit that allows you to repair damaged threads on any wheel stud

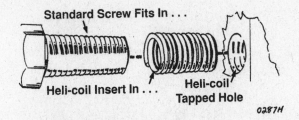

2.109 To install a Heli-Coil, drill out the hole, tap it with the special included tap and screw in the Heli-Coil

Notes

3 Special tools

Many tools the home mechanic will use to repair or maintain the family automobile are designed with one function in mind. Different from a socket set or end wrench set, which are considered the basic hand tools, special tools are used to perform a specific job. Sometimes the tool is designed for one particular function on only one make and model of automobile; if that is the case, it is considered truly a "special tool."

More often than not, though, the unique tools that fall into this category can be used on many different makes or models, although they still perform only one function or job. As an example; many tool companies manufacture a universal shock absorber removal tool, a universal clutch alignment tool, a seal remover tool, a bearing driver set, and so on. They perform one job but they can be used on many different types of vehicles. On the other hand, you may find that to complete a repair on your vehicle you'll need a tool that is specific to your vehicle which cannot be used successfully on any other make or model. Usually, your only choice is to find and purchase the tool.

With the introduction of every new model, the automobile manufacturers design special tools to enable the dealership technicians to repair their vehicles. Occasionally, the only option for obtaining a specific tool you may need is to contact a dealer and try to purchase the "factory tool." Fortunately, there are several tool companies that provide an extensive line of excellent special purpose tools. Many times their tools will perform the job at hand as well as or better than the "factory tool."

It's not possible, here, to list all the special purpose tools manufactured for all the makes and models of automobiles and trucks on the road today. What you will need in your tool box is an assortment of the special tools necessary to maintain your vehicle at a safe and efficient level. Your personal assortment of special tools will depend on your individual skill level, the type of work you perform most often and the type of vehicle(s) you will be working on.

1 General repair tools

There are many tools in this category you'll never know your going to need until the car breaks down and your faced with a repair you've never done before or you don't have the tool(s) for. Let's say your power steering pump is leaking fluid. Removing the pump from the engine is no problem. You have all the necessary sockets and wrenches, but, lo-and-behold, before you can get to the bolts you have to remove the pulley, and that requires a special puller **(see illustration)**! Now your only choice is to: a) take the vehicle to a professional repair shop and pay the big money, or, b) buy the tool and repair it yourself (check with your neighbor first, maybe he has the tool and you can borrow it). Buying the tool is the least expensive of the options in that example, and you'll have the tool if it's needed again.

Depending on your skill level and your frequency of tinkering, there are other special tools you'll use more often. If you do a lot of engine work, you'll need many of the special engine rebuilding tools shown in Chapter 7. For general repair work you could probably use a seal remover and a seal driver **(see illustrations)** which can be used on any type of engine or transmission . If you drive cars with manual transmissions, the need for a clutch alignment tool will be inevitable **(see illustrations)**.

3.1 A special puller is needed to remove the power steering pump pulley on many vehicles

3.2 A seal removal tool makes prying seals out of engines and transmissions easier

3.3 Seal drivers are needed to drive a seal squarely into its bore

3.4 A clutch alignment tool set is used to properly align the clutch disc when installing the clutch assembly onto an engine

3.5 Several different sized inserts are provided in the clutch alignment tool set, which allow the alignment tool to be used on a variety of vehicles

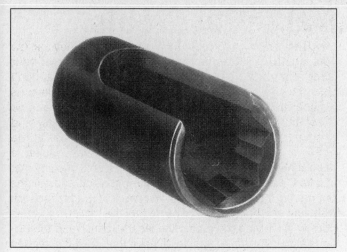

3.6 Special sockets are often needed to remove vacuum switches, the slot in the socket allows the socket to reach the hex nut without damaging the plastic nipples (Lisle tool shown)

3.7 Oil pressure sending units often require special sockets to remove them from the engine (Lisle tool shown)

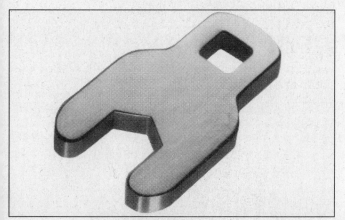

3.8 Here is another oil pressure sending unit wrench, this one grips the small hex under the transducer-type sending unit (Lisle tool shown)

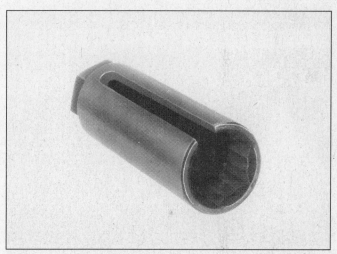

3.9 An oxygen sensor socket has a slot for the electrical lead to pass through (Lisle tool shown)

Many times, especially on newer automobiles, it's next to impossible to reach an engine sensor with normal hand tools. Therefore, there's a multitude of special wrenches and sockets available that make removing vacuum switches, oil pressure senders and emission control sensors possible without damaging the sensitive electrical units **(see illustrations)**. Modern fuel-injected vehicles are often equipped with spring-lock couplings on fuel lines. If it becomes necessary to remove a fuel line from the fuel rail, or in some cases just to replace the fuel filter, you will need the special spring-lock coupling removal tool that fits your specific fuel-injection system **(see illustration)**. Don't even think about removing these special couplings without the proper tools. An attempt to do so could cause serious damage to the fuel line and create, of course, an un-needed expense.

You will need at least two sets of snap-ring pliers. I know, I've already stated in Chapter 2 that pliers are basic hand tools, but these pliers are special. They serve one function, and that is to remove snap-rings. Actually, one of the sets are lock-ring pliers **(see illustration)**. Large, stiff

3.10 Modern fuel injected vehicles are often equipped with spring-lock couplings on the fuel lines - special disconnect tools are absolutely necessary to disconnect the lines without damaging them, spring-lock couplings are also found on air-conditioning lines (Lisle tool shown)

3.11 Lock-rings are usually used to retain a component on a splined shaft, lock-ring pliers are used to spread the lock-ring

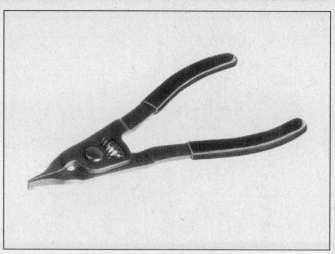

3.12 Lisle lock-ring pliers

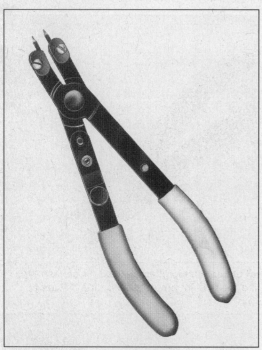

3.13 This set of snap-ring pliers is reversible and can be used on either internal or external snap-rings (Lisle tool shown)

lock-rings are used to hold a component on a splined shaft, and these pliers with their outer gripping jaws are used to expand the ring **(see illustration)**. You may also encounter either internal or external snap-rings and one set of reversible snap-ring pliers is all that's necessary for both **(see illustration)**.

With the advent of front-wheel drive automobiles a whole new tool category has been created. If you need to replace a damaged C-V joint boot (which is a very common repair), first you'll need special removing tools to remove the hub and driveaxle **(see illustration)**. Then a boot remover and installing tool is used **(see illustration)**, and finally a set of C-V joint boot clamp pliers (of which there are several types) or a banding tool is necessary to complete the job **(see illustrations)**.

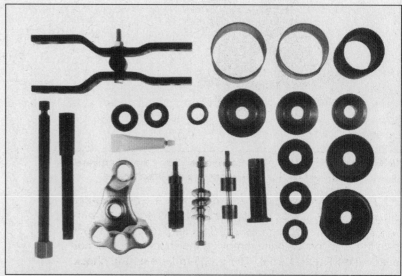

3.14 Several special tools are needed to service the driveaxle on a front wheel drive vehicle - this Lisle tool set is used to pull the hub and bearing assembly from the splined driveaxle on GM vehicles and removes the hub from the bearing and the bearing from the steering knuckle on most domestic made Ford and Chryslers - the tool is also used for reassembly of the components

3.15 This Lisle C-V joint boot driver removes and installs boots on GM vehicles with the stamped retainer rings - it's fast and doesn't damage the boots

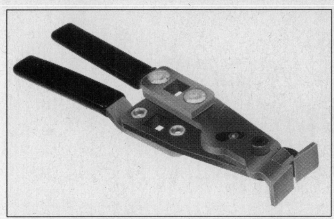

3.16 The manufacturers have used several different types of C-V joint boot clamps - this set of Lisle C-V boot clamp pliers can be used on all ear-type clamps and is designed for use with a torque wrench which is required for stainless steel clamps

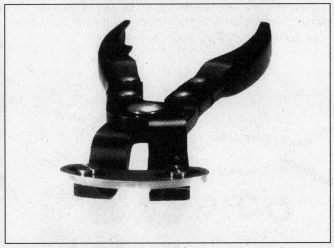

3.18 Offset boot clamp pliers crimps ear-type clamps and are a special set designed to work in a confined space

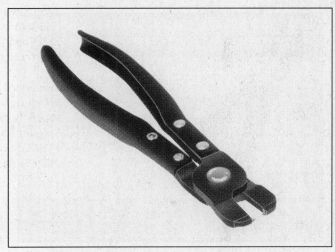

3.17 This set of boot clamp pliers is used on earless-type clamps like the type found on GM inboard C-V joints

Replacing worn shock absorbers is not a cut-and-dry situation either, especially if your vehicle is equipped with MacPherson strut suspension. Special sockets and tool sets are available to make removing the shock absorber nut easier **(see illustrations)**. The problem here is, the shock absorber shaft wants to turn along with the nut, so a method of holding the shaft and turning the nut is needed, and that's exactly what the tool does for you. Now that you've got the strut assembly off the car another special tool is necessary to complete the job. A MacPherson strut spring compressor is needed to separate the spring from

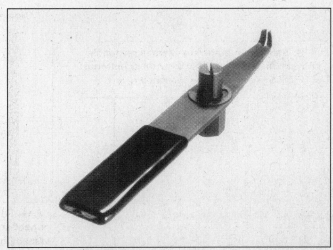

3.19 A CV-joint banding tool is needed for use on all "Band-it" type boot bands - it uses a 5/8-inch socket or wrench to wind and crimp the new band on the boot

3.20 Removing shock absorbers is much easier when you use a special tool such as this Lisle universal shock nut set - use either one of the two different size stem sockets inside the double-ended shock-nut socket to remove the shock nut

3.21 This Lisle universal strut nut remover makes disassembly and assembly of a MacPherson strut easier - the double ended drivers remove the top nut on most all strut applications and work especially well on nuts that are recessed

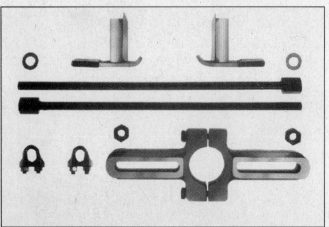

3.22 A MacPherson strut spring compressor is needed to disassemble and assemble the strut - this Lisle compressor is universal and safely handles all strut springs

the shock absorber **(see illustration)**. Because of the high spring pressures required and the possibility of injury involved, this is one area that we recommend professional help if you do not have the experience to safely complete the job.

If you are one of the many who drive and maintain a four-wheel drive truck, you'll need a front wheel bearing lock-nut removal tool **(see illustrations)**. Cleaning the sand, mud or snow from the front hubs and bearings regularly is one of the most important maintenance items on four wheel drive vehicles, and don't forget the spindle bearings **(see illustration)**. They need cleaning too!

3.23 Four wheel drive wheel bearing lock-nut tools are used to remove the front wheel bearing lock-nuts on most domestic four wheel drive vehicles (Lisle tool shown)

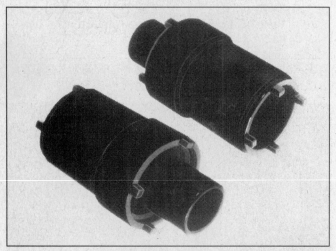

3.24 Late model Ford four wheel drive trucks use ratcheting lock-nuts which require this ratcheting lock-nut tool (Lisle tool shown)

3.25 This four wheel drive spindle puller is necessary to remove the front spindle to access the spindle bearings, it fits all common vehicles (cut-away to show the stepped design)

If you're restoring a classic auto and need to replace all of the hydraulic lines, or if you are just repairing a damaged fuel line in the family car, you'll need several tubing fabrication tools **(see illustrations)**. A tubing cutter is a must - it will be used to cut out damaged tubing or to cut a new section to the proper length. A tubing cutter is absolutely necessary to cut tubing that is to be flared. Don't use a hack saw to cut tubing; you can't make a straight cut and you'll get metal particles from cutting into the tubing. The tubing bender is necessary to form tubing into tight bends without kinking the tubing. Next on the list is a tubing flaring kit **(see illustration)**. Included will be all the necessary adapters to form perfect double-flared fittings. Remember, the lives of you and your loved-ones may be riding on the quality of your flared fittings, whether they are brake or fuel line fittings. Don't cut corners here, follow the tool manufacturers instructions explicitly and form and flare good quality lines.

Now, lets go inside the car. Do you have a GM car or truck? Lets say that you need to replace the turn-signal switch. It should be no problem, right? We have a steering wheel puller, just jerk the steering wheel off and dive in! Wrong! Under the steering wheel is a lock-plate, retained by a locking ring, and a lock-plate depressing tool is needed to push to lock-plate down so you can get the lock-ring off **(see illustrations)**.

3.26 A tubing cutter is used to make a clean straight cut on fuel lines, brake lines, etc. (KD tool shown)

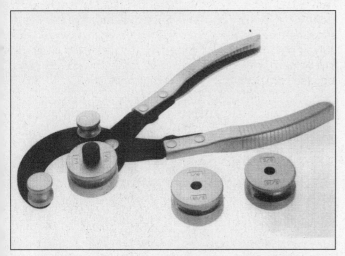

3.27 Tubing benders are used to custom form tubing and are necessary to form kink-free bends (KD tool shown)

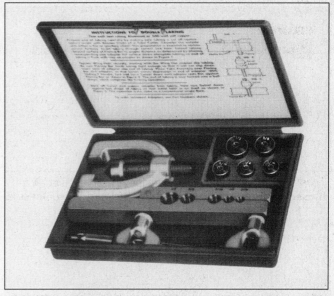

3.28 KD's tubing flaring tool kit comes with everything you'll need to make perfect double-flared fittings

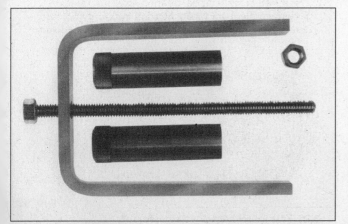

3.29 A steering wheel lock plate tool is needed to remove the lock-plate from a GM steering column

3.30 The lock plate tool depresses, and holds, the lock-plate so you can remove the retaining ring

Automotive Tools Manual

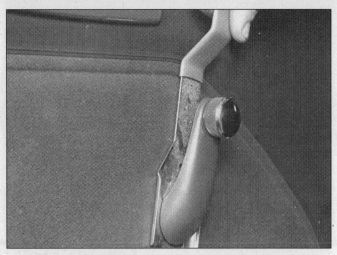

3.31 A special tool is needed to remove the door glass regulator handle on many automobiles

Have you ever looked at a window regulator handle lately. Guess what? There are no screws holding most of them on. Then how do you get them off when its time to remove a door panel? With a special tool? That's correct, a little clip holds the handle on the shaft of the regulator and a special tool is needed to remove it **(see illustrations)**. You'll also need a special door trim panel clip removal tool if you want to remove the door panel without damaging it **(see illustration)**. How about those screws along the base of the windshield? You can't get a screwdriver in there, not even a stubby screwdriver, the shaft is too long! Do you have to remove the windshield to get the dash pad or defroster grille off? No! You can use a little right angle screwdriver to remove the screws from tight areas with limited access **(see illustration)**.

Sometimes the tools that you use most are the simplest

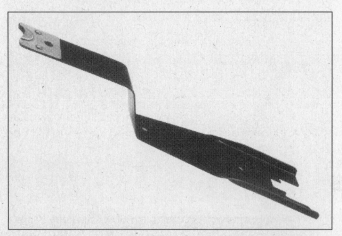

3.32 Lisle's tool has the removing tool on one end and the opposite end holds the clip firmly for easy installation

3.33 The Motormite window crank removal tool comes with extra clips and gaskets

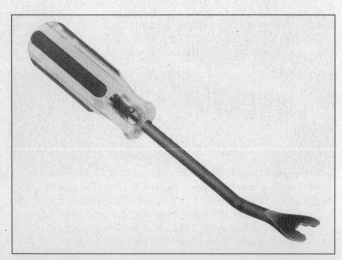

3.34 Special tools are also needed to remove the door panel from the door without damaging the panel - place the tool under the edge of the door panel, insert the fastener into the tool and pry up

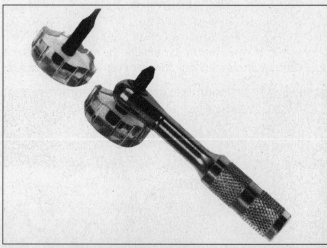

3.35 Lisle's little right angle ratcheting screwdriver is great for getting into tight places

and least expensive tools that you own. The three following tools fall into that category. No tool set is complete without a magnetic pick-up tool and a telescoping inspection mirror **(see illustrations)**. Both of these tools really come in handy when you need to fish a small part out of a crevice or have a look at the underside of a blind area. The magnet saves wear and tear on your back, too, when you use it to reach under the vehicle to retrieve a dropped bolt or tool. The little dental-pick or scribe tool is also a very useful tool also **(see illustration)**. You'll be surprised how often you use this little tool to remove a small retainer, or to scribe a part or component.

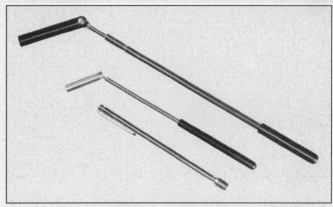

3.36 No tool box should be without a magnetic pick-up tool . . .

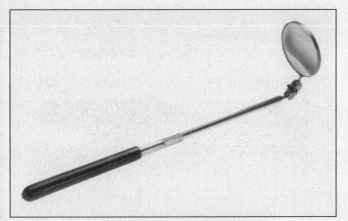

3.37 . . . and a telescoping mirror

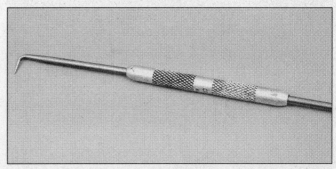

3.38 A little pick\scribe is one of the most useful tools in the tool box

2 Brake service tools

Brake service is one area where many special tools are needed. One of the "cleanest" brake tools available is the Mini-Brake Washer **(see illustration)**. We all know how important it is not to allow ourselves to breathe brake dust. For someone who does a lot of brake work, this little washer could be a very valuable investment.

The first thing you want to do after removing the wheels is check the condition of your rotors and drums. Check the disc thickness **(see illustration)** and drum inside diameter with a micrometer made especially for measuring brake discs and drums and check the rotor run-out with a dial in-

3.39 The Clayton mini-brake washer is great for washing the brake dust out of the drum - by saturating the brakes with the cleaning solution before removing the drum it totally eliminates airborne dust, the cleaning solution is biodegradable so there's no disposal problems

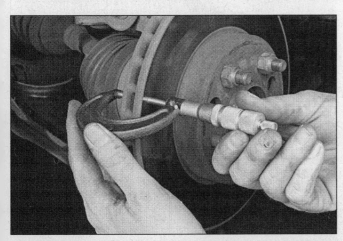

3.40 Before removing the disc during a brake job, first measure the disc thickness with a caliper . . .

3.41 . . . and then check for runout with a dial indicator (see Chapter 7 for more on precision measuring equipment)

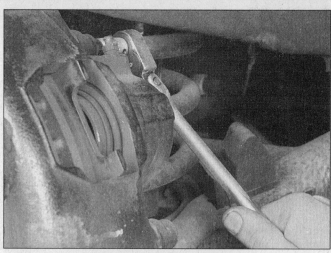

3.42 Most disc brakes use caliper hold-down bolts to attach the caliper and most caliper hold-down bolts have either hex or Torx heads

3.43 Lisle makes a complete set of brake caliper socket/bits that fit most common caliper hold-down bolts

dicator (see illustration) (see Chapter 7 for more information on precision measuring equipment).

Many vehicles require a special bit or socket to remove the brake caliper and special tools are available to press the caliper piston into the bore (see illustrations). Brake drum springs require special removal and installing tools (see illustrations). There are several different types and styles available (see illustrations). Some combine several functions into one tool, and others are made specifically for one type of spring. Most home mechanics will need at least two types; one for use on brake shoe hold-down springs and another for the return springs.

3.44 A disc brake pad spreader can be used to push the caliper piston into the caliper bore

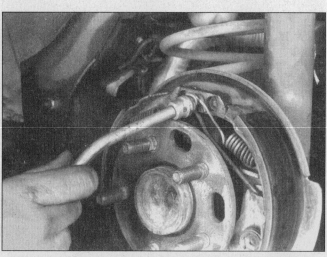

3.45 Drum brakes require special tools to remove the brake springs - a special tool is needed to remove and install the return spring . . .

3.46 . . . and another tool is needed to remove and install the brake shoe hold-down springs

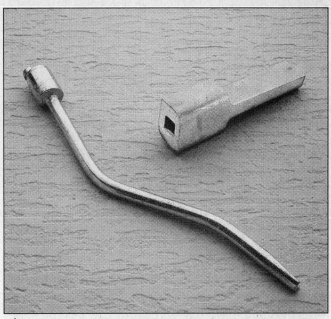

3.47 Here is a Motormite brake shoe spring tool and a disc brake spreader

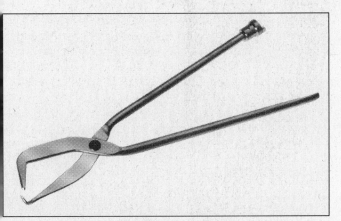

3.48 Lisle's brake spring pliers are double ended so they can remove and install return springs and also install adjuster springs

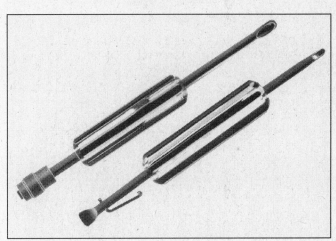

3.49 These two double ended brake spring tools are designed to remove and install brake return springs in special applications

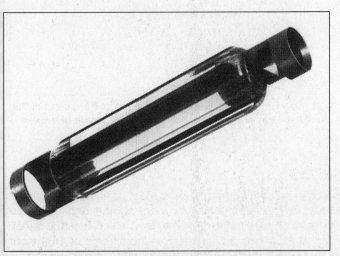

3.50 This double ended brake spring washer tool fits both large and small brake shoe retaining spring washers

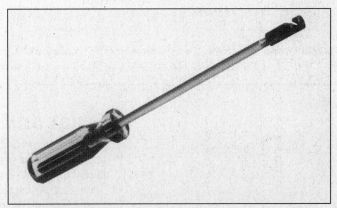

3.51 This Lisle tool is designed to remove and install the small brake return springs found on many import cars

Automotive Tools Manual

3.52 Use a seal driver to seat the boot in the caliper housing bore

If an overhaul of the hydraulic system is in order, several special tools may be needed. There are special caliper seal drivers available for installing the dust boot **(see illustration)**. Many newer model automobiles use a type of lock-ring to retain the rear brake cylinder. Using the retainer remover made especially for its removal makes the job much easier **(see illustration)**. Once the cylinder is disassembled, use a brake hone to renew the bore **(see illustration)**.

There are several new brake bleeding kits on the market today. Most attempt to make brake bleeding a one-man operation, and do a very good job of it. One type uses a hand-held vacuum pump to draw the fluid into a reservoir when the bleeder screw is opened **(see illustration)**. Another type relies on a check valve to keep the air from returning to the system when the operator presses and releases the brake pedal **(see illustration)**. Yet another uses gravity to create a flow of fluid (and air) into a catch container **(see illustration)**.

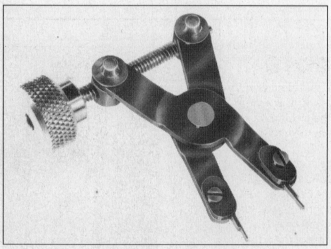

3.53 A special brake cylinder retainer remover is needed to remove the brake cylinders on some GM cars

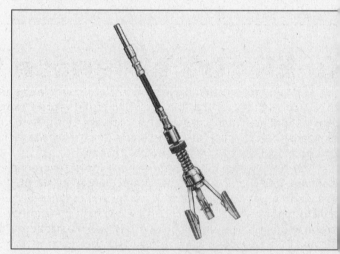

3.54 If you plan to overhaul the brake cylinders you will need a brake cylinder hone

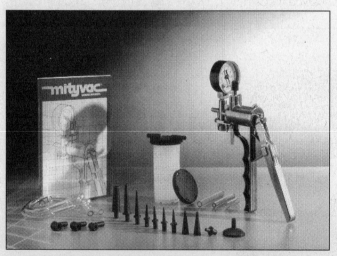

3.55 The Mityvac automotive kit is complete with the necessary attachments for bleeding brakes

3.56 Attach the vacuum pump to the bleeder screw, open the bleeder and using the vacuum pump remove the air from the system

3.57 Lisle's one-man brake bleeder uses a system of check valves to keep air from entering back into the system when you release the brake pedal

3.58 This one-man bleeder simply uses gravity to bleed the system

3 Electrical service tools

The automotive electrical system is a very complex system, making it prone to malfunction. It is vital to the operation of the vehicle, therefore, that even the slightest problem be addressed immediately. If one is to repair the electrical system satisfactorily, there are a few basic electrical service tools that the home mechanic should not be without **(see illustration)**.

The "test light", or automotive circuit tester, is probably the most common electrical tool found in most tool boxes **(see illustration)**. It's used to check for voltage in a circuit while power is connected to the circuit. Test lights are available in several styles, all having three common components; a light bulb, a test probe and a wire lead with a ground clip **(see illustrations)**. On some models, 6, 12, and 24-volt systems may be tested by changing the bulb to one of the appropriate voltage. Although accurate voltage measurements aren't possible with a test light, large differences may be detected by the relative brightness of the glowing bulb. A quick check for available power to a component can be made by

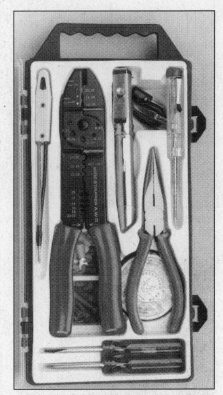

3.59 Everything you need for minor automotive electrical repairs is included in this electrical kit from Thorsen Tools

3.60 A circuit tester is used to probe a circuit, checking for power, ground or continuity

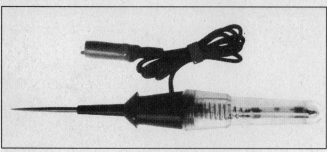

3.61 The basic circuit tester consists of a probe, a ground lead and clip, and a bulb in the handle

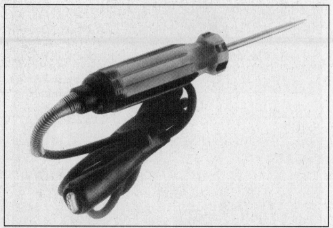

3.62 Lisle's heavy duty circuit testers handle, cord and clamp are reinforced for extra durability

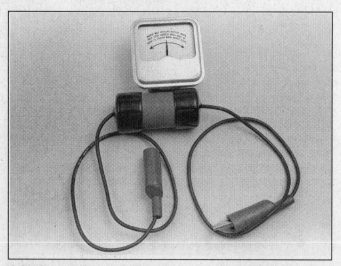

3.64 A great little tool kit for finding shorts is KD Tools "short detector" - consisting of a pulse unit and an electromagnetic meter

connecting the clip to the ground side of the circuit, and probing the power source with the tip. If power in the circuit is present, the bulb contained in handle will glow. One important point to remember; before using the test light for diagnosis, verify that the circuit through the test light is complete by touching the probe to a known good power source such as the battery or fuse box.

Another type of circuit tester is the self-powered test light or continuity tester (see illustration). It is physically similar to an ordinary test light with one exception: it has a self-contained battery in the handle. Self-powered test lights are very useful in checking for open or short circuits. Since they contain their own power source, the circuit in question can be isolated and probed. They can only be used on a circuit that has no power applied to it; vehicle battery power will burn out the low voltage tester bulb. Never use a self-powered continuity tester on a circuit that contains solid-state components because damage to these components may occur.

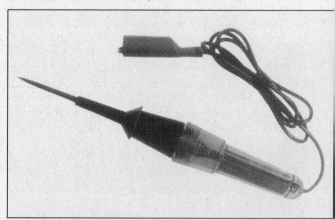

3.63 A continuity tester is very similar to a circuit tester, except it has a battery in the handle, It's great for checking continuity on circuits, fuses and switches - it is not to be used on live circuits or computer sensor feed circuits

Faced with having to find a short circuit is one of the most dreaded situations in automotive electrical repair. Most of the vehicles wiring is hidden in the body or underneath the dash and tying to find the exact point of a short is sometimes very difficult. The electrical overload caused by the short usually causes a fuse to blow repeatedly, and if this is the case, there's an ingenious little device available that just may save the day. The short circuit detector, or "short finder," is an electromagnetic device designed to trace short circuits quickly and easily (see illustration). One component of the short finder is a circuit breaker "pulse unit," which is installed in place of the fuse in the circuit where the short is suspected (see illustration). The other component is a hand held meter which is moved along the suspected wiring harness until the meter deflections indicate the point in the harness where the short is located. The meter takes advantage of the pulsating magnetic field, created in the wiring harness by the pulse unit, to locate the exact point of the short. The beauty of this device is it can detect the pulsations right through the sheet metal panels and body trim.

How to trace a short with a short circuit detector

1   The first step in finding the short is identifying the circuit that has the problem. We are assuming that a fuse has blown. The fuse terminal in the fuse box corresponding to the blown fuse will usually indicate the circuit it protects (i.e. "Int Pnl" for instrument panel), or the vehicle's owners manual will have a fuse box description. A wiring diagram for the vehicle is also very helpful and can be found in the Haynes Automotive Repair Manual for the specific vehicle.

2   Remove the blown fuse, and, leaving the battery connected, connect the pulse unit of the short finder across the fuse terminals **(see illustration)**.

3   Complete the circuit by turning to ON any switches, motors or components in the suspected circuit. The circuit breaker in the pulse unit will begin to open and close if a short is present.

4   Now you will use your knowledge of the suspected circuit to operate the meter. Beginning at a point closest to the fuse panel, slowly move the meter along the suspected wiring harness **(see illustration)**. If you are close to the defective wiring harness and the circuit breaker is pulsing, the needle on the meter will be fluctuating across the face of the meter with each current pulse.

5   Continue with the meter along the harness until you reach a point where the needle stops fluctuating. That point is the area where the short will be found.

6   Remove any components necessary to gain access to the wiring harness and examine the area for the damaged wiring.

7   Repair the damage, using approved methods, and replace the fuse with one of the correct rating.

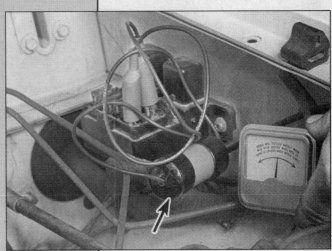

3.65 The short detector pulse unit is connected to the fuse terminals in place of the fuse in the suspected circuit

Multimeters are suited for a variety of test functions requiring the measurement of volts, ohms and amperes, and can be very useful to the home mechanic. Many brands and varieties are available at tool and electronics supply stores.

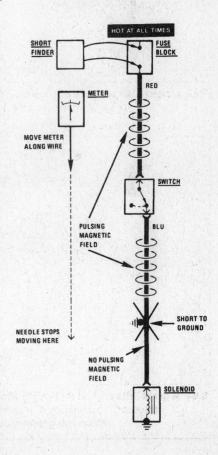

3.66 Move the meter along the wiring harness until the needle pulsation's cease; look for the short in that area

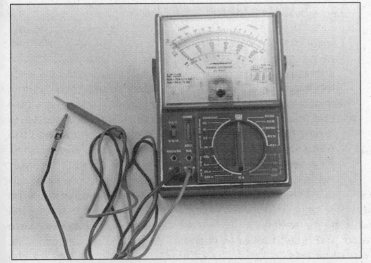

3.67 Analog multimeters can be used to measure volts, amps and ohms in a non-solid state circuit

Automotive Tools Manual

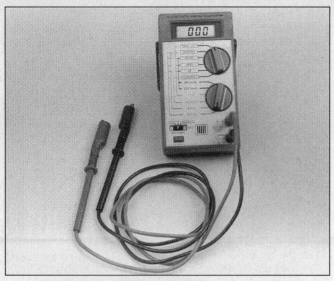

3.68 Digital multimeters can be used for testing all types of circuits

The units offering the most features and scales are usually the most desirable. Analog meters **(see illustration)** have limited use on modern automobiles, they can't be used to test solid state circuits such as computers and modules. If you already own one, by all means, you can use it to perform many tests on non-solid state circuits. However, if you intend to purchase a new multimeter, consider a digital multimeter **(see illustrations)**. Digital multimeters display the measured volts, ohms or amperes with a higher degree of accuracy and are compatible for use on solid-state circuits. See Chapter 6 for more information on digital multimeters and other types of electronic test equipment.

Another handy device is the inductive ammeter **(see illustration)**. This little unit is placed directly over the battery cable and measures the current flow through the cable **(see illustration)**. Inexpensive and easy to use, the inductive ammeter, by itself or in conjunction with a voltmeter, can provide a fast and accurate diagnosis of the charging and starting systems.

3.69 They can make very accurate measurements on computers, modules and sensors (see Chapter 6 for more on digital multimeters)

3.70 Inductive ammeters are great little tools for diagnosing the charging or starting systems

3.71 Just place the meter over a battery cable and the inductive pick-up measures the current flow through the cable

Now that you've located the defective wiring, you'll need a couple of special tools to repair the damage. Wire stripper/crimping tools **(see illustration)** are the first tool to come to mind. They are used to cut the wire, strip the end and crimp on a connector **(see illustrations)**. They are capable tools and offer a fast and easy repair in most situations. Although, crimp-type connections add resistance to the circuit, which is acceptable in most common repairs, there are cases that will require a better connection to be made. Any repair to a low-voltage circuit, such as a sensor or the computer should be soldered. For that you'll need a soldering gun or iron **(see illustration)**. Soldering does require some acquired skills to perform successfully. Before you attempt a delicate wiring repair on your expensive automobile, practice on the bench until you become competent **(see illustration)**. Be sure to follow the soldering gun manufacturer's instructions and use the correct type of solder. Use a 60/40 rosin core solder for electrical repairs, and never use acid core solder or acid flux on electrical connections.

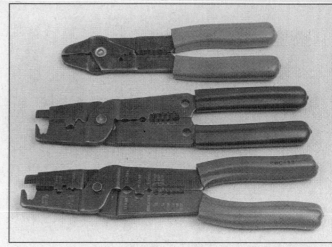

3.72 Wire stripper/crimping tools, like the ones shown here, can be used to cut wire, strip the ends and install crimp connectors

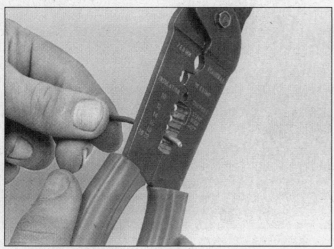

3.73 The tool strips several different size wire, find the correct opening that cuts the insulation and not the wire

3.74 Use the proper section to crimp the connector securely onto the wire

3.75 Soldering guns and irons are available in different sizes and heat ranges - always use rosin-core solder in electrical work

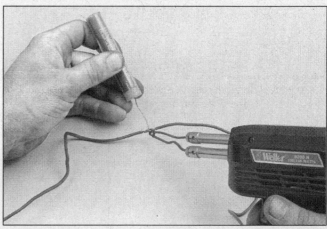

3.76 Soldering a connection takes a certain amount of skill to perform properly - practice soldering a few connections on the bench first!

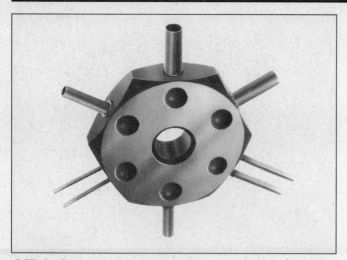

3.77 A wire terminal removal tool is necessary to remove the terminal from the connector without damaging the terminal

Many times it's necessary to remove the individual terminals from an electrical connector. For example, the steering column connector must be disassembled to replace the turn signal switch on early model Ford trucks. Each automobile manufacturer uses several different types of locking terminals in its connectors and all have their own special tools for removal. Universal tools are available that can be used on a variety of terminals **(see illustration)**. Modern computerized cars often experience driving problems that can be traced to a loose or corroded electrical connector of the computer or a sensor. These weather resistant terminals often require tiny little locking tabs to be depressed and can be very difficult to remove for repair or replacement without the special tool.

4 Air-conditioning service tools

Not many people can, or want to, service their own automotive air conditioning system nowadays. But if you do, there are a few basic tools you will need. A set of manifold gauges and hoses are unquestionably the most important tools used in air conditioning servicing **(see illustrations)**, as well as the necessary adapters to hook-up to the system.

For the two types of refrigerant systems used today (R-12 and R-134a), the manifold gauges are used in exactly the same way, but you can't use the same set of gauges for both systems. They use completely different couplers and hoses. The fittings are totally different, so each type of gauge is incompatible with the fittings and hoses used on the other system. The hoses are color-coded, making them easier to keep separated. R-12 low-side hoses are solid blue, high-side hoses are solid red and the utility hose is yellow. R-134a hoses are also blue, red and yellow, but they have a black stripe running the length of each hose. Practically speaking, this means that if you

3.78 A manifold gauge set and hoses are needed to hook to the vehicles air conditioning system

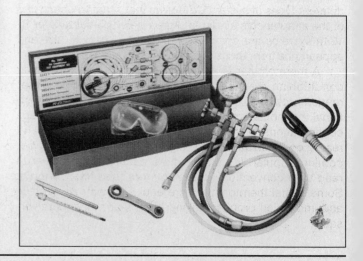

3.79 KD Tools makes this complete set that contains everything you'll need to service the air conditioning system on your vehicle

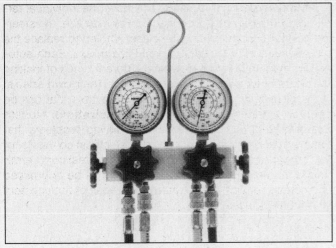

3.80 A manifold gauge set consists of the manifold block, high and low side gauges and the hose fittings and valves

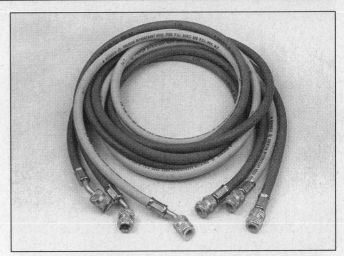

3.81 The hoses are just as important as the manifold gauge set you use with them - they should be high quality hose of the proper length and with the correct fittings for the system you intend to service

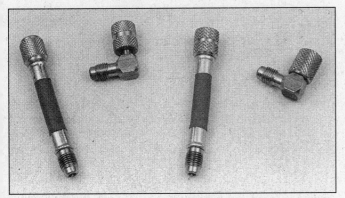

3.82 Many times adapters are needed to hook-up the hoses to the system - you can buy them individually to suit your particular system

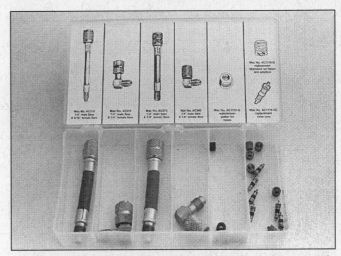

3.83 You can also buy adapter sets that will contain several different types of adapters

wish to service both R-12 and R-134a systems, you will have to obtain two complete sets of gauges and hoses.

Service Adapter fittings are available individually, or in sets **(see illustrations)**. If you will only be servicing the air conditioning system on the family car then you may only need one or two adapters. If you will be servicing several different types of systems, then you may want to obtain one of the adapter sets available. Again, service adapters for R-134a systems are completely different in design, size and appearance from those used on R-12 systems.

A thermometer is an essential tool for heating and air conditioning diagnosis. You'll need a thermometer that ranges between 25 degrees and 125 degrees F. Conventional thermometers are available in standard and dial face configurations, with the dial type being easier to use and read **(see illustration)**. The digital thermometer is fast becoming popular. It's faster, more accurate and easier to read than conventional thermometers **(see illustrations)**. Some digital thermometers are equipped with air, surface and immersion probes, making them that much more versatile.

3.84 This deluxe adapter set contains most of the necessary adapters to service a wide variety of vehicles

Automotive Tools Manual

3.85 When servicing the air conditioning system you'll want to monitor the temperature of the air as it leaves the ducts

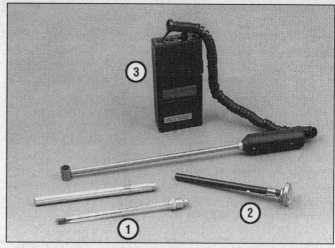

3.86 These are a few of thermometers currently available

1. ***Conventional mercury column thermometer*** - *delicate and hard to read*
2. ***Dial type thermometer*** - *rugged and easy-to-read, the most common type*
3. ***Digital thermometer*** - *acceptably rugged, easy to read, very quick response and very accurate, but expensive*

For the more serious air conditioning technician, a leak detector will be useful to locate and repair the types of subtle leaks often occurring in many automobiles today. When refrigerant was a dollar a can and plentiful and R-12 was considered a harmless substance, finding a leak was more of an annoyance than anything. Now, of course, with the discovery of the holes in the ozone layer over the Arctic and Antarctic - and the fears of scientist that we may be putting ourselves at greater risk of getting skin cancer as a result of ozone depletion - fixing leaks has become much more than an annoyance. Not only is it environmentally responsible to be sure your air conditioning system doesn't leak, it's also a good idea from a dollars-and-cents point of view. With R-12 and R-134a very expensive, you can't afford leaks in your air conditioning system.

The most sophisticated, sensitive and easiest-to-use leak detector is the ion pump halogen leak detector **(see illustrations)**. The most unique feature of this technological marvel is its pumping mechanism. The importance of a suction pump in instruments used for detecting refrigerant gas leaks has been recognized for quite some time. Up until recently, however, the use of bellows, valves and other mechanical moving parts has made suction pump-equipped leak detectors bulky, inefficient and unreliable. These problems are eliminated by the ion pump, which is small, efficient and has no moving parts. The ion pump harnesses the electrical energy generated in the sensing element to produce a precise and reliable flow of air through the sensing element chamber. the air flow rate of the ion pump is self-regulating, enabling it to detect leaks as small as 1/10th of an ounce per year. Although expensive, a halogen leak detector is worth the money if you want a safe, simple and

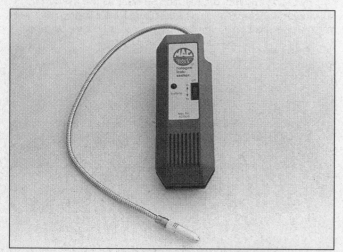

3.87 An ion pump halogen leak detector is the simplest, quickest, most convenient method of finding a refrigerant leak

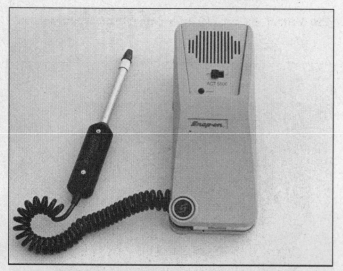

3.88 Electronic leak detectors are safe to use and very accurate at finding small leaks, but they're expensive

sensitive means of finding leaks fast.

If an air conditioning system has had 1) refrigerant removed to service or repair the system, 2) refrigerant loss caused by component failure, 3) shows evidence of refrigerant contamination or 4) is being retrofitted to operate with R-134a, it must be evacuated to get rid of all moisture and air before it can be recharged with refrigerant. Air and moisture are extracted from the system with a vacuum pump. Pumping draws air from within the closed system to create negative pressure, or vacuum. By lowering the pressure inside the system into a vacuum condition, the boiling point of water, or moisture, is also lowered to a point at which evaporation easily occurs, This vaporized moisture is then easily drawn out by the vacuum pump

There are two kinds of vacuum pumps generally available. The venturi type pump is easy to use, maintenance-free and inexpensive, but it requires an air compressor that can pump at least 80 to 90 psi an hour to drive it **(see illustrations)**. And a constantly running air compressor uses a lot of electricity. The rotary vane type pump **(see illustration)**, which has a small electric motor, is considerably more expensive than a venturi type pump and requires some maintenance. But it doesn't require the use of an air compressor to evacuate the system, so it uses a lot less electricity.

Whichever type you choose, remember to follow all the safety rules, wear goggles at all times when servicing an air conditioning system and do not release refrigerant into the atmosphere (see Chapter 1).

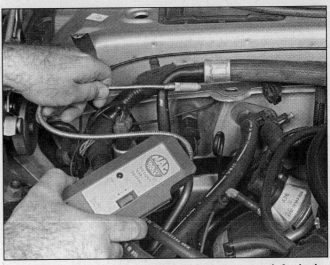

3.89 When using an electronic leak detector, search for leaks by slowly moving the sensing tip near all the systems components, controls, seals and fittings - the instrument will emit an audible alarm when the sensing tip detects the presence of refrigerant gases

3.90 Venturi type vacuum pumps operate on compressed air

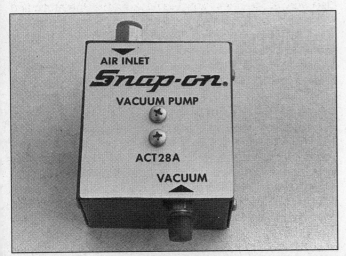

3.91 This type of pump is inexpensive, but requires a lot of electricity to run the compressor

3.92 The rotary vane type pump is powered by an electric motor - it's much more expensive to buy than a venturi type pump but is more economical to operate

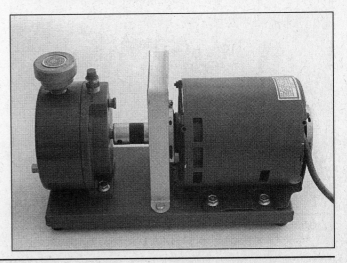

5 Tune-up and maintenance tools

Many of the tools needed for routine tune-up and maintenance are basic hand tools, such as wrenches and sockets. But many more are special tools, such as timing lights, spark plug gapping tools and oil filter wrenches. The special tools are also necessary to complete the proper maintenance of your vehicle. Grouped together here, for ease of illustration, are the tools needed to perform most of the routine maintenance service your vehicle will need **(see illustrations)**.

Maintenance requirements have changed dramatically on many modern automobiles. The use of front wheel drive, distributorless ignition, rack and pinion steering, MacPherson strut suspension, etc. have eliminated many tools that were standard for so long, so you'll need to choose your tools according to your needs. Some will need chassis lubrication tools and timing lights, others will not. All will need, at least for the present, spark plug, oil changing and battery maintenance tools.

There are many different types of oil filter wrenches available. You'll need to choose one that is the easiest to use on your vehicle. Often the location or position of the oil filter will dictate the type of wrench you end up with.

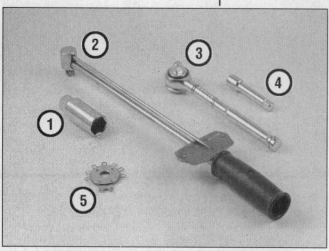

3.93 Tools required for changing spark plugs

1   *Spark plug socket* - This will have special padding inside to protect the spark plug's porcelain insulator
2   *Torque wrench* - Although not mandatory, using this tool is the best way to ensure the plugs are tightened properly
3   *Ratchet* - Standard hand tool to fit the spark plug socket
4   *Extension* - Depending on model and accessories, you may need special extensions and universal joints to reach one or more of the plugs
5   *Spark plug gap gauge* - This gauge for checking the gap comes in a variety of styles. Make sure the gap for your engine is included

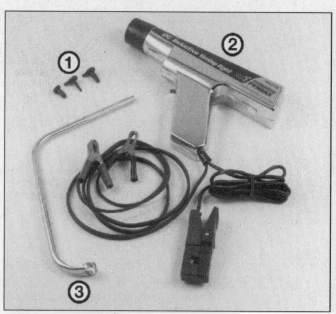

3.94 Tools needed to check and adjust the ignition timing

1   *Vacuum plugs* - Vacuum hoses will, in most cases, have to be disconnected and plugged. Molded plugs in various shapes and sizes are available for this
2   *Inductive pick-up timing light* - Flashes a bright, concentrated beam of light when the number one spark plug fires. Connect the leads according to the instructions supplied with the light
3   *Distributor wrench* - On some models, the hold-down bolt for the distributor is difficult to reach and turn with conventional wrenches or sockets. A special wrench like this must be used

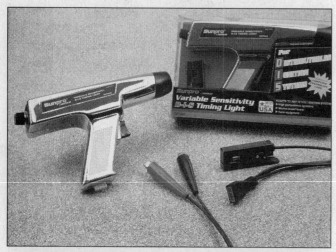

3.95 The timing light enables you to synchronize ignition timing with engine timing - you'll want a stroboscopic type with an inductive pick-up that clamps over the no. 1 spark plug wire

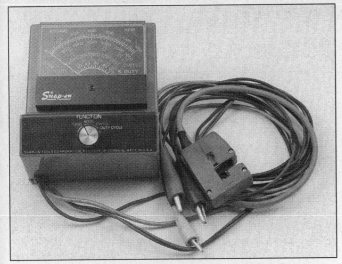

3.96 The tach/dwell meter combines the functions of a tachometer and dwell meter into one package - the tach indicates engine speed in RPM; the dwell meter indicates the degrees of distributor rotation during which the breaker points are closed, the dwell meter can also be used to monitor the duty cycle of an air/fuel mixture control solenoid in a feedback carburetor

3.97 One cannot stress enough the importance of proper spark plug gap - the gauge should slide between the electrodes with a slight drag, if not, adjustment is required

3.98 Here a several spark plug gapping tools manufactured by Lisle - note that each tool has an adjustment lever used to bend the electrode of the spark plug

3.100 A spark plug boot puller is used to remove the boot from the spark plug (which are usually stuck tight) without damage to the wire - never pull on the wire

3.99 This is another very popular gapping tool, the hole in the tool is used to adjust the gap

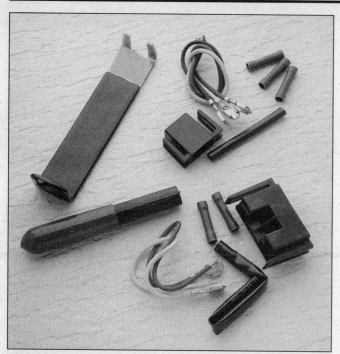

3.101 Another type of boot puller from Motormite and a spark plug starter which is a very handy tool for starting the threads of the park plug into the cylinder head

3.102 Occasionally the spark plug threads in the cylinder head will become damaged (especially on aluminum heads) - this spark plug hole thread chaser from Lisle is used to restore the damaged threads

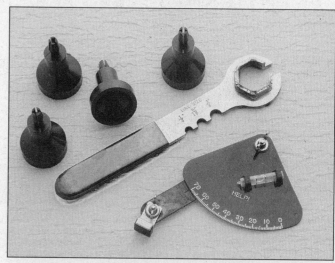

3.103 Three tools from Motormite that are used to tune-up your carburetor - a set of bench mount carburetor feet for working on the carburetor on the bench, a carburetor nut wrench, and a choke angle gauge

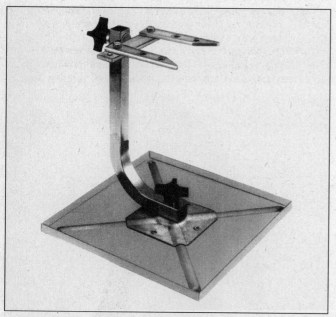

3.104 Lisle's carburetor stand hold the carburetor securely and allows you to rotate the carburetor during a overhaul

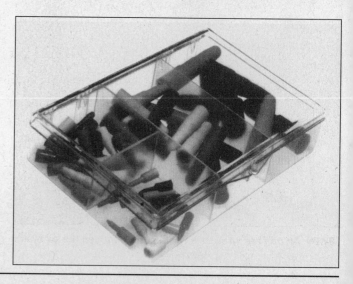

3.105 Lisle's color coded vacuum hose identifiers are very useful in identifying the location of vacuum hoses and fittings when removing the carburetor for service

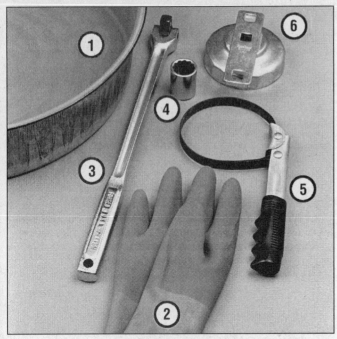

3.106 These tools are required when changing the engine oil and filter

1   **Drain pan** - It should be fairly shallow in depth, but wide to prevent spills
2   **Rubber gloves** - When removing the drain plug and filter, you will get oil on your hands (the gloves will prevent burns)
3   **Breaker bar** - Sometimes the oil drain plug is tight, and a long breaker bar is needed to loosen it
4   **Socket** - To be used with the breaker bar or a ratchet (must be the correct size to fit the drain plug - six-point preferred)
5   **Filter wrench** - This is a metal band-type wrench, which requires clearance around the filter to be effective
6   **Filter wrench** - This type fits on the bottom of the filter and can be turned with a ratchet or breaker bar (different-size wrenches are available for different types of filters)

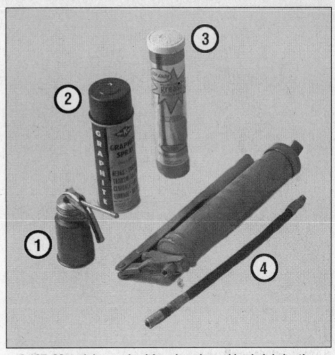

3.107 Materials required for chassis and body lubrication

1   **Engine oil** - Light engine oil in a can like this can be used for door and hood hinges
2   **Graphite spray** - Used to lubricate lock cylinders
3   **Grease** - Grease, in a variety of types and weights, is available for use in a grease gun. Check the Specifications for your requirements
4   **Grease gun** - A common grease gun, shown here with a detachable hose and nozzle, is needed for chassis lubrication. After use, clean it thoroughly

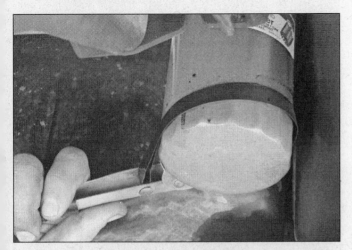

3.108 An oil filter wrench is necessary to loosen the oil filter for removal

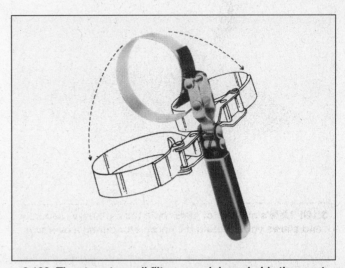

3.109 The strap-type oil filter wrench is probably the most common type used - this Lisle wrench's handle swivels 180 degrees to clear obstructions and is available in three sizes

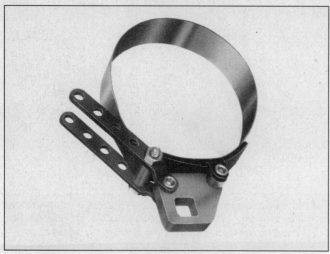

3.110 This Lisle strap type wrench is adjustable to fit many different size oil filters, for use with a 1/2-inch drive ratchet or breaker bar

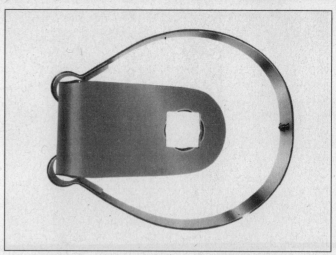

3.111 Lisle's three-inch filter wrench removes all the common 3-inch filters, the 3/8-inch square drive directly under the filter allows it to be used in tight spots

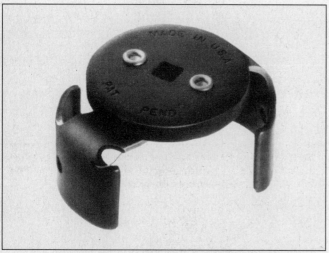

3.112 Lisle's import car filter wrench removes all oil filters from 2 1/2 to 3 1/8-inch in diameter; this range enables the wrench to fit the small import filters plus the common 3-inch filter

3.113 This unique tool from Lisle, removes the 3 1/4-inch drain plug on GM four-cylinder engines where the oil filter is in the oil pan; it works where the original hex on the plug has been rounded-off, a common problem with those engines

3.114 The ultimate oil drain pan and storage container is available from Double Duty Container; it's a 9-quart holding tank under a 6-quart catch basin, all made from recycled plastic, it's only 5 1/2 inches high, so it fits under most cars and the drain holes are designed so that the oil pan plug bolt cannot fall into the dirty oil

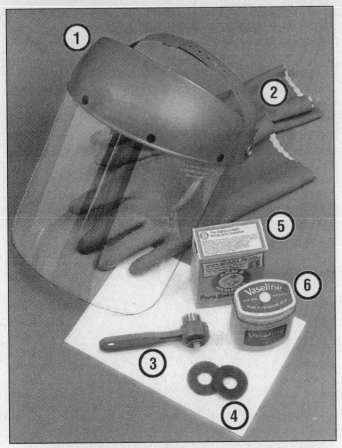

3.115 Tools and materials required for battery maintenance

1 *Face shield/safety goggles* - When removing corrosion with a brush, the acidic particles can easily fly up into your eyes
2 *Rubber gloves* - Another safety item to consider when servicing the battery - remember that's acid inside the battery!
3 *Battery terminal/cable cleaner* - This wire brush cleaning tool will remove all traces of corrosion from the battery and cable
4 *Treated felt washers* - Placing one of these on each terminal, directly under the cable end, will help prevent corrosion (be sure to get the correct type for side-terminal batteries)
5 *Baking soda* - A solution of baking soda and water can be used to neutralize corrosion
6 *Petroleum jelly* - A layer of this on the battery terminal bolts will help prevent corrosion

3.116 Top post battery brush cleans dirt and corrosion from the battery terminals and cable clamps, the external brush cleans cable clamps and the internal brush cleans terminal posts

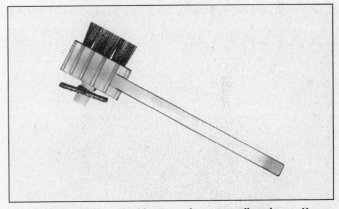

3.117 The side terminal battery cleaners coil spring cutters polish the battery contact surface while the stainless steel brushes clean the cable terminals

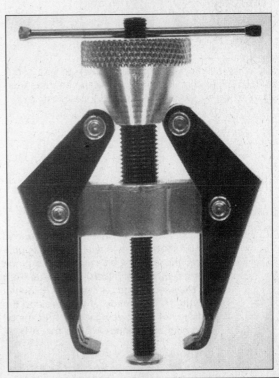

3.118 A battery terminal puller makes it easy to remove cable clamps without breaking or damaging the battery post

Automotive Tools Manual

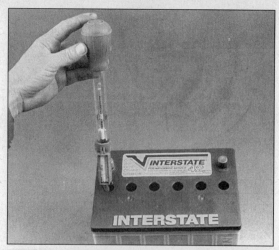

3.119 A battery hydrometer is used to check the condition of each cell

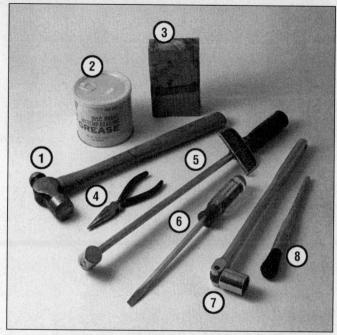

3.120 Tools and materials needed for front wheel bearing maintenance

1   **Hammer** - A common hammer will do just fine
2   **Grease** - High-temperature grease that is formulated specially for front wheel bearings should be used
3   **Wood block** - If you have a scrap piece of 2x4, it can be used to drive the new seal into the hub
4   **Needle-nose pliers** - Used to straighten and remove the cotter pin in the spindle
5   **Torque wrench** - This is very important in this procedure; if the bearing is too tight, the wheel won't turn freely - if it's too loose, the wheel will "wobble" on the spindle. Either way, it could mean extensive damage
6   **Screwdriver** - Used to remove the seal from the hub (a long screwdriver is preferred)
7   **Socket/breaker bar** - Needed to loosen the nut on the spindle if it's extremely tight
8   **Brush** - Together with some clean solvent, this will be used to remove old grease from the hub and spindle

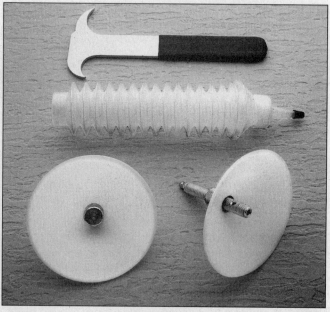

3.121 Motormite's wheel bearing tools include a seal puller and a wheel bearing grease packing tool

3.122 Here is another wheel bearing grease packing tool available from KD Tools

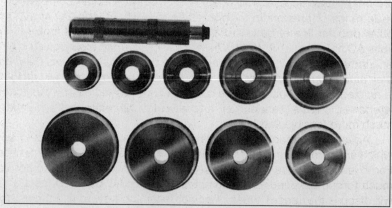

3.123 If any of the wheel bearings need replacing, this bearing driver set is used to install the bearing race into the wheel hub

4 Power tools

Home mechanics who spend a lot of time on their automotive projects will soon discover the very popular line of tools that are powered by electricity or compressed air, referred to as "power tools." This does not mean that all of a sudden you'll have superior control over that rusty ol' classic car you have sitting in the garage, but, instead, power tools can speed up those long, arduous tasks which are quite common with automotive work. Power tools for automotive use are often powered by compressed air. If you have an air compressor, there's a wide range of pneumatic tools to make all sorts of jobs easier and faster. The other popular line of power tools is the electrical powered type which use 110 volts AC house current. **Note:** *There are some electric tools powered by 220 volts AC (three phase), but this manual does not specifically discuss them because of their strict industrial applications.* Really, the only power tool you absolutely need is an electric drill, but, let's face it, a little compressed air and a drawer full of air wrenches, chisels, sanders, air ratchets etc. will make that automotive project much more feasible and faster.

Advanced technology has designed yet another line of electric power tools which are cordless and can be recharged in a special receptacle or charging station overnight. These tools are portable and convenient, but do not develop as much torque or speed as the compressed air or AC powered tools. This chapter will discuss the various types of power tools and how to use them. We will start with the most popular air tools widely used in automotive repairs as well as examine the more unusual and expensive cordless tools now available.

1 Pneumatic tools

Air compressor

An air compressor makes most jobs easier and faster; drying off parts after cleaning them with solvent, blowing out passages in a block or head, running power tools - the list is endless. Once you buy a compressor, you'll wonder how you ever got along without it. Air tools really speed up tedious procedures like removing and installing cylinder head bolts, crankshaft main bearing bolts or vibration damper (crankshaft pulley) bolts.

Air compressors come in all sizes, shapes, capacities and horse-power ratings. There are stand-up air compressors that are designed to be positioned much like a water heater **(see illustration)**. This type is bolted to the cement floor usually in the corner of the garage. Most of these types of air compressors run on 220 volts A/C (single and three phase) and have large capacity air tanks. Stand-up air compressors are intended more for industrial applications. There are also gasoline powered air compressors that have a separate internal combustion engine attached to the air compressor (small, four stroke engine) which pumps up the air in the tank(s) **(see illustrations)**. This type of air compressor is usually used out in the field for mobile mechanical work or even home and commercial construction sites. The most popular type of air compressor designed for portable use inside the garage is the smaller, horizontal tank type **(see illustrations)**. This type of portable air compressor is usually equipped with two large wheels and a large handle bar for easy gripping. It is designed to roll to other stations and plug into another wall socket. Keep in mind when operating this type of air compressor that a long power extension cord will cause a voltage drop which will consequently cause the circuit breaker or fuses in the garage wiring circuit to set or blow. It is advisable to use only the electric cord that is equipped with the air compressor.

4.1 Vertical air compressor - rated at 11.8 CFM at 40 PSI and 9.6 CFM at 90 PSI. The electrical supply is 15 amp with 230 volt single phase outlet

4.2 Portable gasoline air compressor - notice that it is equipped with a wheel and tire in the middle of the tanks used to be pushed much like a wheelbarrow

4.3 This heavy duty gasoline air compressor is used out in the field far from electrical outlets

4.4 This Campbell Hausfeld air compressor is equipped with a 20 gallon tank and it is rated at 8.6 CFM at 40 PSI and 6.3 CFM at 90 PSI

4.5 This DeVilbiss air compressor is rated at 7.6 CFM at 40 PSI and 5.6 CFM at 90 PSI

Another handy tool available to the home mechanic is the portable air tank **(see illustration)**. These small air tanks are great for emergency use and they store enough spare compressed air to fill up a tire, clean off parts or just about any small job around the shop or garage. In the event the home mechanic does not have an air compressor, simply drive down to the local service station, fill up the tank and you are in business. This type of portable air tank has its limits but they are very handy for many emergency situations.

Two other important features of air compressors are the tank capacity and the horse-power ratings. Depending upon what type of job you are planning, it is very important that you have the air capacity and horsepower available to the tool, to allow it to work efficiently and quickly without overloading the air compressor and consequently the wiring circuit in the house. Many home mechanics will invest in a five-gallon, 1-horsepower air compressor for blowing dust off parts, drilling an occasional hole in a piece of

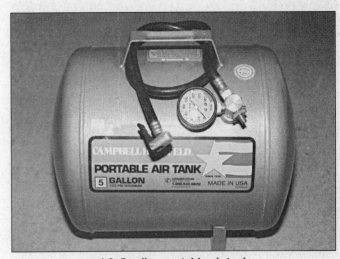

4.6 5 gallon portable air tank

metal or block of wood, but when they want to remove some tough lug bolts from their rusty classic they soon find that the air compressor is not "heavy duty" enough for the job. The air compressor will be forced to cycle on and off constantly to try and make up for the loss of air pressure in the small capacity tank which in turn drops the pressure inside the tank to a point where it will not "break" the lug bolts from the wheels. All of a sudden, the fuse will blow and the unsuspecting do-it-yourselfer is standing in the dark wondering "how come it had to happen to me." Well, there is no mystery, just common sense. This type of situation also happens quite often when the home mechanic decides to use the his small air compressor to do some sanding, priming or painting. The spray gun quickly drains the air volume (capacity) in the tank, thereby dropping the pressure and consequently you end up with a very uneven spray pattern on the body panels.

This type of rating is called CFM; Cubic Feet per Minute. A higher capacity tank with a larger horsepower motor will deliver more compressed air per minute. This capacity ranges from 4.0 CFM to 120.0 CFM. This cubic feet per minute capacity indicates the amount of air that is available to the air tool per minute of use. This important capacity rating will only help the potential buyer to know how much the air compressor will deliver. For example; The home mechanic owns a

3.5 horsepower air compressor that delivers 8.6 CFM at 40 PSI but only 6.3 CFM at 90 PSI. Well, the air impact wrench that the owner wants to work with requires 9.1 CFM to attain 900 ft-lbs. of torque at 90 PSI. The tool will be handicapped and not develop the torque capable of its potential. This by the way is an extreme case. The impact wrench is heavy duty and not often used by the home owner. Most air tools are rated between 1.5 and 6.0 CFM. Therefore, this air compressor size is quite adequate for most jobs that will come up in the garage. The point to this example is that the home mechanic should know the limits of the air compressor and the tools that will be used.

Another important rating to know when discussing air compressors and air tools is the actual CFM rating of the air tool. For example, check the rating of a typical air drill. At 90 PSI, the drill requires 4.0 CFM to operate at the normal torque rating. In other words, the air tool will not deliver the full potential unless the air compressor delivers at least 4.0 CFM at 90 PSI. This a typical situation and most air compressors will have enough strength and horsepower to deliver the necessary air capacity. Check the CFM rating of all the air tools in your tool box and make a note to remember which tools require more air capacity so that when you are actively working in the shop you will avoid fuse blowouts, poor performance or uneven spray patterns on the spray gun or any other tool failure. Operating air tools requires knowledge from the home mechanic so that he/she can combine the limits of the air compressor with the power of the air tool. **Note**: *Most CFM ratings on air tools are given at 90 PSI because that is the pressure setting most commonly used on home air compressor units.*

Before buying an air compressor, it is a good idea to write down all the jobs you would like it to perform. If your shop is only equipped to drill "light duty" holes in wood or metal or even an occasional parts cleaning job, then it will not be necessary to invest in an expensive, large capacity air compressor. If you would like to do some brake jobs, engine overhauls or engine repair work, then it will be necessary to get an air compressor with more capacity and an electric motor with more horsepower. If you are interested in restoring a classic automobile, then, by all means, be sure to invest in a larger air compressor that will develop some horsepower and fill a large capacity tank with the necessary amount of compressed air. The more "air-time" and air tools that will be needed, the larger and more powerful air compressor will be required.

Horsepower ratings and the electric circuit built into your garage or home will be another important consideration. Most homes are wired for 110 volts AC. Now we must consider the amperage this circuit will allow. Many older homes are not wired with the newer gauge standards, and consequently they will not handle large amperage draws. After all the consideration the home mechanic put into buying the air compressor that "fills the bill", the first time they try the "gem" out POP goes the circuit breaker or fuse. Well, then we go to the local hardware store, replace the fuse or reset the breaker and POP goes the fuse. The home owner must research the type of wiring in the garage or home and figure out if it must be rewired or modified. This will most likely require an electrician. If you are a renter, well you're out of luck unless the landlord is willing to invest in some construction costs.

All home mechanics will require the use of pneumatic lines and a gun to blow air **(see illustrations)**. Air lines come in many types and levels of quality. The coiled type is

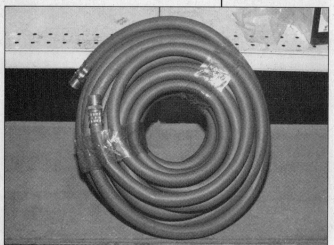

4.7 Rubber air hose is a necessity when using an air compressor - it's usually purchased in 25 or 50 foot lengths

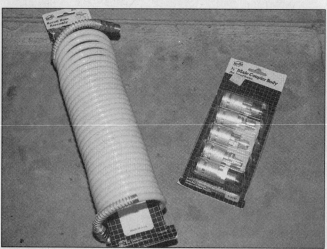

4.8 Coiled air lines are very convenient to use with air tools - the coils retract, keeping the air hose from dragging on the shop floor

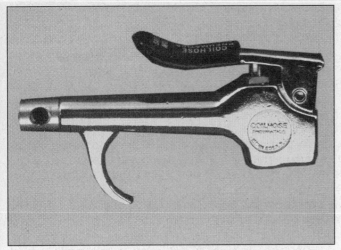

4.9 Coilhose Pneumatics safety blow gun

4.10 Air regulator and lubricator assembly

usually made of resin hardened plastic while other types are made of rubber products. When purchasing air hose, be sure to choose quality line or most likely you will be dissatisfied when the rubber peels off the braided material or the coil loops start to crack and lose compressed air constantly. Also consider a blow gun for your tool collection. No, this is not some kind of voodoo weapon but instead the blow gun is useful when cleaning out passages of carburetors, blowing dust off of parts or cleaning the debris off the trousers and shop coats. Most blow guns are small and compact and can be purchased along with the air compressor.

Another important tool for keeping the air compressor in top shape is the pressure regulator assembly **(see illustration)**. This assembly combines a valve to regulate air pressure, a filter to clean the air coming out of the tank and a lubricating chamber to provide oil to the air tools. Most of these pressure regulator assemblies are not equipped with the lubricator. Oil can be installed into the air tool before use each day. The lubricating chamber is not used in air line systems that spray paint or primers onto body panels or other surfaces.

Impact wrenches

Impact wrenches **(see illustrations)** are made for the fastest removal of lug bolts, body panel bolts, head bolts, etc. The list goes on and on. Impact wrenches must be operated with great care or physical harm could come to the home mechanic. Many of the impact wrenches are designed for large torque and heavy duty applications. The most common usage is for removing lug bolts from the wheels when performing brake jobs, tire rotations, front end work etc. Although the work position may be awkward, strict control of the impact wrench or "air gun" must be maintained. The socket must not angle down or up against the lug bolt or it will strip the bolt immediately upon triggering the tool. Get a "feel" for the gun by gently squeezing the trigger a few times to allow yourself the comfort of the grip and the control of the tool. If the lug bolts do not spin off at first, be sure to use a regular size socket or lug socket without an extension. The extension will only lose leverage. Also, do not use a long, over-extended air hose from the air compressor or it will lose pressure over the long distance to the air tank. In the event that there is absolutely NO WAY to

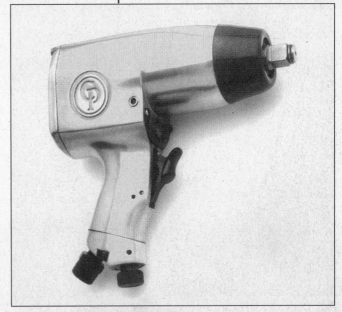

4.11 Chicago Pneumatic 1/2 inch air impact wrench is rated at 250 ft-lbs. of torque at 90 PSI

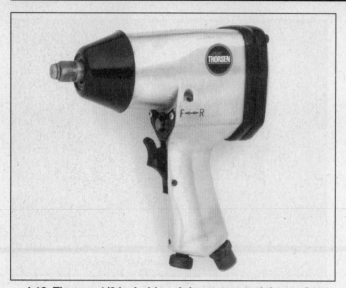

4.12 Thorsen 1/2 inch drive air impact wrench is rated at 230 ft-lbs. of torque at 90 PSI using 4.5 CFM

get the air compressor next to the job (or vice-versa), it is preferable to use an extended air line rather than try running a long extension chord to the electrical outlet on the other side of the garage. It is better to lose air pressure than cause a circuit overload.

Air impacts come in many sizes and varieties and have many applications. The most common air impact is the 1/2 inch drive, medium duty impact for all-purpose use. This type can usually develop almost 300 ft-lbs. torque with the maximum amount of air pressure which is most often 90 PSI. The next step up is the 3/4 inch drive which can develop approximately 500 ft-lbs. torque. This is a larger gun and is most often used in truck applications. Of course there is the 1 inch drive impact wrench which must be gripped by two hands. This gun is used for removing lug bolts from deep inside the wheel recess on large semi-truck trailers and heavy duty truck applications. This type of gun develops approximately 900 ft-lbs. of torque so be very careful when handling the tool because of the extraordinary amount of "twist" on contact with the bolt head.

Next on down the line is the lighter duty and high rpm air impact wrenches. These are usually used for smaller bolt heads and for jobs that do not require such large torque specifications on the bolts or nuts. These guns come in a variety of sizes and shapes for ease and handling qualities.

Air ratchets

Air ratchets are basically speed wrenches powered by compressed air **(see illustration)**. Air ratchets rotate clockwise (tighten) or counter clockwise (loosen) and they are designed to reach into tight places within the engine compartment while working on water pumps, exhaust manifolds, brake work etc. Don't think that these smaller tools cannot hurt you because they definitely develop the torque and power available that could easily twist your wrist or smash a knuckle. It is always a good idea and much safer to "break" a bolt or nut loose first with a breaker bar before using the air ratchet to spin it off. The sudden grab of the power tool on the bolt head can pull your hand, wrist or finger directly into a fan blade or some other engine component.

Air ratchets come in different sizes and torque ratings for various job applications **(see illustrations)**. The most common air ratchet is the 3/8 inch drive that develops approximately 40 to 50 ft-lbs. of torque. There are also the 1/4 inch drive air ratchets that can reach into tight corners in the engine compartment or

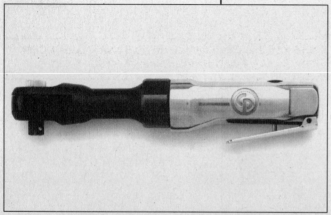

4.13 Chicago Pneumatic 3/8 inch drive air ratchet is rated at 10 to 50 ft-lbs. of torque at 90 PSI

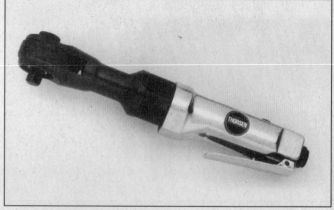

4.14 Thorsen 3/8 inch drive air ratchet is rated at 10 to 50 ft-lbs. of torque at 90 PSI using 4 CFM

under the dashboard. This smaller tool does not develop the torque or power, but instead it is lighter and quicker than the other sizes. The 1/4 inch drive ratchets usually develop 20 to 30 ft-lbs. of torque. These air ratchets are also handy because they can be switched over to reverse, and, because of their lighter touch, they are easily used for tightening bolts without breaking them or over-torquing them.

The butterfly type uses a trigger that can be quickly pivoted to remove or install bolts while holding it in the palm of your hand **(see illustration)**. The pistol grip type is compact and develops slightly more torque than the butterfly type which is approximately 90 to 125 ft-lbs. of torque with maximum air (90 PSI) at the line head. It is best to try out these types of air impacts before purchasing them to find out if they are comfortable and fit your needs.

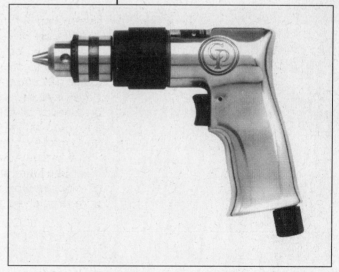

4.15 This 3/8 inch drive butterfly air impact wrench is rated at 75 ft-lbs with 2 1/2 CFM at 90 PSI

Air drills

Air powered drills **(see illustrations)** are very similar to the electric powered drills that are discussed later in this chapter. The basic difference is the amount of rpm the air powered drill delivers. Air powered drills are more trigger sensitive and they can develop up to 1,500 to 5,000 rpm with the proper air pressure. This is very handy in drilling hard metal, broken off bolts in exhaust manifolds, thick steel etc. Air drills develop high rpm levels without losing the torque. Electric powered drills develop torque without the high rpm. Both types work just as well for various applications. Air drills are more commonly used in automotive applications because of the hardened steel and metal alloys that drills must penetrate. Electric drills are commonly used for the home repair (wood, ceramic, tile etc.). **Note**: *Torque ranges for air drills are measured in inch/pounds (in-lbs.) because of their lighter duty.*

Air drills come in different sizes and types. The most important difference is "chuck range." This range designates how small or how large a drill bit will fit down into the chuck. Smaller air drills will fit only 1/64 inch to 1/4 inch diameter drill bits (or any other type tool, grinding wheel, polisher etc.). Larger chuck ranges include 1/16 to 3/8 inch diameter. Be sure to check this before buying an expensive air drill or some of your drill bits may not even fit.

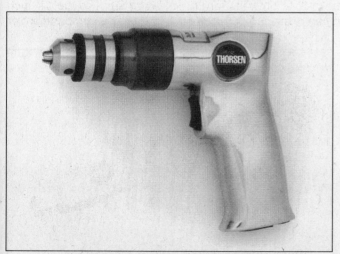

4.17 Thorsen planetary gear air drill, 3/8 chuck, capable of 2600 to 2800 rpm at 90 PSI using 4 CFM

4.16 Chicago Pneumatic air drill, 3/8 chuck, uses 4 CFM, 2,600 rpm (maximum) at 90 PSI

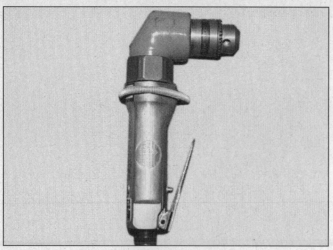

4.18 Angled air drill, 3/8 inch chuck, rated 4.0 CFM at 1,800 rpm at 90 PSI

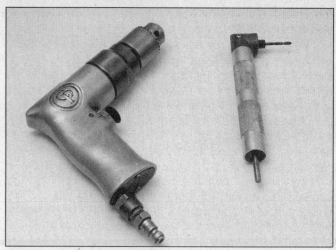

4.19 Special adapters are available that install into the air drill chuck and convert the angle to 90 degrees

4.20 Thorsen air chisel set along with the various bits delivers 4500 blows per minute with a 1 5/8 stroke at 90 PSI using 4 CFM

Also, air drills are available in angled models (usually 90 degrees), compact models and reversible models **(see illustrations)**. These features will largely be an added expense when purchasing them.

Air hammers or air chisels

Air chisels **(see illustration)** are used largely in metal work, dismantling exhaust systems, cutting sheet metal, knocking off stubborn ball joints etc. Air chisels operate much like a jackhammer against bedrock or asphalt. The blade or bit jigs up and down at a tremendous frequency allowing the material to snap under the cutting pressure. Here again, this type of power tool must be used with extreme caution to avoid any physical harm.

Air chisels are rated differently than other air tools. Heavy duty models use slower, more powerful blows against the metal and consequently are rated about 2,000 to 2,500 blows per minute. Lighter duty air hammers are rated 3,000 to 3,500 blows per minute as they operate quickly and not so severely.

Air chisels usually come with a variety of bits to perform many different functions. There are cutting bits, chisels and even a hammer head to push or bend metal. Be extremely careful when operating these tools because of their tremendous power and the tendency to allow your hands to lose their grip from the constant vibration.

Air sanders

Air sanders **(see illustrations)** are used mostly in automotive body and metal preparation. Air sanders are used to take the paint down to the metal, grind the surface rust off older body panels and to smooth out large areas of body filler. Air sanders come in different sizes and shapes and they are commonly rated in maximum rpm. Some larger sanders are rated 800 to 2,000 rpm while smaller, faster sanders are rated up to 9,000 to 10,000 rpm. Here again, the type of sander and the rotational velocity it will attain is an important consideration depending upon what type of job you are trying to accomplish.

Air sanders also come in single action or dual action. Single action will allow only one, circular motion while dual action provides orbital and random pad movement. Random movement is more like vibrational movement for less abrasive cutting action on the disc pad.

When working the sander, be sure to experiment with different degrees of sandpaper grit for different metal finishes. Start out with light or fine sandpaper to test how much cutting action the sander will perform. It is a good idea to know the range of operation the sander has in order to avoid cutting down into the metal initially.

Air sanders come in various sizes and shapes depending upon what type of job. The most common type of sander is the compact disc sander. This type of sander cuts through automotive paint to reach metal, rounds off rough corners and is good for all around general use. Disc sanders are available in dual action or single action. This type of sander is also available with an angled degree to help with the grip and to access tougher surfaces. They are most often equipped with an extra handle (or sometimes two handles) to allow for a steady grip. Orbital air sanders develop high rpm and torque, so it is imperative that the operator grip the tool and steadily hold it over the surface of the metal. It is very common to apply too much weight onto the surface of the metal, quickly damaging the area. Angled air sanders do not develop the high rpm of the compact disc sander, but they are ready for more heavy-duty applications.

The next most common air sander is the jitterbug. Much like the old dance of the 1950s, the jitterbug sander uses a vibrational pattern, moving the pad up and back quickly with short strokes. The jitterbug sander is used for light duty jobs where it is important not to damage the surface. The jitterbug sander is great for finishing type jobs. This sander is rated in oscillations per minute. Capable of tremendous speed (up to 8,000 oscillations per minute), the surface can be cut quickly and precisely.

Another popular type of sander is the in-line sander or air file. This tool is used primarily for cutting body filler down to workable size or cutting the surface down quickly and efficiently in tight corners or hard to reach areas of the body panels.

This sander is also rated in oscillations per minute. Only capable of speeds up to 1,500 to 2,000 oscillations per minute, the air file is for much rougher surfaces that need material removed

4.21 Thorsen dual action sander runs at 7500 to 9500 rpm at 60 PSI using 4 CFM

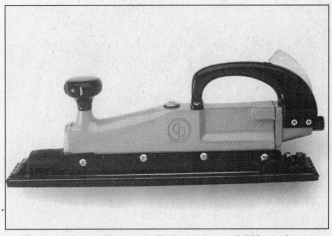

4.22 Air inline sander or air file operates at 3,500 strokes per minute at 90 PSI using 7 CFM

Die-grinders

Die grinders (see illustrations) are used primarily to cut down metal either for removing chunks of unwanted slag, for rounding off jagged edges of metal or a variety of metal fabrication jobs. This tool operates at a high rpm level thereby cutting the metal very quickly. Some of the better quality die grinders can attain approximately 23,000 rpm. This tool is rarely used for any type of finishing work but, instead, are useful when removing large pieces of unnecessary or unwanted metal.

Die grinders are used primarily in automotive metal work, but they are also quite often used in metal fabrication, welding and other manufacturing processes. This tool develops extremely high rpm and therefore is a dangerous

4.23 Die grinders are capable of reaching rpm of 23,000 at 3 CFM

tool capable of releasing hot metal chips in all directions. Beware of danger to the face and eyes. Take all the necessary precautions such as eye goggles, long sleeve shirts and even a welding mask when working up close. It is easy to let yourself concentrate on the actual grinding process and not notice the metal chips flying everywhere. Take all the precautions to avoid any harm.

Air buffers and polishers

Air polishers or buffers are used to polish the wax surface on the body panels or to cut the lacquer surface off certain types of paint jobs to lay down a lasting finish. These tools are rated according to their rpm level. The air powered buffers typically reach a higher rpm than electric powered buffers. The air buffer is much more versatile but requires an air compressor and air lines. Air buffers come equipped with a buffing pad that must be kept clean while in service. These tools rotate at a high rpm to quickly remove wax build-up or lacquer finishes. Make sure when operating air buffers that the pad is clean and not worn through to expose the rubber blade.

Air Saws, Nibblers, Shears

There are many varieties of air tools (**see illustrations**) that speed-up the process of cutting, edging, and sheet metal fabrication. These tools are called shears, air saws, and nibblers. Consult with a metal shop concerning the nature and the exact type of tools necessary for this type of work. Caution should be used when operating these tools because of the hot metal chips that become air-borne during operation.

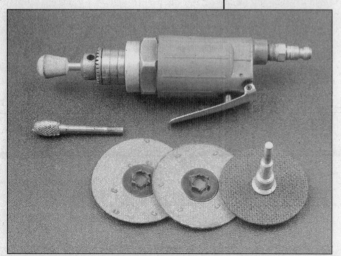

4.24 A good die grinder will deburr engine blocks, radius piston domes, chamfer oil holes and do a lot of other little jobs that would be tedious if done manually

4.25 Pistol grip air shears rated 4.0 CFM, 2,800 rpm at 90 PSI

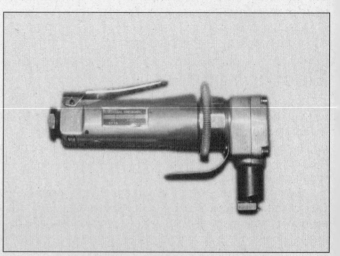

4.26 Air nibbler rated at 4.0 CFM at 90 PSI

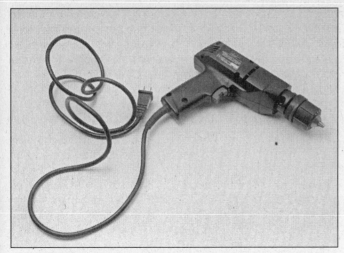

4.27 Electric drill; variable speed, reversible with a 3/8 inch keyless chuck

4.28 Get a set of good quality drill bits for drilling holes and wire brushes of various sizes for cleaning up metal parts - make sure the bits are designed for drilling in metal

2 Electric power tools - household voltage

Electric drills

Countersinking bolt holes, enlarging oil passages, honing cylinder bores, removing rusted or broken fasteners, drilling or enlarging holes and fabricating small parts - electric drills **(see illustration)** are indispensable for automotive work. Electric drills are often used to attach honing tools for cylinder wall restoration. Electric drills come in 1/4, 3/8 or 1/2 inch diameter chuck sizes. A 3/8-inch chuck (drill bit holder) will handle most jobs. Collect several different wire brushes to use in the drill and make sure you have a complete set of sharp metal drill bits **(see illustration)**.

Electric drills are versatile tools that are adequate for most home repair jobs without the additional requirement of an air compressor. Because electric motors do not develop the same rpm, the rotation at the drill bit and the cutting power are reduced. Electric drills can perform most repair jobs but they require slightly more patience and dexterity than air drills.

Electric drills are equipped with variable speed triggers, reversible modes and extra handles to allow for a firm grip.

Electric sanders

Electric sanders are versatile tools that are adequate for home repair jobs without the additional requirement of an air compressor. Because electric motors do not develop the same rpm as air powered sanders, the rotation of the sanding pad is reduced. The amount of rpm lost is minimal for most sanding jobs around the shop. Electric sanders are often used for finishing body panels or taking the rough edges off metal.

Electric sanders, like air sanders, come in many different sizes and shapes. Orbital sanders provide circular pad movement with the ability to strip body panels down to the metal very quickly. As with air sanders, do not underestimate the cutting power of the pad when course sandpaper is attached. Applying too much weight onto the tool while operating will quickly damage the surface. These tools are usually heavy and require good balance and dexterity for good results.

Another handy electric sander is the hand sander or jitterbug sander. This small, hand-size electric tool oscillates back and forth producing rapid but short strokes for fine finishing work. This type of sander must be kept moving constantly over the working surface to ensure smooth results.

Electric impact wrenches

Electric impact wrenches are not as common as the air impact wrenches, but good quality models deliver adequate torque and power for most home applications. Some larger electric impact wrenches deliver about 240 to 260 ft-lbs of torque without an air compressor!

Electric Dremel tools

Electric Dremel tools are used most often for carving, engraving or grinding small pieces of metal off hard-to-reach areas.

Dremel tools usually come equipped with a variety of bits that can be exchanged on the chuck much like a drill. There are various specialty bits for sanding, buffing wheels, router bits, grinding bits and even tiny drill bits for extremely small diameter holes. This tool develops high rpm, so take all the precautions necessary to prevent an accident. Use eye-wear or goggles with a long sleeve shirt when working around metal.

Bench-mounted grinder

A bench grinder is also handy. With a wire wheel on one end and a grinding wheel on the other, it's great for cleaning up fasteners, sharpening tools and removing rust. Make sure the grinder is fastened securely to the bench or stand, always wear eye protection when operating it and never grind aluminum parts on the grinding wheel. See Chapter 1 for more information.

3 Electric rechargeable power tools

Cordless power tools are used for all types of automotive repair jobs because of the added advantage of not requiring a bothersome electric power cord or a twisted air line wrapped around your legs while trying to work on your vehicle. Cordless tools have a few disadvantages, but here again it is important to remember what types of repair jobs they will be best suited for. Cordless ratchets will squeeze between the fan and the radiator to quickly remove those water pump bolts. Cordless screwdrivers are great for removing lens covers from the truck sitting in the driveway. Cordless drills handle drilling holes in dash panels for the "larger" speakers that you are trying to install. Here are a few tips for using cordless tools at home.

Cordless drills

Cordless drills are extremely versatile because they don't force you to work near an outlet. They're also handy to have around for a variety of non-mechanical jobs. Technology has changed cordless drills over the years and it is important to know the differences in the design and the power ratings. Some of the first cordless drills were rated on the 6.0 volt system and then they added the 9.6 volt system **(see illustration)**. With each increase in the chargeable voltage, the power and torque

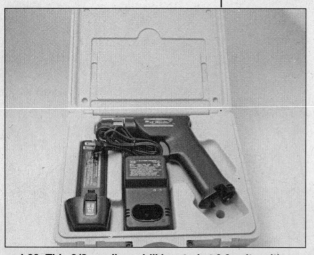

4.29 This 3/8 cordless drill is rated at 9.6 volts with a keyless chuck and reversible and variable speeds

ratings increased also. Now, the most recent cordless drills are rated at 12 volt and they also are equipped with the keyless chuck **(see illustrations)**. With each increase in voltage and power comes an increase in the price. Check each brand of cordless drill very carefully and rate them for durability, torque, length of battery charge and power.

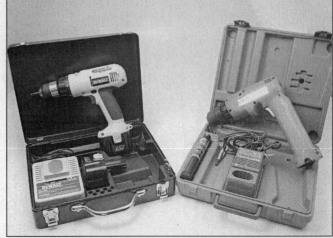

4.31 A 12 volt cordless drill, like the one on the left, develops considerably more torque and power than the 9.6 volt cordless drill on the right

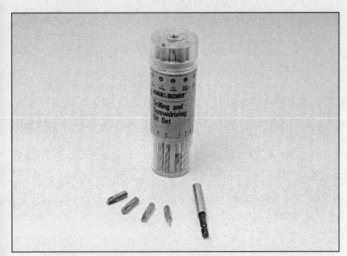

4.30 Here is a kit that includes all the necessary screw tips and the magnetic adapter to install into the chuck

Cordless ratchets

Cordless ratchets are very handy for most repair work in the engine compartment **(see illustration)**. These cordless tools do not develop the same torque or rpm that air ratchets develop but they are great for quick, easy jobs. Many times it will be necessary to "break loose" the bolts manually from the engine and then use the cordless ratchet to zip them off without any straining effort. These tools are great for difficult angles and for working under the dashboard.

Cordless screwdrivers

Cordless screwdrivers **(see illustration)** are used for all types of screws: dashboard screws, cover-plate screws, inset screws etc. These tools do not develop the rpm that air drills develop, but they are handy and completely portable.

4.32 1/4 inch 6.0 volt cordless ratchet with the charging adapter

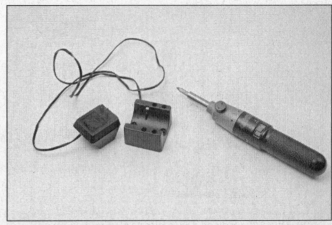

4.33 6.0 volt cordless screwdriver and charging adapter

4 Twist drills and drilling equipment

Drilling operations are done with twist drills, either in a hand drill or a drill press. Twist drills (or drill bits, as they're usually called) consist of a round shank with spiral flutes formed into the upper two-thirds to clear the waste produced while drilling, keep the drill centered in the hole and finish the sides of the hole.

The lower portion of the shank is left plain and used to hold the drill in the chuck. In this section, we will discuss only normal parallel shank drills **(see illustration)**. There is another type of bit with the plain end formed into a special size taper designed to fit directly into a corresponding socket in a heavy-duty drill press. These drills are known as Morse Taper drills and are used primarily in machine shops.

At the cutting end of the drill, two edges are ground to form a conical point. They're generally angled at about 60-degrees from the drill axis, but they can be reground to other angles for specific applications.

When buying drills, purchase a good-quality set (sizes 1/16 to 3/8-inch). Make sure the drills are marked -"High Speed Steel" or "HSS." This indicates they're hard enough to withstand continual use in metal; many cheaper, un-marked drills are suitable only for use in wood or other soft materials. Buying a set ensures the right size bit will be available when it's needed.

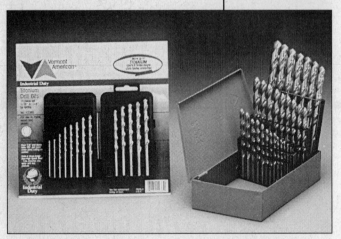

4.34 Complete drill set, note the titanium bits on the left, they're used for drilling into tempered steel and other tough drilling jobs

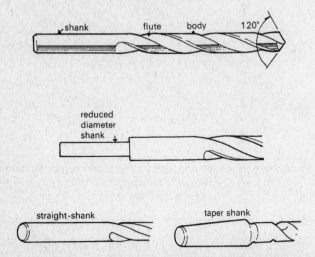

4.35 A typical drill bit (top), a reduced shank bit (center) and a tapered shank bit (bottom right)

4.36 Reversible drills remove metal material from a cut in the opposite direction to allow for easier extraction of broken bolts or studs

Twist drill sizes

Twist drills are available in a vast array of sizes, most of which you'll never need. There are three basic drill sizing systems: fractional, number and letter **(see illustration)** (We won't get involved with the fourth system, which is metric sizes).

Fractional sizes start at 1/64-inch and increase in increments of 1/64-inch. Number drills range in descending order from 80 (0.0135-inch), the smallest, to 1 (0.2280-inch), the largest. Letter sizes start with A (0.234-inch), the smallest, and go through Z (0.413-inch), the largest.

This bewildering range of sizes means it's possible to drill an accurate hole of almost any size within reason. In practice, you'll be limited by the size of chuck on your drill (normally 3/8 or 1/2-inch). In addition, very few stores stock the entire range of possible sizes, so you'll have to shop around for the nearest available size to the one you require.

Sharpening twist drills

Like any tool with a cutting edge, twist drills will eventually get dull **(see illustration)**. How often they'll need sharpening depends to some extent on whether they're used correctly. A dull twist drill will soon make itself known. A good indication of the condition of the cutting edges is to watch the waste emerging from the hole being drilled. If the tip is in good condition, two even spirals of waste metal will be produced; if this fails to happen or the tip gets hot, it's safe to assume that sharpening is required.

With smaller size drills - under about 1/8-inch - it's easier and more economical to throw the worn drill away and buy another one. With larger (more expensive) sizes, sharpening is a better bet. When sharpening twist drills, the included angle of the cutting edge must be maintained at the original 120-degrees and the small chisel edge at the tip must be retained. With some practice, sharpening can be done freehand on a bench grinder, but it should be noted that it's very easy to make mistakes. For most home mechanics, a sharpening jig that mounts next to the grinding wheel should be used so the drill is clamped at the correct angle **(see illustration)**.

4.37 Drill bits in the range most commonly used are available in fractional sizes (left) and number sizes (right) so almost any size hole can be drilled

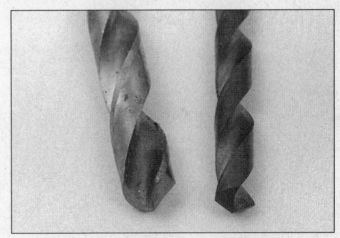

4.38 If a bit gets dull (left), discard it or resharpen it so it looks like the drill bit on the right

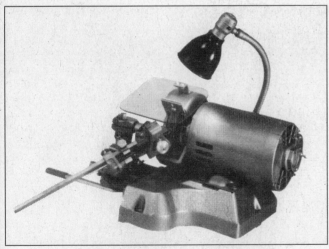

4.39 Lisle drill bit sharpener; bench mounted, this unit sharpens drill bits to "new" condition

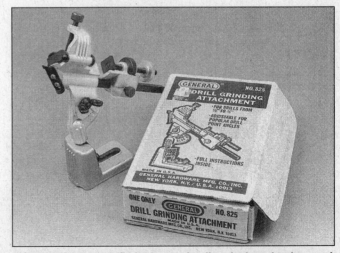

4.40 Inexpensive drill bit sharpening jigs designed to be used with a bench grinder are widely available - even if you only use it to resharpen drill bits, it will pay for itself quickly

Drilling equipment

Tools to hold and turn drill bits range from simple, inexpensive hand-operated or electric drills to sophisticated and expensive drill presses. Ideally, all drilling should be done on a drill press with the work-piece clamped solidly in a vise. These machines are expensive and take up a lot of bench or floor space, so they're out of the question for many do-it-yourselfers. An additional problem is the fact that many of the drilling jobs you end up doing will be on the engine itself or the equipment it's mounted on, in which case the tool has to be taken to the work.

The best tool for the home shop is an electric drill with a 3/8-inch chuck. Both cordless and AC drills are available. If you're purchasing one for the first time, look for a well-known, reputable brand name and variable speed as minimum requirements. A 1/4-inch chuck, single-speed drill will work, but it's worth paying a little more for the larger, variable speed type.

All drills require a key to lock the bit in the chuck. When removing or installing a bit, make sure the cord is unplugged to avoid accidents. Initially, tighten the chuck by hand, checking to see if the bit is centered correctly. This is especially important when using small drill bits which can get caught between the jaws. Once the chuck is hand tight, use the key to tighten it securely - remember to remove the key afterwards!

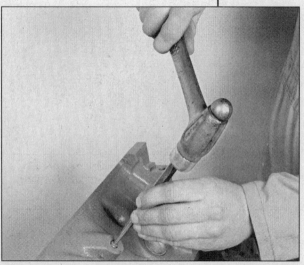

4.41 Before you drill a hole, use a centerpunch to make an indentation for the drill bit so it will not wander

Drilling and finishing holes

Preparation for drilling

If possible, make sure the part you intend to drill in is securely clamped in a vise. If it's impossible to get the work to a vise, make sure it's stable and secure. Twist drills often dig in during drilling - this can be dangerous, particularly if the work suddenly starts spinning on the end of the drill. Obviously, there's little chance of a complete engine or piece of equipment doing this, but you should make sure it's supported securely.

Start by locating the center of the hole you're drilling. Use a center punch to make an indentation for the drill bit so it won't wander. If you're drilling out a broken-off bolt, be sure to position the punch in the exact center of the bolt **(see illustration)**.

If you're drilling a large hole (above 1/4-inch), you may want to make a pilot hole first. As the name suggests, it will guide the larger drill bit and minimize drill bit wandering. Before actually drilling a hole, make sure the area immediately behind the bit is clear of anything you don't want drilled.

Drilling

When drilling steel, especially with smaller bits, no lubrication is needed. If a large bit is involved, oil can be used to ensure a clean cut and prevent overheating of the drill tip. When drilling aluminum, which tends to smear around the cutting edges and clog the drill bit flutes, use kerosene as a lubricant.

Wear safety goggles or a face shield and assume a comfortable, stable stance so you can control the pressure on the drill easily. Position the drill tip in the punch mark and make sure, if you're drilling by hand, the bit is perpendicular to the surface of the work-piece. Start drilling without applying much pressure until you're sure the hole is positioned correctly. If the hole starts off center, it can be very difficult to correct. You can try angling the bit slightly so the hole center moves in the opposite direction, but this must be done before the flutes of the bit have entered the hole. It's at the starting point that a variable-speed drill is invaluable; the low speed allows fine adjustments to be made before it's too late. Continue drilling until the desired hole depth is reached or until the drill tip emerges at the other side of the work-piece.

Cutting speed and pressure are important - as a general rule, the larger the diameter of the drill bit, the slower the drilling speed should be. With a single-speed drill, there's little that can be done to control it, but two-speed or variable speed drills can be controlled. If the drilling speed is too high, the cutting edges of the bit will tend to overheat and dull. Pressure should be varied during drilling. Start with light pressure until the drill tip has located properly in the work. Gradually increase pressure so the bit cuts evenly. If the tip is sharp and the pressure correct, two distinct spirals of metal will emerge from the bit flutes. If the pressure is too light, the bit won't cut properly, while excessive pressure will overheat the tip.

Decrease pressure as the bit breaks through the work-piece. If this isn't done, the bit may jam in the hole; if you're using a hand-held drill, it could be jerked out of your hands, especially when using larger size bits.

Once a pilot hole has been made, install the larger bit in the chuck and enlarge the hole. The second bit will follow the pilot hole - there's no need to attempt to guide it (If you do, the bit may break off). It is important, however, to hold the drill at the correct angle.

After the hole has been drilled to the correct size, remove the burrs left around the edges of the hole. This can be done with a small round file, or by chamfering the opening with a larger bit or a countersink **(see illustration)**. Use a drill bit that's several sizes larger than the hole and simply twist it around each opening by hand until any rough edges are removed.

Enlarging and reshaping holes

The biggest practical size for bits used in a hand drill is about 1/2-inch. This is partly determined by the capacity of the chuck (although it's possible to buy larger drills with stepped shanks). The real limit is the difficulty of controlling large bits by hand; drills over 1/2-inch tend to be too much to handle in anything other than a drill press. If you have to make a larger hole, or if a shape other than round is involved, different techniques are required.

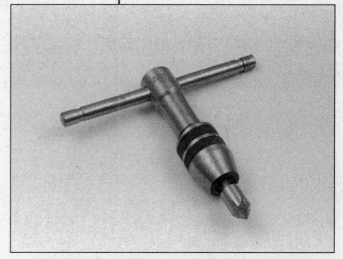

4.42 Use a large drill bit or a countersink mounted in a tap wrench to remove burrs from a hole after drilling or enlarging it

If a hole simply must be enlarged slightly, a round file is probably the best tool to use. If the hole must be very large, a hole saw will be needed, but they can only be used in sheet metal.

Large or irregular-shaped holes can also be made in sheet metal and other thin materials by drilling a series of small holes very close together. In this case the desired hole size and shape must be marked with a scribe. The next step depends on the size bit to be used; the idea is to drill a series of almost touching holes just inside the outline of the large hole. Center punch each location, then drill the small holes. A cold chisel can then be used to knock out the waste material at the center of the hole, which can then be filed to size. This is a time consuming process, but it's the only practical approach for the home shop. Success is dependent on accuracy when marking the hole shape and using the center punch.

A good die grinder will enlarge or reshape a hole ten times as fast as you can do any of these jobs by hand. Refer to the section above on die-grinders for additional information.

Notes

5 Tool storage

1 Tool boxes and chests

Home mechanics that cherish their tools often find themselves purchasing a tool box to lock up their "gems." Some home mechanics try to make you think that the tools inside the box are not worth much by purchasing a beat-up, old tool box that still locks perfectly well. Other tool enthusiasts find themselves buying a streamlined tool box that shines from top to bottom and is so heavy, no one without a crane or a lifting dolly could remove it from the garage. Professional mechanics **(see illustration)** go to great lengths to make sure all the tools of their trade are top quality and are secured properly. Home mechanics do not earn their living "turning wrenches," but it is a good idea to take care of the tools you own to make them last and to keep them organized. No matter what decision or tastes the tool owner has, the bottom line is: does the toolbox hold all the tools and does it lock securely?

Let's take a look at some of the more common tool boxes and how to arrange them in your shop. The most common tool box, and the one most home mechanics will use, is the portable tool box with the handle on the top **(see illustrations)**. This type is made of plastic or metal and usually has a lift-out tool tray

5.1 Here's how the professional mechanic does it - his fully equipped tool boxes contain every type of tool imaginable

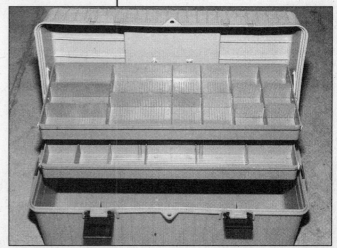

5.2 The small plastic tool box with pull-up drawers is handy for keeping a small assortment of tools and small parts

5.3 A medium sized Craftsman metal tool box with a lift out tool tray will hold a large selection of basic hand tools

5.4 The pull-out drawers of this Craftsman box allow for easier access to tools that would normally be at the bottom of the box

or small dividers under the top. Even if you have a large tool box in the shop, these little boxes are handy for carrying extra tools in your vehicle. Plastic tool boxes are durable and resistant to rust and to breaking open during a sudden impact. Some of the larger models are equipped with pull-out drawers, similar to a full sized tool chest, that allow for easy tool access from the side (see illustration).

The most common type of professional tool box is the combination of the roller cabinet or "bottom box," the tool chest or "top box" and the hang on cabinet or "side box." It is much easier and convenient to own tool boxes that stack upon each other (see illustrations). In the event the mechanic needs to move, the boxes can be lifted separately onto a truck or lifting dolly and away they go. Tool chests and roller cabinets are available in many different sizes and drawer configurations. The roller cabinet can be had with a large bottom storage space or all drawers. You could opt to go with just one or the other also. A nice sized tool chest could be set on a work bench or all your tools could be stored in a roller cabinet for mobility, and the top of the cabinet makes a convenient work surface also.

5.5 Stack-On combination tool box sets are available in many different sizes and drawer configurations

5.6 This Craftsmen top and bottom box combination is the perfect size for the serious home mechanic and would allow for ample storage of the tools suggested by this manual

The bottom box is usually equipped with roller wheels and large drawers for big tools and specialty items **(see illustration)**. The heavier tools should be sitting near the bottom drawers to help keep the tool box balanced. It is not a good idea to allow a tool box to become "top heavy." Arrange the tools and specialty items in such a way that they are easy and convenient to find and tuck away when the job is completed. Here is a list of suggestions for arranging the bottom box. For example; pick out a drawer in the bottom box for electrical testing equipment. Place tools such as the timing light, volt/ohm-meter, ignition system testing equipment, scan tools or whatever tools that are required for checking the electrical systems. Next, pick out a drawer for specialty equipment such as breaker bars, crowbars, tire irons, pipe wrenches, adjustable wrenches etc. This drawer will become quite heavy, so pick one in the lower sections of the tool box. Next, pick out a drawer for sockets. Include all the large sockets such as four-wheel drive front end sockets, large six-point sockets for heavy duty use, lug sockets and any other sockets that are very large and weigh considerably more than the average 3/8 and 1/2 inch drive sockets that will be arranged in their own drawer. Of course if necessary , the heavy sockets can be mixed together with the other smaller sockets if there are not so many to worry about. Well, the remaining drawers are pretty much for the owner to choose. You could make a drawer full of only air tools, or a drawer full of drill bits and drilling equipment. You could make a drawer for only large extensions and ratchets or even a drawer full of specialty equipment such as solder flux, gasket sealers, tapes, etc. One important drawer in my opinion is the specialty tool drawer. Here, I place all special tools designed by the manufacturer for repairing their particular transmission or front end. These tools might include spring lock coupling tools for the fuel lines, fan bolt wrenches to remove the large nut on the water pump, valve adjusting tools, adapters for charging the air conditioning system. The list goes on and on. Keep all these tools in order and easily accessible for those unique repair jobs.

The top box is used to store the tools that will be used the most **(see illustration)**. These tools should be handy and quickly accessible into the mechanic's hand and then back again into the drawers. Top box includes a drawer for the open-end wrenches, another drawer for the box-end wrenches, another drawer for the offset wrenches, the 1/4, 3/8 and 1/2 inch drive sockets, the brake line wrenches, all the ratchets, the extensions for the sockets, and any other frequently used items. The most important point to remember when arranging the top box is that it should be organized in such a way that the home mechanic has thought out a storage plan rather than just throw all the tools together. By organizing the tools, the mechanic will have more time to think about the job at hand instead of where that 12 point, 16 mm socket is hiding.

The side box is used mainly for extraneous tools and miscellaneous items. The side box might include cans of aerosol penetrating oil, carb cleaner and brake cleaner or receipts for automotive parts. Many home mechanics store extra parts or specialty parts they can use for testing such as ignition modules, coils, test harnesses etc. The side box

5.7 **International Tool Boxes 5 drawer roller cabinet is 27 inches wide, 18 3/4 inches deep and 35 5/8 inches high**

5.8 **This International Tool Box 10 drawer chest with pull-out drawers and locking slide bars has 8,883 cu. in. of storage space**

is also handy for placing the job on the rubber pad directly over the box and working very close to the tools. The side box can be great for repairing carburetors, distributors, dashboard parts, and other small components that are easily held on the surface. The top of the box should be covered with a rubber cover to help grip any components or tools that are moving around.

Another important member in the tool box family is the "middle box" or insert box. This tool box is usually inserted between the top and bottom for the purpose of adding drawer space or cubic feet to the household. This middle drawer quite often stores incredible socket collections or amazing wrenches of all sizes and lengths. This tool box is usually added after years and years of collecting and arranging tools. It is a good idea to make sure when you get ready to add a middle box, purchase one that is the same brand as the other boxes or at least have the same type handles on the drawers.

There is yet another type of tool box that is becoming more and more popular and they are considered all-purpose tool boxes. These units are a work bench and tool box combined to fit into the garage, extra room, shop or even in the kitchen. Most of these combination workbench//toolboxes come with two sides; one side is equipped with a few larger drawers while the other side is equipped with six to eight smaller drawers. This arrangement is much like the bottom and top box set side-by-side. The workbench itself is usually made of one inch thick wood. These combo tool boxes are never equipped with wheels (unless custom ordered) and they are designed to load heavy objects on the top.

Another distant type of tool box is the tool cart or tool tray **(see illustrations)**. Tool carts hold all the tools that are currently being used for the project. They can easily be laid out and accessed. The other tiers can be used to hold car parts or specialty tools that must be used frequently during the day. In the evening when the job is completed, the tool cart can be rolled over to the tool box and the tools can be put away.

5.9 The Three layered tool cart is handy for carrying tools to and from the work site

5.10 Professional tool cart with permanently mounted tool organizers

2 Tool organizers

Tool box organizers come in many brands, sizes and shapes designed to help arrange the tools in an organized manner. Tool organizers can be plastic, metal or even magnetic based, to allow the tools to become attached to any iron based metal object such as the tool box, refrigerator, body panels etc. Here is a brief description along with some helpful hints concerning tool box organizers.

Tool racks

Tool racks are constructed of plastic, metal or magnetic based metal. These racks serve as holders for the various wrenches that must be organized within the tool box **(see illustrations)**. Be sure the tool racks that you purchase fit into the drawer of the toolbox without catching on the sides, top or back of the tool box.

Magnetic tool holders

Magnetic tool holders come in many sizes, shapes, types and brands depending upon the application. These tool holders are used pri-

5.11 Metal wrench tool rack equipped with a handle for easy carrying

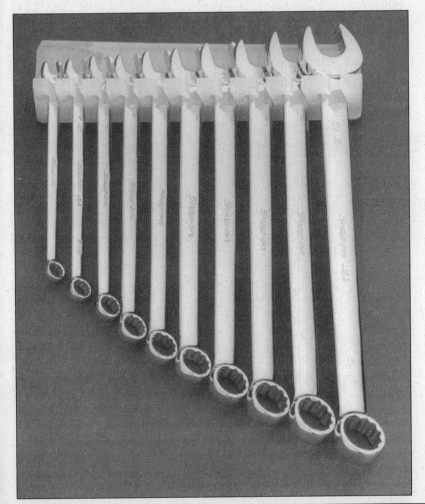

5.12 This MTS magnetic based tool rack can be placed onto the side of the box, on top of the tool cart or inside the box to provide easy accessibility

Automotive Tools Manual

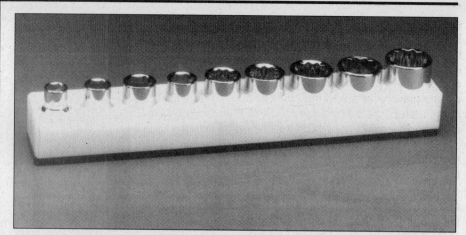

5.13 This 3/8 inch drive socket magnetic tool holder will accommodate shallow and deep sockets

5.14 This 1/4 inch drive bi-level organizer allows you to store shallow and deep sockets into one space-saving tool holder

marily for removing complete sets of sockets, screwdrivers etc. from the tool box and placing them on a metal surface such as a tool cart, side tool box or work bench and letting the magnetic bind keep the tools stationary and in order during the duration of the repair. Then the tools can be installed back into the tool box as a complete unit when the job is completed. The most popular type of magnetic tool holder is the socket holder and the wrench holder **(see illustrations)**. Some are designed for single socket sets others are designed for deep and shallow sets and oth-

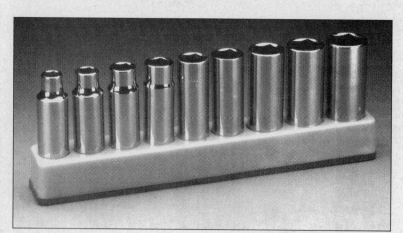

5.15 These deep sockets also fit in a magnetic tool holder designed for shallow sockets

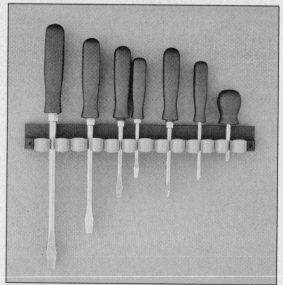

5.16 This MTS magnetic tool holder is designed for screwdrivers as well as wrenches, clippers, scissors and many other tools. The expandable loops will accommodate different socket handles also

ers are designed for swivel socket sets. Deep sockets can be installed into holders that are made for shallow sockets because of the magnetic properties of the holder. The magnetic tool holders are great for allowing the home mechanic keep the tools organized and clean and ready for the next job.

There are other types of magnetic tool holders that allow articles such as fire extinguishers, buffing compounds, coffee cups etc. to be mounted nearby on refrigerators, fenders or tool boxes **(see illustrations)**. These magnetic tool holders keep the material close by and handy for the immediate job.

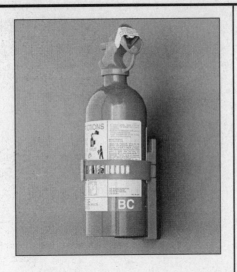

5.17 This multi purpose magnetic tool holder secures containers that need to be close to where you are working. The adjustable strap allows a safe and secure fit for containers up to 3 inches in diameter

5.18 Place a can of spray lubricant on the side of your tool box with an MTS magnetic tool holder

5.19 The multi-purpose holder is a very convenient way of keeping wax or rubbing compound handy by placing them on the fenders while buffing

Notes

Haynes Techbook Manual

6 Diagnostic tools and equipment

This Chapter is devoted to the tools and equipment needed to perform many of the diagnostic tasks necessary on the automotive engine and its sub-systems. Correct diagnosis is an essential part of every repair; without it you can only cure the problem by accident.

If you are concerned about the condition of your engine because of decreased performance or fuel economy, or maybe it's making some unusual noises or leaking fluid, you'll need to perform some basic tests to reach the proper diagnosis. You may want to perform a vacuum test, a power balance test or a compression test. Whatever diagnostic steps you are willing to take, you will need the proper tools.

Modern engines with computer-controlled fuel, emission and ignition systems will have their own related problems. If an engine won't start or runs poorly, you may want to begin your diagnosis by checking the fuel pressure or the spark voltage. You'll need the proper diagnostic tools again. If you need to continue on to the electronic engine management systems, there are lots of interesting high-tech pieces of equipment available to you for testing the computer and the sensors.

It's not always easy to diagnose an engine problem. A number of factors must be considered before even beginning. The tools and equipment in this chapter will help you to perform those special diagnostic tasks and are indispensable for determining the cause of your engine problem. Anything from a broken piston ring to a defective fuel injector can be properly diagnosed using these tools.

1 Engine diagnostic tools

The tools in this section will be used to determine the mechanical condition of your engine. They will help you decide if your engine needs a major overhaul or help pin-point the location of a problem, such as a misfiring cylinder, an unusual noise or a fluid leak. All of the tools and equipment discussed here are generally available at auto parts stores, with the exception of a few specialty pieces that may be found only at specialty tool stores or tool dealers. Granted, not every item will be used frequently enough for the home mechanic to justify its cost, but, if you do a lot of engine repair work, most of the tools will be needed sooner or later.

Stethoscope

Every moving part in the vehicle can make noise. Determining the source of the noise can be made easier by using a mechanic's stethoscope (see illustration). It looks just like the one your doctor uses, except that it's equipped with a noise attenuator to dampen the harsh sounds of the engine. Use it by placing the ear-pieces in your ears and probing the suspected area of the engine or component with the tip (see illustration). Move the listening device around until the sound is loudest. Depending on the problem, you may even want to short out the spark plug of each cylinder and note how that affects the sound. Think about what components are in the area of the noise and how they could produce the offensive sound.

Knocking or ticking noises are the most common types of internal engine noise. Noises that occur at crankshaft speed are usually caused by crankshaft, connecting rod and bearing problems, so begin your search on the lower part of the engine. Noises that occur at half of crankshaft speed usually involve the camshaft, lifters, rocker arms, valves, springs and mechanical fuel pump pushrod. Listen for these sounds near the top of the engine.

A stethoscope can be used to diagnose a faulty electronic fuel injector also. Much can be determined about the condition of the fuel injectors by listening to the clicking sound the solenoid contained in each injector is making. Place the tip of the stethoscope on each injector and listen for one that is abnormal from all the rest, or is not making any clicking noise at all, indicating an open circuit in the solenoid windings.

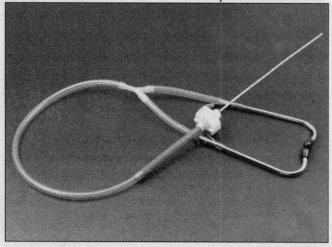

6.1 The stethoscope amplifies engine sounds, allowing you to pinpoint possible sources of pending trouble

6.2 Using a mechanics stethoscope, listen for changes in engine noise as you probe the various components or area of suspected trouble

Compression gauge

Good compression is vital for the operation of any internal combustion engine. A compression gauge (see illustrations) measures the compression, in pounds-per-square inch (psi), of each individual cylinder and is used to check the condition of the pistons, piston rings, valves, valve seats and head gaskets. Specifically, it can tell you if your engine's compression is low due to leakage caused by worn piston rings, a burned valve or valve seat or a blown head gasket. The gauge is installed in the spark plug hole, after the spark plug has been removed, and the engine is rotated while watching the gauge for the readings (see illustration).

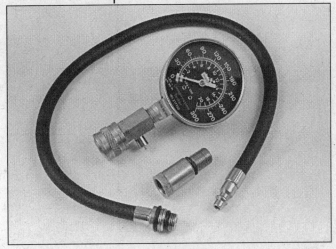

6.3 The compression gauge indicates combustion chamber pressure in pounds-per-square inch - this type threads directly into the spark plug hole

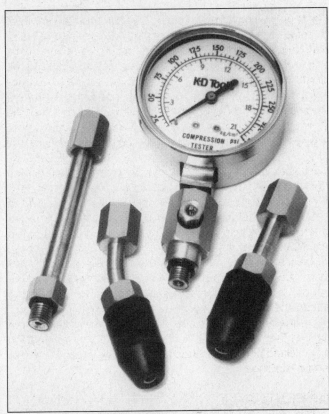

6.4 This compression tester doesn't thread into the spark plug hole; you simply push it into the hole and the rubber tip seals the compression - it's especially useful on small engines

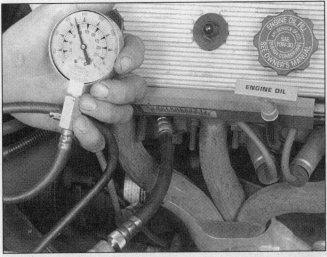

6.5 The compression gauge often is equipped with a quick-disconnect fitting, allowing you to thread the lower hose into the engine before connecting the gauge

How to take and read a compression check

Note: *The engine should be at normal operating temperature and the battery must be fully charged for this check.*

1   Begin by cleaning the area around the spark plugs to prevent dirt from entering the cylinders when the plugs are removed and the gauge installed. Compressed air is best for this, if available.

2   Remove all of the spark plugs from the engine. Be sure to keep them in order if they are to be re-installed.

3   Block the throttle wide-open (necessary to allow air into the cylinders to get an accurate reading).

How to take and read a compression check (continued)

4   Detach the coil wire from the center of the distributor cap and ground it on the engine block. If the engine is fuel injected, disable the fuel pump by removing the power to the circuit (remove the fuel pump fuse on most models).

5   Install the compression gauge into one of the spark plug holes.

6   Using the starter, crank the engine over at least five compression strokes and watch the gauge. The compression should build up quickly in a healthy engine. Low compression on the first stroke, followed by gradually increasing pressure on successive strokes, indicates worn piston rings. A low compression reading on the first stroke, which doesn't build up during successive strokes, indicates leaking valves or a blown head gasket (a cracked head or hole in the piston could also be the cause). Record the highest gauge reading obtained.

7   Repeat the procedure for the remaining cylinders. Record the readings and compare them with the compression test percentage chart (see illustration). If the readings differ by more than twenty percent among cylinders, internal engine components are damaged or excessively worn.

8   If any of the readings are low, remove the gauge and add about three squirts of engine oil from an oil can through the spark plug hole. Install the gauge and repeat the test.

9   If the compression increases after the oil is added, the piston rings are probably worn. If the compression does not increase significantly, the leakage is most likely occurring at the valves or head gasket. Leakage past the valves may be caused by burned valves and/or seats, warped or cracked valve faces, or a bent valve head or stem.

10   If two adjacent cylinders have equally low compression, there's a strong possibility that the head gasket between the cylinders in blown open. The appearance of coolant in the combustion chamber or the crankcase would verify this condition.

11   If one cylinder is about twenty percent lower than the others, and the engine has a slightly rough idle and/or backfires, a worn camshaft lobe could be the cause.

12   If the compression is unusually high, the combustion chambers are probably coated with carbon deposits and should be de-carbonized.

13   If the compression is very low or varies greatly between cylinders, it would be a good idea to perform a leak-down test to locate the exact point where leakage is occurring.

COMPRESSION TEST PERCENTAGE CHART

Maximum kPa (PSI)	Minimum kPa (PSI)	Maximum kPa (PSI)	Minimum kPa (PSI)	Maximum kPa (PSI)	Minimum kPa (PSI)	Maximum kPa (PSI)	Minimum kPa (PSI)
923.23 (134)	696.40 (101)	1130.78 (164)	848.09 (123)	1337.63 (194)	999.78 (145)	1544.48 (224)	1158.36 (168)
937.72 (136)	703.29 (102)	1144.57 (166)	858.98 (124)	1351.42 (196)	1013.57 (147)	1558.27 (226)	1165.26 (169)
951.51 (138)	717.08 (104)	1158.36 (168)	868.77 (126)	1365.21 (198)	1020.46 (148)	1572.06 (228)	1179.65 (171)
965.30 (140)	723.98 (105)	1172.15 (170)	875.67 (127)	1379.00 (200)	1034.25 (150)	1585.85 (230)	1185.94 (172)
979.09 (142)	737.77 (107)	1185.94 (172)	889.46 (129)	1392.79 (202)	1041.15 (151)	1599.64 (232)	1199.23 (174)
992.88 (144)	744.66 (108)	1199.73 (174)	903.25 (131)	1406.58 (204)	1054.94 (153)	1613.43 (234)	1206.63 (175)
1006.67 (146)	758.45 (110)	1206.63 (176)	910.14 (132)	1420.37 (206)	1061.83 (154)	1627.22 (236)	1220.42 (177)
1020.46 (148)	765.35 (111)	1227.31 (178)	917.04 (133)	1434.16 (208)	1075.62 (156)	1641.01 (238)	1227.31 (178)
1034.25 (150)	779.14 (113)	1241.10 (180)	930.83 (135)	1447.95 (210)	1082.52 (157)	1654.80 (240)	1241.10 (180)
1048.04 (152)	786.03 (114)	1254.89 (182)	937.72 (136)	1461.74 (212)	1089.41 (158)	1668.59 (242)	1248.00 (181)
1061.83 (154)	792.93 (115)	1268.68 (184)	951.51 (138)	1475.53 (214)	1103.20 (160)	1682.38 (244)	1261.79 (183)
1075.62 (156)	806.72 (117)	1282.47 (186)	965.30 (140)	1489.32 (216)	1116.99 (162)	1696.17 (246)	1268.68 (184)
1089.41 (158)	813.61 (118)	1296.26 (188)	972.20 (141)	1503.11 (218)	1123.89 (163)	1709.96 (248)	1282.47 (186)
1103.20 (160)	827.40 (120)	1310.05 (190)	979.09 (142)	1560.90 (220)	1137.68 (165)	1723.75 (250)	1289.37 (187)
1116.99 (162)	834.30 (121)	1323.84 (192)	992.88 (144)	1530.69 (222)	1144.57 (166)		

6.6 Locate your maximum compression reading on the chart and look to the right to find the minimum acceptable compression, then compare it to your lowest reading

Remote starter switch

A remote starter switch (see illustration) allows you to operate the starter from outside the vehicle. It's leads are hooked up to the starter solenoid and the battery and energizes the starter when the switch is depressed (see illustration). It can be used any time remote operation of the starter is required and is especially useful during a compression test. Make sure the leads are heavy enough to handle the current draw of the starter circuit and do not operate the starter for more than 15-seconds or overheating and damage to the starter motor can occur.

6.7 A remote starter switch is an invaluable tool to use anytime remote starter operation is desired, especially during a compression test

6.8 Connect the remote starter switch electrical leads to the starter solenoid and the positive battery terminal, then depress the switch to operate the starter - make certain you have disabled the ignition before using a remote starter or the engine may start

Cylinder leak-down tester

Cylinder leak-down testers (see illustration) are installed into the spark plug hole, much like a compression gauge, and pressurize the cylinder with compressed air supplied by an air compressor. Air is forced into the cylinder with the valves closed and the rate of leakage is measured as a percentage.

Used in conjunction with a compression test, which may identify one or more weak cylinders, the leak-down test better determines exactly where the problem lies. A cylinder leak-down test can locate problems like a blown head gasket, leaking exhaust valves, cracked cylinder walls and heads, and faulty pistons or rings. With the cylinder pressurized, air will leak past the worn or defective parts. By listening for the escaping air, you can tell exactly where it's coming from. If air is heard out the tail pipe, the exhaust valve is leaking; air coming from the intake manifold indicates a leaking intake valve. Remove the oil filler cap and listen for sounds of air coming from the crankcase, which indicates blow-by past the piston rings or a damaged piston.

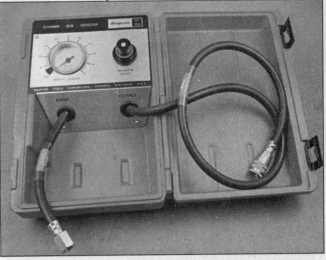

6.9 The leak-down tester indicates the rate at which pressure leaks past the piston rings, valves or head gasket in the combustion chamber

A leak-down test determines the overall condition of an engines cylinder walls, piston rings and valve sealing capabilities better than a compression test. In a compression test, you are comparing the readings from all cylinders with the highest reading, looking for noticeable differences. A leak-down test checks each cylinder individually and compares the percentage of leakage with a set value. A leakage rate of ten percent is considered normal and the engine in good condition. If a cylinder leakage rate is twenty percent or more it is considered excessive and repairs should be made.

Block-tester

If your engine has been severely overheated and is running poorly with a loss of power, a blown head gasket may be the cause. Sometimes difficult to diagnose by other methods, the combustion leak block-tester can diagnose a cracked cylinder block, cylinder head or blown head gasket by detecting exhaust gases in the cooling system, which indicates a compression leak from a cylinder into the coolant.

The block-tester consists of a large bulb-type syringe and bottle of test fluid **(see illustration)**. A measured amount of the fluid is added to the syringe. The syringe is placed over the radiator filler neck, and with the engine running, the bulb is squeezed and a sample of the gases present in the top of the radiator are drawn up through the test fluid **(see illustration)**. If any combustion gases are present in the sample taken, the test fluid will change color.

If the block-test indicates combustion gas is present in the cooling system, you can be sure that the engine has a blown head gasket or a crack in the cylinder head or block, and will require disassembly to repair. Block-testers and extra test fluid are readily available from most auto parts stores.

6.10 The combustion leak block tester kit consists of a bulb, syringe and test fluid and tests for cracked blocks or heads and leaking head gaskets by detecting combustion gases in the coolant

6.11 Place the tester over the radiator filler neck and use the syringe bulb to draw a sample into the tester

Vacuum gauge

A vacuum gauge **(see illustration)** provides fast, easy and valuable information on the condition of the engine. You can check for worn piston rings or cylinder walls, leaking cylinder head or intake manifold gaskets, incorrect carburetor adjustments, restricted exhaust system, stuck or burned valves, weak valve springs, improper ignition timing and other ignition problems. Unfortunately, vacuum gauge readings are easy to misinterpret, so they should be used in conjunction with other tests to confirm the diagnosis.

Both the absolute readings and the rate of needle movement are important for accurate interpretation. Most gauges measure vacuum in inches-of-mercury (in-Hg). As a point of reference, normal atmospheric pressure at sea level is about 30 in-Hg. As altitude increases (or atmospheric pressure decreases), the reading will decrease. For every 1,000 foot increase in elevation, over 3,000 feet, the gauge readings will decrease about one inch-of-mercury.

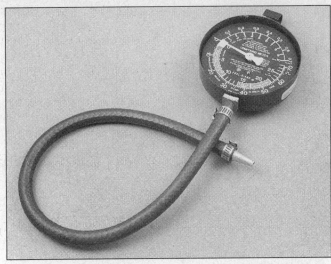

6.12 The vacuum gauge indicates intake manifold vacuum in inches-of-mercury (in-Hg) - it can tell you if the engine is producing good intake vacuum, help you determine if the catalytic converter is blocked and also aid in diagnosing a wide variety of engine related problems

How to use a vacuum gauge to diagnose engine problems

Connect the vacuum gauge directly to an intake manifold vacuum source, not to ported vacuum (carburetor or throttle body) **(see illustration)**. Make sure no hoses are left disconnected during the test or false readings will result.

Start the engine and allow it to warm up completely (upper radiator hose hot). Block the wheels and set the parking brake.

With the engine idling, read the vacuum gauge; a healthy engine should produce about 15 to 20 in-Hg, at sea level, with the needle on the gauge holding fairly steady.

Refer to the following vacuum gauge readings and the indicated engine diagnosis:

6.13 Connect the vacuum gauge to a good source of intake manifold vacuum

Low steady reading

This usually indicates a leaking gasket between the intake manifold and carburetor or throttle body, a leaking vacuum hose, late ignition timing or incorrect camshaft timing **(see illustration)**. Check ignition timing with a timing light and eliminate all other possible causes.

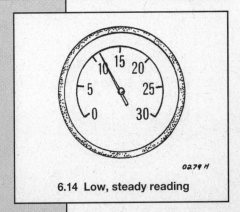

6.14 Low, steady reading

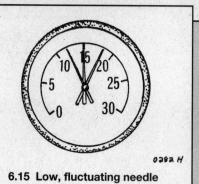

6.15 Low, fluctuating needle

Low, fluctuating reading

If the needle fluctuates about three to eight inches below normal **(see illustration)**, suspect an intake manifold gasket leak at an intake port or a faulty fuel injector on multi-port fuel injected models.

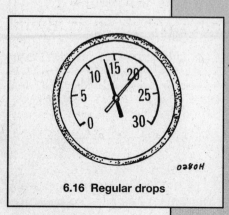

6.16 Regular drops

Regular drops

If the needle drops about two to four inches at a steady rate **(see illustration)**, the valves are probably leaking. Perform a compression check and/or a leak-down test to confirm.

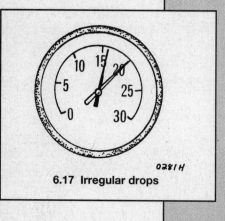

6.17 Irregular drops

Irregular drops

An irregular down-flick of the needle **(see illustration)** can be caused by a sticking valve or an ignition misfire. Perform a compression test and/or a leak-down test and check the ignition system.

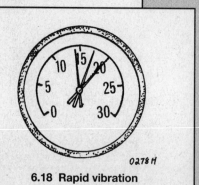

6.18 Rapid vibration

Rapid vibration

A rapid four in-Hg, or more, vibration at idle **(see illustration)** combined with exhaust smoke indicates worn valve guides. Perform a leak-down test to confirm. If the rapid vibration occurs with an increase in engine speed, check for a leaking intake manifold gasket or head gasket, weak valve springs, burned valves or an ignition misfire.

Slight fluctuation

A slight fluctuation of about one in-Hg up and down, may indicate an ignition problem. Check all the usual tune-up items and, if necessary, perform additional ignition system diagnosis.

Large fluctuation

A large fluctuation indicates a weak or dead cylinder, or a blown head gasket. Perform a compression and/or a leak-down test to confirm **(see illustration)**.

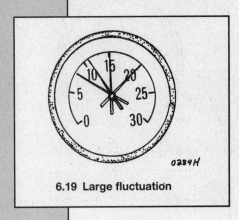

6.19 Large fluctuation

Slow hunting

If the needle moves slowly through a wide range, check for a clogged PCV system, incorrect idle fuel mixture, carburetor/throttle body or intake manifold gasket leaks.

Slow return after revving

Quickly open the throttle until the engine speed reaches approximately 2,500 rpm and let it snap shut. Normally the reading should drop to near zero, rise above normal idle reading (about 5 in-Hg over) and then return to the previous idle reading **(see illustration)**. If the vacuum returns slowly and doesn't peak when the throttle is snapped shut, the piston rings may be worn. If there's a long delay, look for a restricted exhaust system (often the muffler or catalytic converter). An easy method of confirming this is to temporarily disconnect the exhaust ahead of the suspected component and perform the test again.

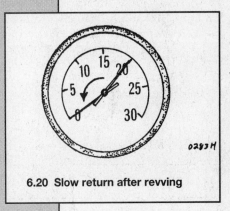

6.20 Slow return after revving

Oil pressure gauge

An oil pressure gauge **(see illustration)** provides a fairly good indication of the condition of the engine bearings and oil pump. As bearing surfaces wear, oil clearances increase. This increased clearance allows oil to flow through the bearings more readily, which results in lower oil pressure. Oil pumps also wear which causes an additional loss of pressure.

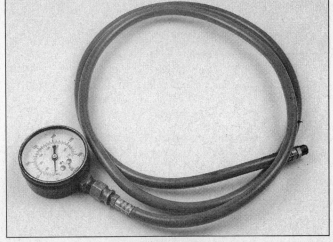

6.21 The oil pressure gauge indicates the oil pressure, in psi, of the lubrication system

If the oil pressure warning light comes on while driving, or if the vehicle gauge reads dangerously low, check the engine oil pressure with a mechanical gauge. To install the gauge in the engine, remove the oil pressure sending unit and install the gauge hose fitting in its place **(see illustration)**. Sometimes an adapter is needed to match the threads. Start the engine and allow it to reach normal operating temperature. Read the oil pressure gauge; if the pressure is extremely low, the bearings and/or oil pump are probably worn or the oil pump pressure regulator valve is stuck. As a general rule, an engine should produce about ten psi of oil pressure for each 1,000 rpm of engine speed. If the mechanical gauge reads normal during the test, suspect a faulty oil pressure sending unit, faulty wiring or a defective warning light or dash gauge.

6.22 Thread the oil pressure gauge hose fitting in place of the oil pressure sending unit

Vacuum/pressure pump

Most engines are equipped with all sorts of vacuum operated devices that depend on a good source of vacuum for proper operation. This vacuum comes from the intake manifold. These devices could be part of the emissions system, such as an EGR valve, or an accessory such as a vacuum operated cruise control servo. Most carburetors are equipped with a vacuum operated choke pull-off diaphragm, and many engines are equipped with one or more thermo-vacuum switches.

To check these devices, you will need a hand operated vacuum pump **(see illustration)**. With this instrument, you can apply a specific amount of vacuum to a device and test its ability to operate properly or hold vacuum for a specific period of time **(see illustration)**. An integral part on all but the least expensive vacuum pumps is the gauge.

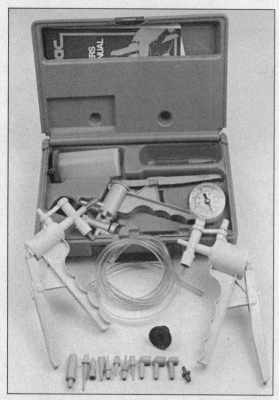

6.23 A hand operated vacuum pump and gauge is indispensable for troubleshooting emissions systems components; it can help you trace vacuum leaks and test all sorts of vacuum operated devices - Mityvac pumps (shown) are available as inexpensive plastic models, like the two in the foreground (one of which can be purchased without a gauge), and sturdier metal units like the one in the box. Kits come with a variety of fittings and adapters, and can be used for a host of other applications besides emissions tests

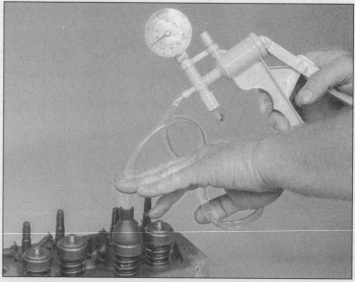

6.24 Many special adapters are available for use with a vacuum pump, like the adapter shown here, used to check the O-ring valve stem seal for leaks

The gauge measures the amount of vacuum applied to the circuit or device which is crucial for diagnostic purposes.

Many accessories are becoming available for the top-of-the-line vacuum pumps. Converters are available which allow the pump to create and read either vacuum or pressure at the flick of a switch (see illustration). Brake bleeding kits (see Chapter 3) are one of the most popular accessories. Mityvac has recently introduced a leak-down checker kit for use with a hand-held vacuum pump. Also available are the turbocharger wastegate test kit and a cooling system pressure tester (see **Cooling system pressure tester**).

Fuel pressure gauge

Checking fuel pressure is a critical factor in diagnosing any fuel-related problem. Fuel pressure readings reflect the health of the fuel system. Without the correct pressure, performance and fuel economy will inevitably suffer.

Before the widespread appearance of fuel-injected engines, checking fuel pump pressure was a simple matter. One would remove the fuel line to the carburetor, install the gauge on the line, crank the engine and read the pressure. Most vacuum gauges (see **Vacuum gauge**) also measured low pressure and could be used to check the output of a mechanical fuel pump, which was normally in the 5 to 7 psi range for a good pump.

Fuel injection created a whole new ball game. Fuel injection requires high fuel-system pressure to operate. Electric fuel pumps are required. They are often mounted inside the fuel tank and require gauges capable of reading higher pressures for diagnosis. Throttle-body fuel injection (one or two injectors spraying into a manifold) generally operate in the 15 to 20 psi range, while multi-port fuel injection systems (one injector for each cylinder) operate in the 30 to 40 psi range. Some continuous injection systems (CIS) operate at even higher pressures. As you can see, you can't use that old low pressure gauge you've had in your tool box for so long to check your new fuel-injected car or truck.

Installing the fuel pressure gauge into the system is another problem. First and foremost, relieve the fuel system pressure before opening any fuel line connections on a fuel injected engine. Remember, the system operates under high pressure and its possible for fuel to spray out, creating a very unsafe condition, especially if the engine is still hot. Consult a *Haynes Automotive Repair Manual* or the *Haynes Fuel Injection Diagnostic Manual* for fuel relief procedures. Some manufacturers have made installing a gauge very easy by providing schrader valve-type test ports on their vehicles. After relieving fuel pressure, simply thread the gauge hose on the test port. Other models do not provide test ports, and therefore some type of adapter will be needed to tap into the fuel system. Adapters are a large part of any fuel injection test kit (see illustrations).

6.25 The Mityvac Dual converter, when installed on a hand-held vacuum pump, quickly converts from vacuum to pressure with the twist of a knob

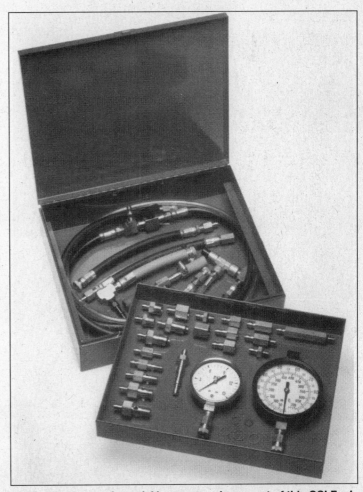

6.26 Adapters and special hoses are a large part of this GSI Fuel Injection Test Kit; they are necessary to allow the gauges to be used on most all foreign and domestic fuel injection systems - this kit is complete with a low pressure gauge (0 to 15 psi) and a high pressure gauge (0 to 100 psi) which feature a quick-coupling system for connecting the adapter/hoses to the gauge heads

6.27 Here is how a fuel pressure gauge is inserted into a fuel line - Unless your vehicle is equipped with a test-port, it will be absolutely necessary to obtain the correct hoses and fittings before a safe fuel pressure check can be made

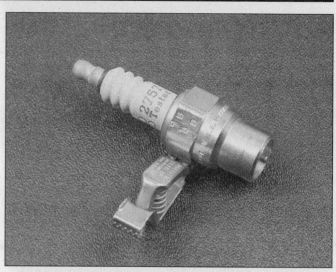

6.28 This spark tester looks like a spark plug. If sufficient voltage is reaching the tester, a nice blue spark will jump the gap when the engine is cranked

Calibrated spark tester

The best troubleshooting tool for simple ignition problems is a spark tester **(see illustration)**. Inexpensive and easy to use, a spark tester provides instant diagnosis of ignition coils, spark plug wires and spark plugs. Just remove the boot from the spark plug and plug it into the grounded tester and crank the engine **(see illustration)**. If the coil and plug wire are good the spark will jump the gap of the tester. If no spark is present, check the plug wire with an ohmmeter **(see illustration)**. If the wire checks out OK, further diagnosis of the coil and primary ignition circuit may be necessary.

6.29 To use the spark tester, disconnect a spark plug wire and connect it to the tester, attach the tester ground clip to the engine and watch for spark as you operate the starter

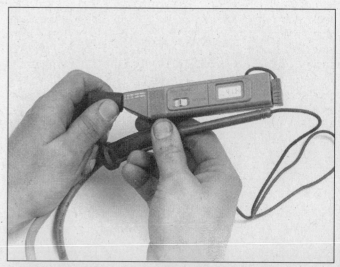

6.30 If no spark is present at the tester, check the spark plug wire for continuity with an ohmmeter - as a rule-of-thumb, no wire should have a resistance of more than 30,000 ohms

Certain models of spark plug testers are calibrated for electronic "high energy" ignition, while another tester will be needed to check conventional points-type ignition. There is one model available that is adjustable from 0 to 40,000 volts, allowing it to be used on standard, electronic and distributorless ignition systems **(see illustration)**. It is also part of a distributorless ignition test kit which is able to perform quick and easy power-balance tests on distributorless ignition systems **(see illustration)**.

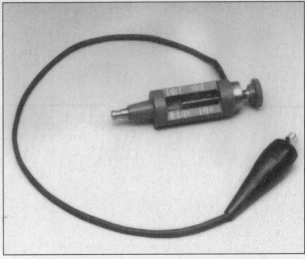

6.31 PRI's spark tester is adjustable from 0 to 40,000 ohms, allowing it to be used on all types of ignition systems

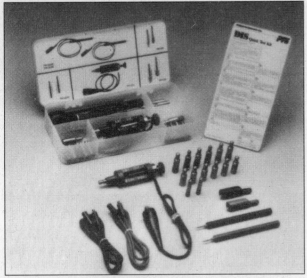

6.32 PRI's Distributorless Ignition System Quick Test Kit comes with all the necessary pieces to perform a quick, easy and safe power balance test on a distributorless ignition system

Cooling system pressure tester

The cooling system and engine can be checked for leaks with a cooling system pressure tester **(see illustrations)**. Install the pump onto the radiator filler neck, and pump up the system to the operating pressure rating found on the radiator cap, usually about 8 to 15 psi **(see illustration)**. If there are any leak points present, coolant will be expelled through the opening immediately. It will find leaks in the radiator, hoses, water pump, heater core and engine gaskets. It can be pumped up to pressure and left on the system to locate a nagging slow leak. Adapters are also available to check the pressure rating of the radiator cap.

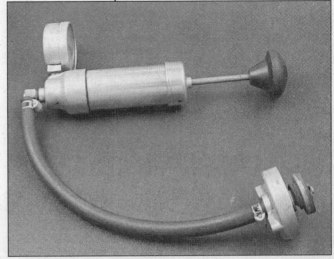

6.33 This is the most common cooling system pressure tester, consisting of a pump, gauge and radiator filler neck adapter

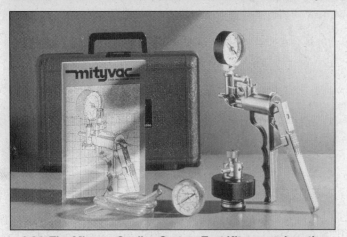

6.34 The Mityvac Cooling System Test Kit pressurizes the cooling system using their popular hand-held pump and comes with a temperature probe to determine the operating temperature of the cooling system; a wide range of adapters are also available to test radiators on most foreign and domestic vehicles

6.35 To use the cooling system pressure tester, install the pump onto the radiator filler neck, pump up the system to the pressure indicated on the radiator cap (usually 8 to 15 psi); inspect for leaks and watch the gauge on the tester, looking for a pressure drop

UV-Fluorescent leak detector

One of the newest innovations in leak detection is the ultra-violet/fluorescent leak detection system **(see illustration)**. It is the best method of pinpointing the exact location of a fluid leak in an automotive engine or transmission. This method of leak detection is used and approved by most major auto manufacturers. Here's how it works:

A measured amount of dye is added to the system being checked **(see illustration)**. Dyes are available for all types of systems; engine, transmission, cooling system, air conditioning, etc. The dye is totally compatible with the systems fluid and will not damage any internal engine or system components.

Run the engine to circulate the dye throughout the system. If added to the engine or transmission it might be a good idea to drive the vehicle for a few miles. If added to the cooling system or air conditioning system driving is not necessary, but don't forget to turn on the air conditioning or heater.

After you're satisfied it has run long enough for the leak to present itself, stop the engine and begin scanning every possible leak point with the ultra-violet lamp **(see illustration)**. The leak will show up under the lamp as a bright fluorescent glow and you'll be able to trace the leak directly to its source.

This method is extremely valuable in locating engine oil leaks. Often the leak has been present for some time and the engine is covered with old oil, sludge and grime. The leak will show up under the UV lamp without having to completely steam clean the engine, which would be necessary to locate the leak otherwise. Also, you may have a slow leak that is next to impossible to locate using conventional methods. With the UV detector, add the dye and drive the vehicle as long as necessary before inspecting with the lamp. This method also works well for locating slow refrigerant leaks in the air conditioning system.

6.36 Tracer products UV-Fluorescent Leak Detection Master Kit contains a 120-watt self-ballasted high intensity UV inspection lamp, six tracer-stick capsules, two control valves and a quick-coupler for R-12 air conditioning systems, eight bottles of gasoline engine oil dye, two bottles of automatic transmission dye, two bottles of engine coolant dye, and a pair of UV-absorbing glasses all in a plastic carrying/storage case

This system is a bit expensive for the home mechanic to justify buying. But now you know how it works, and if you are plagued with a nagging leak that no one can seem to find you may want to seek out a professional who uses a UV/fluorescent leak detector.

6.37 To use the UV-Fluorescent leak detection kit, first add the dye to the system being checked - here the dye is being added to the air conditioning system using the Tracer-Stick capsule

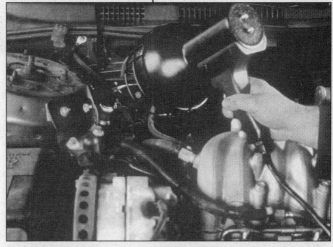

6.38 Next, shine the High-intensity UV lamp over all the points of possible leakage until the leak is located by its fluorescent glow

2 Electronic diagnostic tools and test equipment

A large part of the diagnostic work performed in shops, garages and dealerships around the country today is focused on the complicated electronic engine management systems found on modern automobiles. The computerized fuel, emissions and ignition systems are vital to the efficient operation of any modern vehicle. Even a minor malfunction of one of the electronic systems will cause the vehicle to run poorly, or not run at all, and will need to be diagnosed and repaired immediately if you wish to return the vehicle to service.

The tools in this section are used mostly in the diagnosis of computerized engine management systems. The system components are comprised of solid-state electronic devices and micro-processors, and many of the tools used in their diagnosis are, likewise, electronic devices.

Many of the tools in this section are very expensive and will never be needed or purchased by the average home mechanic but are included to give you an idea of what is available and what direction the industry is headed. Many of the tools are very difficult to use; they require at least some knowledge of basic electronics and some level of skill to operate successfully. But, fortunately, a new piece of test equipment will include detailed instructions on its use and often more! For instance, a computer scan tool will include a small booklet of instructions and diagnostic information, often detailing symptoms you will typically encounter and instructions for complete diagnosis and repair.

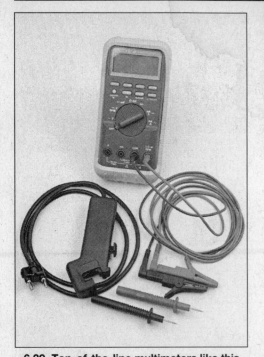

6.39 Top-of-the-line multimeters like this Fluke Model 88 can do a lot of things besides measure volts, amps and ohms - using a wide array of adapters and cables, most of which are included in the basic kit, they can check the status of all the important information sensors, measure the duty-cycle of feedback carburetors and idle air control motors, and even measure the pulse width of the fuel injectors

Digital multimeter

The digital multimeter **(see illustrations)** is one tool everyone should have in their workshop if they plan to work on modern automobiles. The term "multimeter" is used because the meter performs multiple functions; it measures voltage (volts), resistance (ohms) and current (amperes). It can be used not only on the computerized engine management system but also on accessories like cruise control, air conditioning, power windows and door locks. The meter can be used, as well, to check the charging system and current draws on the battery.

A digital multimeter measures volts, ohms and amperes with a high degree of accuracy. It displays its measurements in tenths, hundredths and even thousandths of a volt, ohm or ampere. When working with modern electronic circuits, which are often very low-voltage, this kind of reading is essential for a meaningful diagnosis. A digital meter is somewhat more expensive than an analog unit, but it is absolutely necessary if you want to troubleshoot electronic circuits and devices. That's because a digital meter has a *high-impedance* circuit inside; the resistance of a digital meter's internal circuitry is 10 million ohms (10 M-ohms). Because a voltmeter must be hooked up in parallel to the circuit or load being tested, it's vital that none of the voltage measured be allowed to travel the parallel path set up by the meter itself. This is exactly what happens to analog meters (most of which don't have this high-impedance circuitry) when they're used to measure low voltage circuits. If a fraction of a volt goes through the meter when you're measuring a 12-volt circuit, it doesn't much matter; your reading is still close enough to be considered accurate. But, if you are measuring an extremely low-voltage circuit, an oxygen sensor for example, a fraction of a volt may be a significant portion of what your working with. Allowing any voltage to sneak through the meter will upset the accuracy of your reading. That's why a digital meter is essential for accurate measurements on many of the circuits you'll be working with.

6.40 Alltest 3520 Digital Multimeter performs any electrical or electronic check required on any system, on any car and is versatile enough to do many other jobs around the shop or home

6.41 Sunpro CP7678 Digital Multimeter performs complete tune-up and troubleshooting tests on computer controlled, as well as older vehicles; including automotive tests such as tach and dwell - it features a gasketed and watertight high impact ABS housing

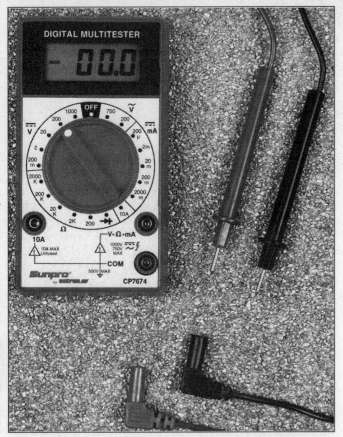

6.42 Digital multimeters do not have to be expensive - this Sunpro CP7674 is an economical multitester for home or shop use, it is computer safe and includes instructions in English and Spanish

6.43 Sunpro Sensor Tester Plus is a versatile tool designed to test computer sensors and ignition modules - it tests most sensors on or off the vehicle and tests ignition modules for GM, Ford and Chrysler

Sensor tester

The computerized engine management systems used on today's automobiles rely on sensors of various types to monitor the actual working conditions of the engine. A faulty sensor, a defect in the wiring or a problem in the computer itself is often the cause of an engine performance problem and is usually very hard to identify. Unfortunately, one of the most common methods of attempting to repair these difficult problems is simply replacing the suspected sensor or component with a new unit and hoping for the best. This type of action, more often than not, results in the wrong diagnosis being made and much time and money wasted.

A new group of tools on the market today are sensor simulators or testers **(see illustrations)**. The testers have the capability of testing the sensors both on or off the vehicle and can simulate a good sensor signal back through the wiring harness to the computer circuit. By simulating various sensor inputs, you can verify whether or not the sensors signal is getting through to the computer, and whether the computer is reading what it should and is making the appropriate response.

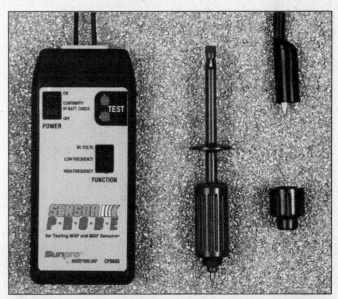

6.44 Sunpro Sensor Probe was designed for quick and easy testing of the Manifold Absolute Pressure, Mass Air Flow and Vane Air Flow sensors - its unique probe design allows for *in circuit testing* for accurate diagnosis

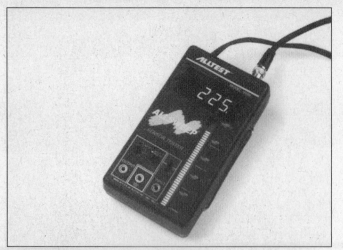

6.45 Alltest Model 9100 Allsweep is a versatile hand-held tester capable of testing a sensor both on or off the vehicle and can simulate a known good sensor signal back through the harness to the computer circuit - it features a labscope interface that allows digital readings on any labscope via a BNC connector

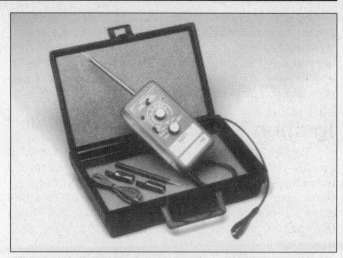

6.47 Products Research, Inc. offers a complete line of quality sensor simulator/testers starting with the SST which can simulate any Oxygen, Knock, Mass Air Flow, Manifold Air Pressure or Barometric Pressure sensor, any variable resistance type sensor (coolant or air temperature) and any three wire Throttle Position sensor

The top-of-the-line models have the capability of testing virtually all sensors in any modern car or truck. Essentially these tools provide a complete inventory of sensors in one convenient box.

6.46 Alltest Model 5300 oxygen Sensor Tester and Simulator is capable of simulating an oxygen sensor on any vehicle - it can accurately measure the output of any oxygen sensor as well as simulate a rich or lean condition back through the harness to the computer circuit to verify the wiring harness and the computer operation

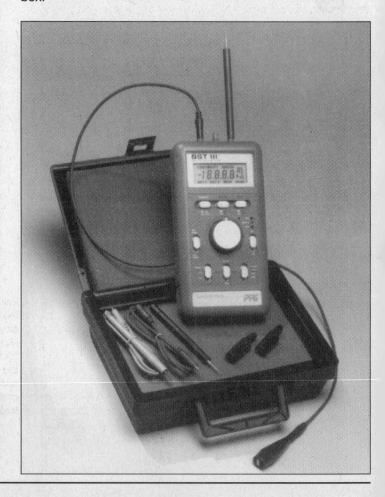

6.48 PRI's top-of-the-line SST III Sensor Simulator/Tester can simulate and test all sensors on any vehicle - it features a built-in digital Volt/Ohm meter to measure the output of any sensor and an AC voltage output to simulate Vehicle Speed sensors, Camshaft or Crankshaft Position sensors and ignition reluctors

By actually simulating the working conditions of any sensor without removing it from the vehicle, the sensor tester allows the correct diagnosis to be made, eliminating unnecessary replacement of non-defective sensors. Finally, an all-in-one tool that will tell you if the sensor, sensor harness and computer circuits are good!

Ignition tester

Electronic ignition systems have long since replaced breaker-point style ignition as the system of choice for the automotive industry. Using solid state circuitry, the electronic ignition module is, however, prone to failure and is another component that is very difficult to test. Often falling into the "diagnosis by substitution" category, many good modules are replaced needlessly.

The professional way to check an electronic ignition module is by testing it, not substituting it. For that you'll use an Electronic Ignition Tester (see illustration). The electronic ignition tester provides a fast , simple and accurate pass/fail indication, finding out if the module is at fault without removing it from the vehicle. They're capable of testing a wide range of domestic and imported modules.

Another very capable ignition tester is the Peak KV Analyzer (see illustration). It's a hand held tester that measures the ignition system performance on any vehicle. The inductive pick-up is placed on a spark plug wire and as the engine is cranked or started. The unit reads the firing voltage of the cylinder immediately. It will quickly help you locate problems such as; fouled, worn or incorrectly gapped

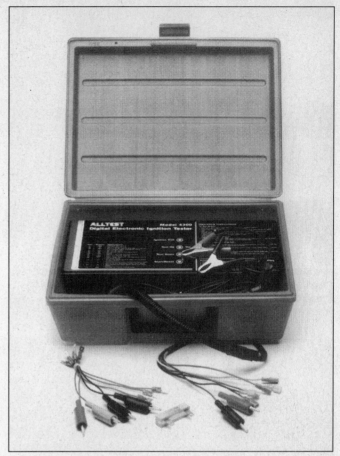

6.49 Alltest Model 4300 Digital Electronic Ignition Tester tests a wide range of domestic and imported ignition modules with the module still on the car - besides testing ignition modules it can perform primary voltage tests, distributor pick-up tests and ignition coil spark tests by actually firing the coil - test results are given as pass/fail indications, so there's no need to interpret any values or use any manuals

6.50 Alltest Model 5400 Peak KV analyzer is a hand-held tester capable of measuring ignition system performance on any vehicle and any type of ignition system - next to a full-sized "scope" the Peak KV tester is the best method available for providing peak KV's (kilo-volts) for each cylinder, allowing the user to troubleshoot a faulty coil, coil lead, cap and rotor, spark plug wire or spark plug; it will also help you locate problems with low compression, ignition timing, vacuum leaks, fuel mixture or a computer sensor

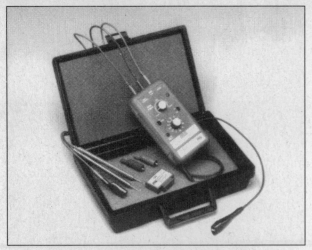

6.51 PRI's new Ignition System Simulator/Tester tests ignition modules, coil packs, cam or crank sensors on all standard, electronic or distributorless ignition systems on any vehicle using interchangeable software modules

spark plugs, open or shorted spark plug wires, faulty coil, coil lead or cap and rotor. It can also aid in diagnosing cylinder compression problems, fuel-mixture or injector problems and faulty sensors.

Many modern vehicles are now equipped with Distributorless Ignition Systems (DIS). The DIS consists of solid state modules and cam and/or crankshaft position sensors which cannot be tested using conventional methods. New testers have been developed that can simulate the cam or crank sensor providing complete diagnostic troubleshooting capabilities by inputting a good signal directly to the ignition module **(see illustration)**. This tester simulates the engine running, so all relays and fuel injectors will operate during ignition tests, making it possible to check fuel-injection timing at the same time.

Engine analyzers

The large console-type engine analyzers are obviously out of the price range of the home mechanic and will not be covered here. What we will show you are the various hand held units and a couple of modular units on the market today. Some of these units may not have the capabilities of testing all systems like the big analyzers, but, using smart diagnostic procedures and a little common sense, you'll be surprised at what you can accomplish.

Hand-held units

The hand-held Digital Engine Analyzer is rugged, dependable and accurate **(see illustrations)**. You can run extensive test sequences on all types of vehicles. A long list of basic tests can be performed on starting, charging, electrical and fuel systems. They include a tachometer, dwell meter, voltmeter, ohmmeter, ammeter and are capable of performing cranking amps test, alternator voltage and amperage test, idle speed and power balance tests and much more.

Additional hand-held units are available to adapt the engine analyzer for use on diesel engines **(see illustration)**. Other units are used to analyze the charging system only.

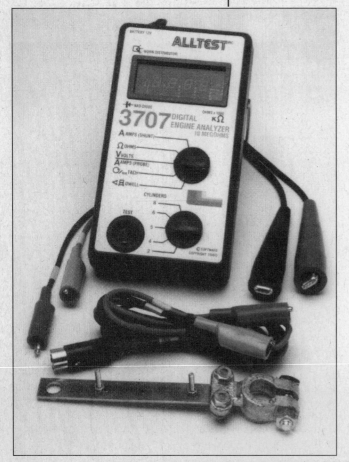

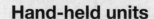

6.52 Alltest Model 3707 Digital Engine Analyzer can run basic starting, charging, ignition and fuel systems tests on all types of vehicles

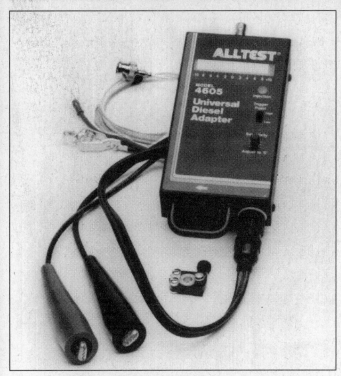

6.53 Alltest Universal Diesel Adapter converts Alltest Analyzers for use with diesel engines

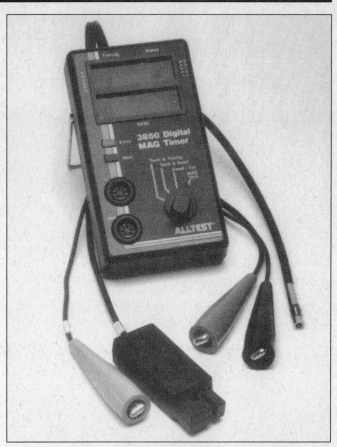

6.54 Alltest Model 3850 Digital Mag Timer takes RPM timing and dwell readings on any engine with a magnetic timing socket

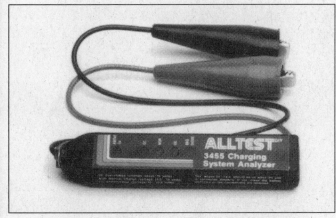

6.55 Alltest Model 3455 Charging System Analyzer performs a quick check of the battery and alternator condition to determine whether in depth tests are needed or if the alternator is in a failure state

Modular units

Modular engine analyzers offer all the capabilities of the large console type analyzers, but in a smaller package **(see illustration)**. They use a scope to display primary and secondary ignition patterns as well as injector pulse width and other sensor or actuator outputs. Many modular units are also transportable, they can be taken on a road test with the vehicle.

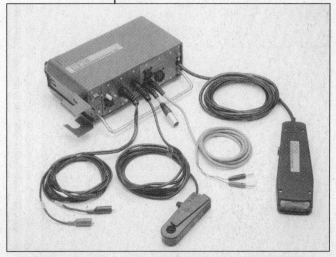

6.56 Micro Processor Systems, Inc. Engine Analyzer Module (EAM) connects to any 286/386/486 or Pentium PC giving you the power of intelligent diagnosis and the ability to perform like an expert - the EAM features all the functions of a full-sized console-based engine analyzer, *and more*

The modular gas analyzer **(see illustration)** interfaces with the modular engine analyzer. The gas analyzer takes tailpipe readings to provide emission information that can tell you exactly how the engine is running. At a glance, you can tell whether the engine, ignition, fuel systems and emissions controls are operating correctly and make the necessary adjustments for peak performance.

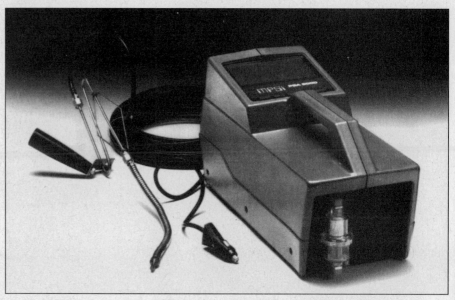

6.57 MPSI's Performance Gas Analyzer (PGA) is a portable emissions analyzer module capable of measuring 4-gas readings to BAR 90 standards

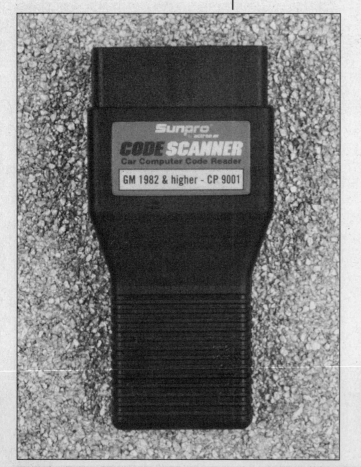

Code scanners

The on-board computers used on modern automobiles have some self-diagnostic capabilities. If the computer senses a problem with itself or one of the sensors it triggers a dashboard light to come on, warning the operator of possible impending trouble. At the same time a code is set in the computer memory. Accessing this code with a code scanner **(see illustrations)** allows you to "read" the diagnostic trouble code, you may then opt to attempt the repairs yourself or take your vehicle to a repair center.

Each auto manufacturer has equipped their vehicles with their own test connector access point and set of trouble codes. There are code scanners available for most all systems that are accessible.

6.58 Sunpro GM Code Scanner plugs into the on-board computer's diagnostic connector and trouble codes flash on the dashboard "Check Engine" light

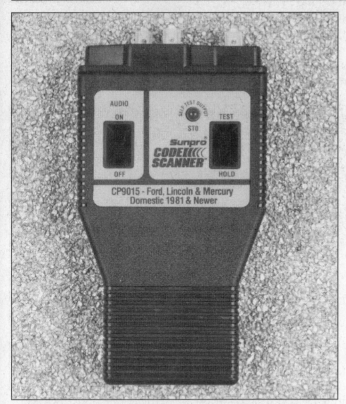

6.59 Sunpro Ford Code Scanner has a built-in battery and audio and visual indicators for reading codes - it accesses Ford's Self-Test system and allows the user to perform operator input tests like the Cylinder Balance Test

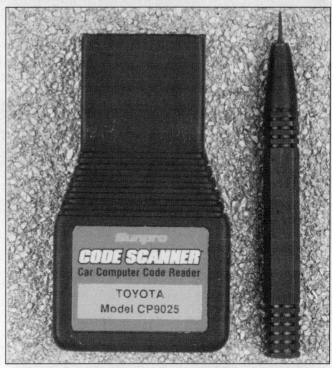

6.60 Sunpro Toyota/Honda/Nissan Code Scanner accesses the on-board computer and trouble codes flash on the dashboard "Check Engine" light or computer module

Computer scan tool

Hand-held digital computer scanners are powerful and versatile tools for analyzing computerized engine management systems **(see illustrations)**. These tools do more than just access codes; they provide the user with a window into the computer system.

A scan tool interfaces with the on-board computer, and the actual operating conditions of the sensors are displayed on the scan tool's digital display. Armed with that information, you can quickly tell if an oxygen sensor, throttle position sensor or any other sensor is operating out-of-range. Depending on the model of vehicle, a power balance test may be performed using a scan tool. The anti-lock brake system, speed control system, automatic ride control system, etc. may be accessed as well.

A scan tool will come complete with the necessary cables to hook up to one or more systems, but you may need adapters and other cartridges to be able to use the tool on different makes of automobiles. They will always include complete operating instructions and a comprehensive diagnostic guide for the make and models the tool is purchased for.

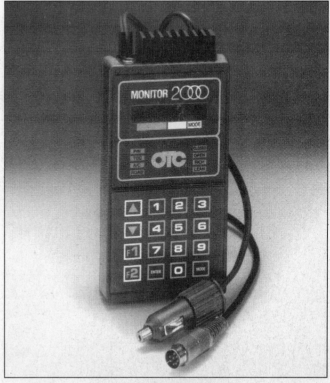

6.61 Scan tools like the OTC Monitor 2000 are powerful diagnostic aids - using software cartridges programmed with comprehensive diagnostic information for your vehicle, they can tell you just about anything you want to know about your engine management system

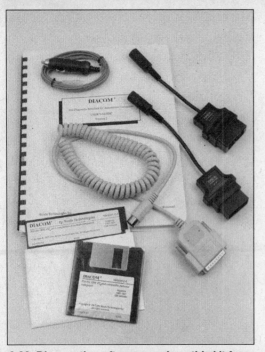

6.62 Diagnostic software, such as this kit from Diacom, turns your IBM PC or compatible into a scan tool, saving you the extra cost of buying a scanner but providing you with all the same information

6.63 In 1980 Micro Processor Systems, Inc. introduced the automotive industry's *first* scan tool; today they claim to have the most expandable and affordable on-board computer diagnostic tester available - the Pro-Link 9000 - the Pro-Link works on a wide variety of automotive and heavy duty applications; specifics for each manufacturer are stored in the Pro-Link cartridge

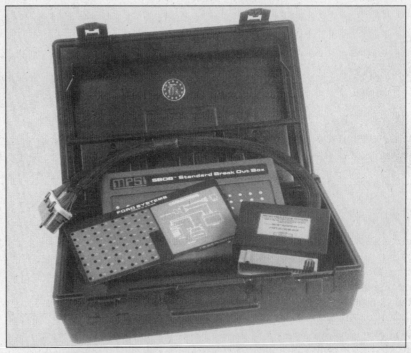

6.64 The MPSI Breakout Box is used in conjunction with a scan tool and provides access to the computer, sensors and actuators through the wiring harness for even more diagnostic information

7 Engine repair and rebuilding tools

The home mechanic is faced with a number of options when the time comes for an engine overhaul. The decision to replace the block or rebuild the block; to re-bore or re-ring will depend on a number of factors. One must consider the value of the vehicle, the cost of the overhaul, parts availability and access to machine shop facilities. The time required to complete the project and the skill level of the home mechanic are also factors.

If the decision is made to overhaul the engine, familiarize yourself with the scope and requirements of the job before beginning the engine overhaul. Overhauling an engine isn't extremely difficult if you follow all of the instructions carefully, have the necessary tools and equipment and pay close attention to all the specifications and details.

Most of the work is done with ordinary hand tools, but, depending on the scope and requirements of the job, you may need one or more of the special rebuilding or precision measuring tools shown in this Chapter.

1 Engine repair and rebuilding tools

Cylinder ridge reamer

If the engine has accumulated a lot of hard miles, upon removal of the cylinder head you will notice the compression rings have worn the cylinder walls and created a ridge at the top of each cylinder. The ridge is actually the unworn portion of the bore that the rings do not travel on. If you were to attempt to remove the pistons, without removing the ridge first, the piston rings would catch on the ridge and further efforts would damage the ring lands of the piston and possibly even break the piston. The ridge reamer (see illustrations) cuts away the ridge so you can remove the piston from the cylinder block.

The ridge reamer is a self-centering device, meaning that as it is installed in the cylinder and tightened, it centers itself in the bore. After properly adjusting, turn the reamer with a wrench and the machine tool bits will shave the ridge down to the diameter of the remainder of the cylinder walls. You can then slide the piston out of the bore without damage.

If a cylinder (or cylinders) is found to have a large ridge, re-boring of the block will almost certainly be necessary.

7.1 The ridge reamer cuts away the ridge from the top of the cylinder bore so the pistons can be removed without damage

7.2 After installing the ridge reamer into the cylinder, adjust the cutting bits and turn with a wrench until the ridge is removed

Piston ring expander

Piston rings are sized to fit snugly in the grooves of the piston and getting them on and off the piston without damaging the ring or the piston can be difficult. The ends of the rings are very sharp and under a lot of tension. They will easily scratch the soft aluminum piston and cannot be bent out-of-shape or the rings sealing capabilities will be lost.

A piston ring expander is a pliers-like tool (see illustrations) used to grip and expand the ring, allowing you to slip it over the top of the piston. They can be used to remove or install a compression ring but are not necessary to remove

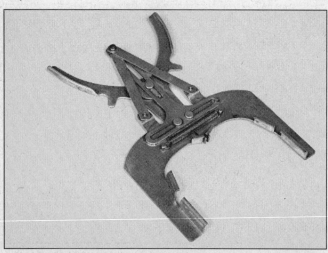

7.3 The piston ring expander pushes the ends of each compression ring apart so you can slip it over the piston crown and into its groove without scratching the piston or damaging the ring

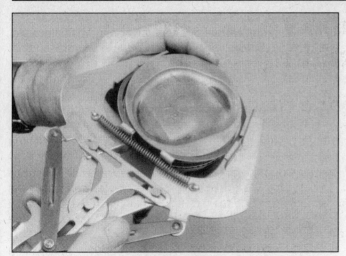

7.4 To use the piston ring installer, expand the ring just enough to clear the top of the piston

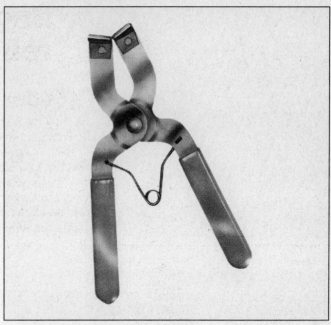

7.5 This Lisle piston ring installer is a very inexpensive and easy to use tool for installing piston rings

or install the oil control rings. When expanding a new ring for installation, expand it just enough to clear the piston. Over-expanding a ring will remove some of the tension and could damage the ring.

Piston ring groove cleaner

Often during a overhaul or repair job, it's not necessary to re-bore the cylinder block. The original pistons can be cleaned, re-ringed and installed back into the original cylinder bores (after honing, of course). The areas of the piston that requires special attention to cleaning are the ring grooves. Carbon builds up behind the rings and must be removed before the new rings are installed.

The piston ring groove cleaner **(see illustrations)** is specially designed to fit into the ring groove and scrape away the carbon as it is rotated around the piston. Several different sized bits are provided and can be selected by loosening the retaining knob. You must be very careful when cleaning the ring grooves. The cutter will dig into the soft aluminum and actually remove some of the piston material, if allowed. Watch closely and remove only the carbon. Stop the process if you notice any metal shavings appearing around the cutter.

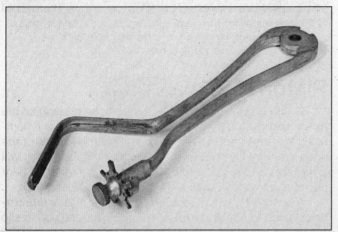

7.6 The piston ring groove cleaner is an odd-shaped tool with several cutting bits that fit different sized ring grooves

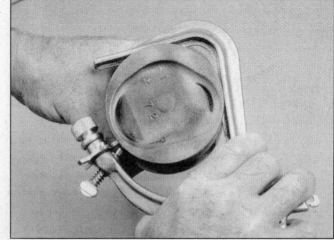

7.7 After selecting the proper bit and adjusting the depth stop, clamp the ring groove cleaner on the piston and rotate it around the piston; if the connecting rod is still installed on the piston, clamp the assembly in a vise to hold it securely

7.8 This pliers-type piston ring compressor manufactured by K-D Tools is used to install pistons 2 1/8 to 5 inches in diameter; to accommodate different bore sizes, insert the appropriate band into the pliers

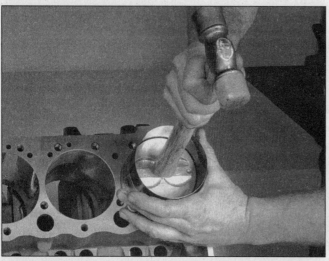

7.10 Once the rings are compressed, align the piston in the bore and gently tap the top of the piston with a hammer handle, driving the piston out of the ring compressor and into the cylinder bore

Piston ring compressor

A piston ring compressor **(see illustrations)** is necessary for any job requiring the pistons to be installed into the cylinder block. Its almost impossible to install pistons without a ring compressor. The ring compressor clamps around the piston, seating the rings in their grooves and allowing the piston and ring assembly to slide into the bore without damage to the piston or rings.

They're relatively inexpensive and easy to use. Several different types and sizes are available to accommodate different bore sizes.

7.9 This inexpensive K-D piston ring compressor is used to install pistons 3 1/2 to 6 1/2 inches in diameter; slip the tool over the piston and tighten with the L-shaped wrench to compress piston rings into the piston grooves

Cylinder surfacing hone

Honing the cylinders is necessary anytime a cylinder is re-bored or new piston rings are to be installed in the original bore. If the cylinders were bored, the machine shop will normally perform the honing procedure on a special "power hone". If you're replacing your own piston rings, you can hone the cylinders yourself using a surfacing hone and an electric or air powered drill. Cylinder surfacing hones **(see illustrations)** are designed to remove or "break" the glaze of a used cylinder so the new rings can "seat", or seal against the cylinder wall.

Two different types of hones are available; the conventional stone-type hone and the Flex-Hone which consists of stone balls in a "bottle brush" type configuration. The conventional-type hone fits a wide range of bore sizes and has an adjustment for contact pressure. The stones can be replaced when worn and different grit stones can be installed for rings requiring a specific finish.

The bottle brush hone has become very popular. It's easy to use and produces a very nice finish. On the other hand, you have to be very careful when using a bottle brush hone, the grit is generally coarse and it removes material quickly. Although they do last a long time (up to 1,000 cylinders, according to the manufacturer), once worn-out they must be discarded.

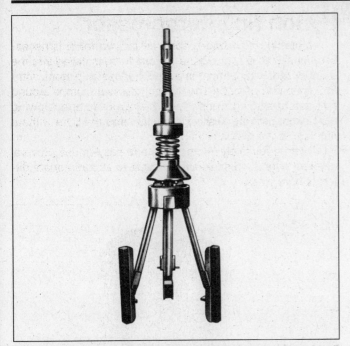

7.11 Lisle's stone-type Glaze Breaker hone ranges from 2 to 7 inches - the furnished general purpose 220 grit stone can be replaced with other grit stones if desired

7.12 K-D's Flex-Hone is a bottle-brush type hone available in three standard sizes and five heavy-duty sizes

7.13 Insert the hone into the bore and operate at a slow speed while moving it up-and-down - use plenty of lubrication during the honing operation

How to hone a cylinder

1   If the crankshaft is removed, install the main bearing caps and tighten the bolts to the specified torque.

2   Mount the hone in a drill motor, compress the stones and slip the hone into the first cylinder **(see illustration)**. Be sure to wear safety goggles or a face shield!

3   Lubricate the cylinder and the hone with cleaning solvent. Operate the drill motor a low speed and move the hone up-and-down in the cylinder at a pace that will produce a crosshatch pattern on the cylinder walls. Ideally, the crosshatch lines should intersect at approximately a 60-degree angle **(see illustration)**. Be sure to use plenty of lubricant, and don't take off any more material than is necessary.

4   Don't withdraw the hone from the cylinder while the drill is running. Instead, shut off the drill (continue moving the hone until it comes to a complete stop), compress the stones and withdraw the hone.

5   Wipe out the cylinder just completed and repeat the procedure for the remaining cylinders.

6   After the honing is complete, chamfer the top edges of the cylinder bores with a small file so the rings won't catch when the pistons are installed. Be very careful not to nick the cylinder walls with the file.

7   Wash the cylinders, very thoroughly with a towel and warm, soapy water to remove all traces of abrasive grit from the honing operation. The bores can be considered clean when a white cloth, dampened with clean engine oil, is used to wipe the bore and doesn't pick up any gray honing residue.

8   After a final rinse with clean water, dry the block and apply a light coat of engine oil to prevent rust.

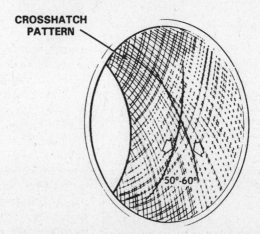

CROSSHATCH PATTERN

50°-60°

7.14 The cylinder hone should leave a smooth, cross-hatch pattern with the lines intersecting at approximately a 60-degree angle

7.15 If the engine is sludged-up the lifters may be difficult to remove - a hydraulic lifter removal tool may be needed to pull them out

Hydraulic lifter remover

Often the valve lifters, in an engine with high mileage, become gummed up with sludge and varnish and become stuck in their lifter bores. The lifters are made of a very hard alloy so pliers won't grip, besides there usually isn't enough showing to grab a hold of anyway. A valve lifter tool **(see illustrations)** will be needed to get them out.

In other instances, such as in a camshaft replacement procedure, you may need to remove the hydraulic lifters with the engine and cylinder heads still installed in the vehicle. In this case the tool is used to reach down through the access in the cylinder head to grip and remove the lifter.

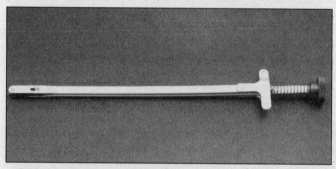

7.16 A typical hydraulic lifter removal tool grips the lifters using spring pressure - it is quick and easy to use but will not remove lifters that are really stuck

7.17 This Lisle Hydraulic lifter puller removes stuck lifters - the expanding collet firmly grips the lifter and the slide-hammer design jars the lifter loose

Camshaft bearing remover/installer

Camshaft bearings are usually replaced during a complete engine overhaul or at times when the camshaft has become defective and has damaged the engine bearings. Normally done in a machine shop, camshaft bearings could be installed by the home mechanic wishing to invest in the proper tool **(see illustration)**.

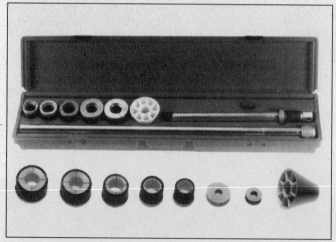

7.18 Lisle's Universal Camshaft Bearing Tool is a complete set that will remove or install camshaft bearings in nearly all engines

Valve spring compressor

The valve spring compressor compresses the valve springs, removing the tension from the keepers and retainers, and ultimately allowing you to remove the valve springs and valves. If the cylinder head is removed from the vehicle, the C-clamp style compressor **(see illustration)** is the fastest and easiest to use. With the valve springs removed, the valves, valve seats and valve seals may be serviced.

Other types of valve spring compressors are available that allow for spring removal on or off the vehicle **(see illustrations)**. They will most often be used with the cylinder head installed in the vehicle when replacement of the valve seals or springs become necessary. The lever type is inexpensive and can be used on any engine with rocker arm studs or bolts. The universal type can be used on any type of overhead valve and is usually the choice of home mechanics wanting a valve spring compressor that can be used on any vehicle with the cylinder head on or off the engine. When a valve spring is removed with the cylinder head installed on the engine, some method of holding the valves must be employed or else they will fall into the cylinder. The most common method is to use an air hose adapter **(see illustrations)** to pressurize the cylinder with compressed air, holding the valves in their closed position.

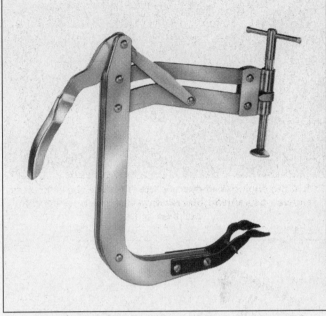

7.19 The most common and easiest to use valve spring compressor is the C-clamp type like this K-D Tools model

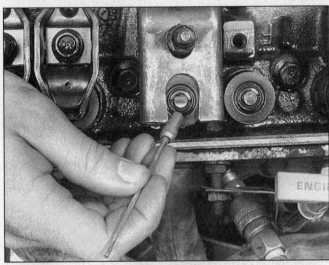

7.20 The K-D Universal Overhead Valve Spring Compressor removes valve springs on most vehicles with the cylinder head on or off the engine

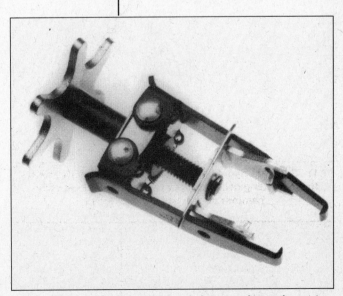

7.21 The lever-type compressor is inexpensive and easy to use on engines with rocker arm studs or bolts

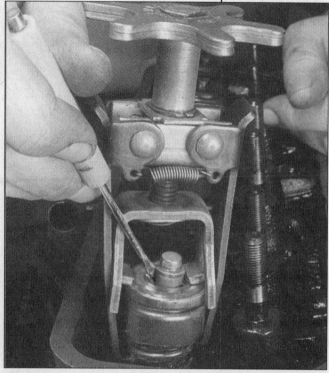

7.22 When removing the valve spring with the cylinder head on the vehicle . . .

7.23 . . . use compressed air with a air hose adapter (arrow) threaded into the spark plug hole

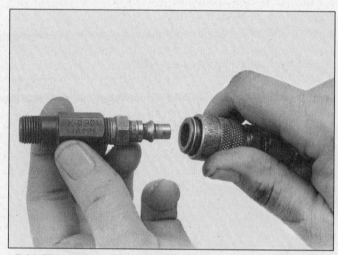

7.24 This is the air hose adapter that threads into the spark plug hole - they're commonly available from auto parts or tool specialty stores

7.25 Lisle's Valve Seat Cutter uses carbide cutters to cut three seat angles at once - this tool will cut virtually all import and domestic automobile and truck valve seats with 30 or 45 degree angles, ranging from 1 to 2 1/2 inches in diameter

Valve seat cutter

Valve jobs are very expensive, and, if you're restoring an antique automobile, or perhaps you just prefer to *do-it-yourself,* a low cost valve seat cutter set might be the ticket. The valve seat cutter **(see illustration)** is an accurate hand tool that cuts new seats eliminating the need for grinding stones and other related equipment.

Valve lapper

Occasionally a valve may not need replacement or machine grinding and a simple hand lapping will do. You can hand lap small and large head valves with a valve lapper **(see illustration)**. Place a small amount of grinding compound on the valve face, place it into its seat, put the suction cup on the valve head and turn the handle between your hands.

Valve guide knurler

You can recondition worn valve guides back to their original size with a valve guide knurler. Resizing the valve guides allows you to install standard size replacement valves without the extra expense of having a machine shop install new valve guides or inserts. No metal is removed from the cylinder head during the knurling process. You will need a 1/2 inch drive drill capable of 550 RPM or less to complete the operation.

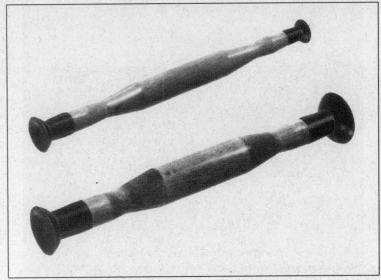

7.26 Valve Lappers for hand lapping valves have 1 1/8 and 1 3/8 inch diameter cups for larger valves or 5/8 and 13/16 inch cups for smaller valves

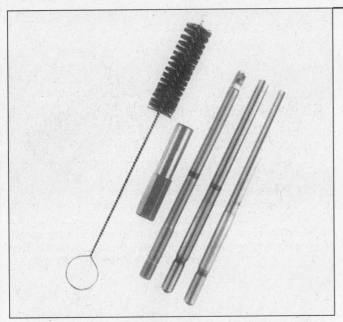

7.27 Lisle's Valve Guide Knurler Kits are available in three standard sets to fit most popular valve sizes - each set includes a knurling tap, knurling tap driver, resizer and cleaning brush

Miscellaneous tools

Of course it is not possible to list all of the miscellaneous tools that might be needed during a major repair operation or engine overhaul, but here are a few of the most common and widely used tools that come to mind:

Many new car manufacturers are switching the torque-angle method of tightening critical fasteners. Instead of simply tightening the head bolts, for example, to the specified torque, the new method requires you to rotate the bolt a specific number of degrees after an initial torque is reached. The torque-angle method of tightening fasteners doesn't necessarily mean that all the bolts are go-

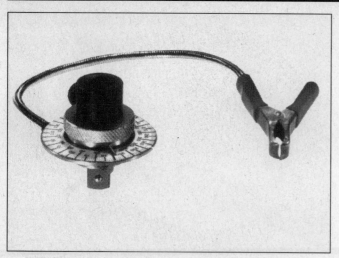

7.28 The torque angle meter is needed to tighten those critical fasteners on today's modern vehicles which specify the torque-angle method of tightening

ing to be more accurately tightened, but that all the fasteners will be more *evenly* tightened across the component. To properly attain the specified angles, a torque-angle meter **(see illustration)** is used in conjunction with your torque wrench.

You can bet that sometime during a major repair or overhaul it's going to be necessary to either turn the crankshaft from underneath the vehicle or to hold the crankshaft securely. A flexplate wrench **(see illustration)** grips the starter ring gear teeth and can be used to rotate the flexplate or flywheel when it's time to remove the bolts. A harmonic balancer holding tool **(see illustration)** can also be used to rotate the balancer or hold it steady while you remove the large center bolt. Of course, you'll need a harmonic balancer puller **(see illustration)** also to remove the balancer from the end of the crankshaft.

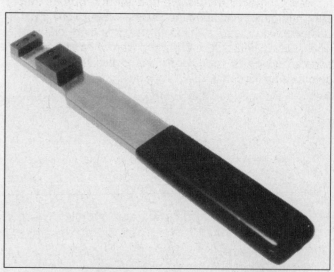

7.29 A Flexplate wrench is a handy tool for rotating the flexplate or flywheel from underneath the vehicle

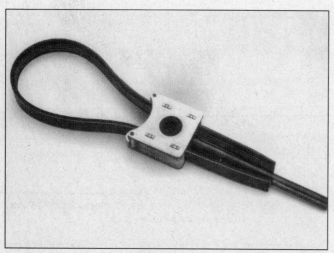

7.30 K-D's Harmonic Balancer Holding Tool is designed to allow the crankshaft, camshaft and other such pulleys to be rotated or held while removing the fastener that holds them in place

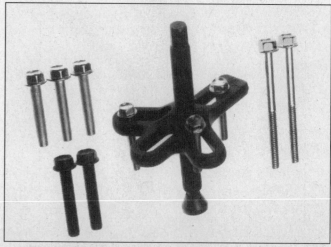

7.31 K-D's Harmonic Balancer puller removes balancers, pulleys and gears with tapped holes

Cleaning tools

Any time a major engine repair or overhaul is undertaken, there will be a certain amount of cleaning necessary. A shallow pan, some cleaning solvent and a few parts cleaning brushes **(see illustrations)** are about the minimum you can get by with.

You'll need a gasket scraper **(see illustrations)** to remove the old gasket material from cylinder heads, intake manifolds and other cylinder block gasket sealing surfaces. Be very careful in their use, especially on aluminum components; you don't want to gouge the sealing surface, or your hand. Wire cup or end brushes **(see illustration)** used with an electric or air powered drill can also be used to clean heavy duty jobs such as baked on cylinder head gaskets and carbon from metal surfaces.

Most importantly, always use the appropriate safety equipment and a little common sense when cleaning parts. Use goggles or a face shield when operating a drill with a wire brush installed. Use rubber gloves when cleaning parts in solvent. Never use gasoline to clean parts, and dispose of your dirty solvent in an environmentally safe manner.

7.32 A shallow pan for cleaning parts with solvent, a wire brush and a medium sized funnel should be part of your repair tool kit

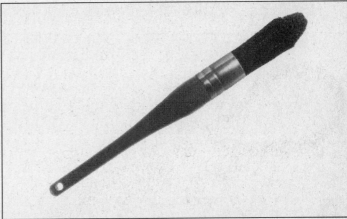

7.33 A parts cleaning brush removes dirt and grease from motors, machinery and metal parts

7.34 Wire scratch brushes remove rust, scale, paint and solder from metal surfaces - their also useful for cleaning threads and files

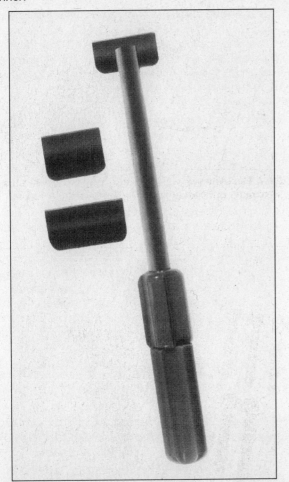

7.35 The sharp, hardened steel blades of this Lisle Heavy Duty Scraper removes carbon, old gasket material, adhesives, sludge and other hard to clean substances from blocks, heads, etc.

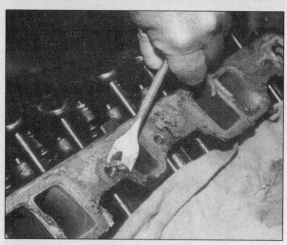

7.36 When removing gasket material, only remove the material, don't gouge the gasket sealing surface or leaks might develop

7.37 Wire cup brush (left), knotted end brush (middle) and crimped end brush (right) are used with a power tool to remove gaskets, carbon, scale, rust, paint and corrosion from metal surfaces

Engine hoist

If you plan on doing a lot of engine repair and overhaul work some sort of engine hoist will make the job much more convenient and safe. Of course, a cable winch or chain hoist can be supported from a beam or rafter, but is it really safe? When it comes time to pull an engine, most of us will probably go down to the local rental yard and rent a "cherry-picker" type engine crane. That is probably the smartest thing to do, but wouldn't a nice new portable engine crane (see illustration) of your very own be nice?

Engine cranes are available in many different weight ratings, when using one make sure its capable of lifting the weight you require. They also are available in models that partially disassemble for easy storage when limited space is a factor.

One important accessory for use with any type of engine hoist is the engine attachment mechanism. It can be nothing more than a section of chain (again make sure its large enough to handle the weight) or any one of the commercial adapters available. The adjustable adapters are nice, they allow you to adjust the engine so it's hanging perfectly level or make minute adjustments to mate the engine to the transmission on installation. Whichever method used, always bolt the chain to the engine securely. You don't even want to think about the possibility of dropping an engine.

7.38 Use an engine crane that's rated high enough to easily lift your engine in and out of the engine compartment - an adapter, like the one shown (arrow), can be used to change the angle of the engine as it's being removed or installed

Engine hanger

Many front wheel drive vehicles require an engine hanger (see illustration) to support the engine from above when performing certain repairs. I hate to think about all the times a home mechanic has used a 2X4 or a section of pipe in place of this important tool. An engine hanger has the strength to hold the engine securely and provides adjustments to assure that the engine remains in the proper position for remounting after the repair has been completed.

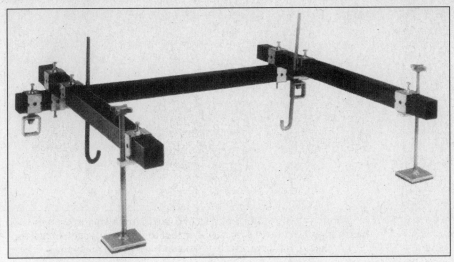

7.39 Lisle's Engine Hanger supports and holds the engine in position on front wheel drive vehicles when the transaxle or engine mounts are disconnected

Engine stand

An engine stand is used to position the engine block at a comfortable work height **(see illustration)**. The engine can be rotated and securely locked in position allowing for easy installation of the crankshaft and bearings. The complete engine can be "built" on the stand, then removed and installed in the vehicle when ready.

Engine stands are available in different weight ratings, so be sure to use one safely rated above the actual weight of the complete engine you will be using it for. Engine stands with the lower weight ratings are usually equipped with three wheels and should only be used with four cylinder engines or lightweight aluminum V6 engines. Heavy duty four wheel models are needed for larger V6 engines and V8 engines.

7.40 An engine stand secures the cylinder block at a comfortable work height

2 Precision measuring tools

Think of the tools in the following list as the final stage of your tool collection. If you're planning to rebuild an engine, you've probably already accumulated all the screwdrivers, wrenches, sockets, pliers and other everyday hand tools that you need. You've also probably collected all the special-purpose tools necessary to tune and service your specific engine. Now it's time to round up the stuff you'll need to do your own measurements when you rebuild that engine.

It would be great to own every precision measuring tool listed here, but you don't really need a machinist's chest crammed with exotic calipers and micrometers. Even most professional engine builders use only four tools 95 percent of the time: a feeler gauge set, a one-inch outside micrometer, a dial indicator and a six-inch dial caliper. So start your collection with these four items.

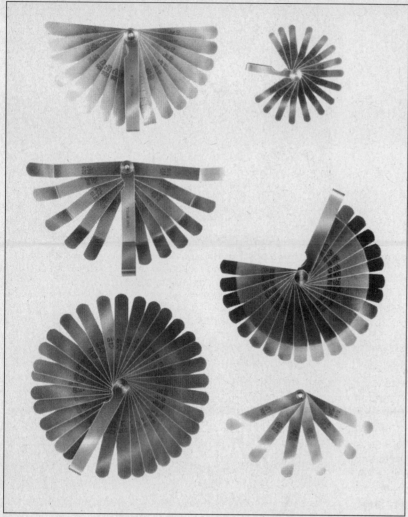

7.41 Feeler gauge sets are available in many different sizes

Feeler gauge

Feeler gauges are the most common precision measuring tool in the mechanics tool box **(see illustration)**. They have been used by mechanics for many years to measure valve tappet clearance and breaker-point gap. Feeler gauges have many other uses around the automotive engine during rebuild time. They can be used to measure piston ring end gap, crankshaft end play and connecting rod side clearance, just to name a few. Feeler gauges are often used, along with a precision straight edge, to check a cylinder head for warpage **(see illustration)**.

Feeler gauges usually come in sets that contain many different size blades. Most blade sizes range from 0.0015 to 0.035 inch. Brass blades are also available for use in adjusting reluctor air gap on electronic ignition systems, where non-magnetic blades are required.

Micrometers

When you're rebuilding an engine, you need to know the exact thickness of a sizable number of pieces. Whether you're measuring the diameter of a wrist pin or the thickness of a valve spring shim or a thrust washer, your tool of choice should be the trusty one-inch outside micrometer **(see illustrations)**.

Insist on accuracy to within one ten–thousandths of an inch (0.0001 inch) when you shop for a micrometer. You'll probably never need that kind of precision, but the extra decimal place will help you decide which way to round off a close measurement.

7.42 Check the cylinder head surface for warpage by slipping a feeler gauge under the straightedge

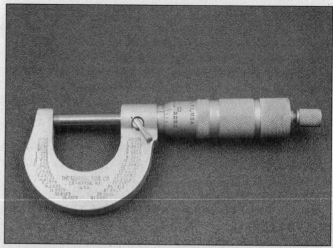

7.43 The one-inch micrometer is an essential precision measuring device for determining the dimensions of a wrist pin, valve spring shim, thrust washer, etc.

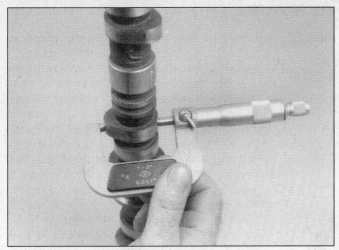

7.44 Here's how you use a micrometer to measure camshaft lobe height

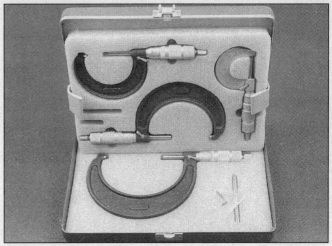

7.45 Get a good-quality micrometer set if you can afford it - this set has four micrometers ranging in size from one to four inches

High quality micrometers have a range of one inch. Eventually, you'll want a set **(see illustration)** that spans four, or even five, ranges: 0 to 1 inch, 1 to 2 inch, 2 to 3 inch and 3 to-4 inch. On engines bigger than about 350 cu. in., you'll also probably need a 4 to-5 inch. These five micrometers will measure the thickness of any part that needs to be measured for an engine rebuild. You don't have to run out and buy all five of these babies at once. Start with the one-inch model; then, when you have the money, get the next size you need (the 3 to 4 inch size or 4 to 5 inch is a good second choice - both of these measure piston diameters).

An affordable alternative to a micrometer set is the range micrometer with interchangeable anvil extensions **(see illustration)**. Furnished with several extensions, a single micrometer will range from 0 to 6 inches. It's a little harder to use, especially when measuring small parts, and changing the anvil can be bothersome. Used carefully, however, the range micrometer should be just as accurate as a standard micrometer.

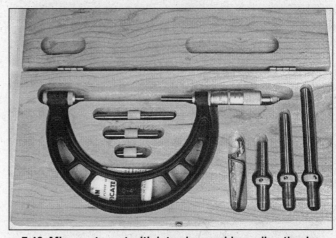

7.46 Micrometer set with interchangeable anvils - they're awkward to use when measuring small parts and changing the anvils is a hassle, but they're an affordable alternative to a complete micrometer set

How to read a micrometer

The outside micrometer is without a doubt the most widely used precision measuring tool. It can be used to make a variety of highly accurate measurements without much possibility of error through misreading, a problem associated with other measuring instruments such as vernier calipers.

Like any slide caliper, the outside micrometer uses the "double contact" of its spindle and anvil **(see illustration)** touching the object to be measured to determine that object's dimensions. Unlike a caliper, however, the micrometer also features a unique precision screw adjustment which can be read with a great deal more accuracy than calipers.

Why is this screw adjustment so accurate? Because years ago toolmakers discovered that a screw with 40

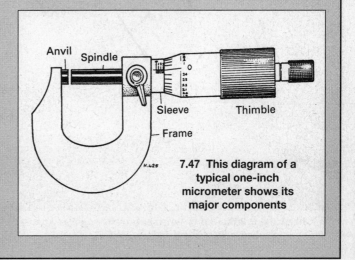

7.47 This diagram of a typical one-inch micrometer shows its major components

precision machined threads to the inch will advance one–fortieth (0.025) of an inch with each complete turn. The screw threads on the spindle revolve inside a fixed nut concealed by a sleeve.

On a one-inch micrometer, this sleeve is engraved longitudinally with exactly 40 lines to the inch, to correspond with the number of threads on the spindle. Every fourth line is made longer and is numbered one-tenth inch, two-tenths, etc. The other lines are often staggered to make them easier to read.

The thimble (the barrel which moves up and down the sleeve as it rotates) is divided into 25 divisions around the circumference of its beveled edge and is numbered from zero to 25. Close the micrometer spindle till it touches the anvil: You should see nothing but the zero line on the sleeve next to the beveled edge of the thimble. And the zero line of the thimble should be aligned with the horizontal (or axial) line on the sleeve. Remember: Each full revolution of the spindle from zero to zero advances or retracts the spindle one-fortieth or 0.025 inch. Therefore, if you rotate the thimble from zero on the beveled edge to the first graduation, you will move the spindle 1/25th of 1/40th, or 1/25th of 25/1000ths, which equals 1/1000th, or 0.001 inch.

Remember: Each numbered graduation on the sleeve represents 0.1 inch, each of the other sleeve graduations represents 0.025 inch, and each graduation on the thimble represents 0.001 inch. Remember those three and you're halfway there.

For example: Suppose the 4 line is visible on the sleeve. This represents 0.400 inch. Then suppose there are an additional three lines (the short ones without numbers) showing. These marks are worth 0.025 inch each, or 0.075 inch. Finally, there are also two marks on the beveled edge of the thimble beyond the zero mark, each good for 0.001 inch, or a total of 0.002 inch. Add it all up and you get 0.400 plus 0.075 plus 0.002, which equals 0.477 inch.

Some beginners use a "dollars, quarters and cents" analogy to simplify reading a micrometer. Add up the bucks and change, then put a decimal point instead of a dollar sign in front of the sum!

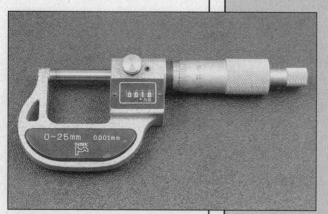

7.48 Digital micrometers are easier to read than conventional micrometers, are just as accurate and are finally starting to become affordable

Digital micrometers

Digital micrometers **(see illustration)** display the measurement in a digital readout as well as on the thimble. They're easier to read than conventional micrometers, are just as accurate and are finally starting to become affordable. If you're uncomfortable reading a conventional micrometer, then get a digital.

Dial indicators

The dial indicator **(see illustrations)** is another measuring mainstay. It's indispensable for degreeing camshafts, measuring valve lift, piston deck clearances, crankshaft endplay and all kinds of other little measurements. Make sure the dial indicator you buy has a probe with at least one inch of travel, graduated in 0.001–inch increments. And get a good assortment of probe extensions up to about six inches long. Sometimes, you need to screw a bunch of

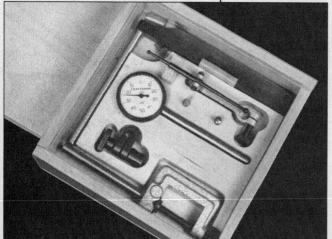

7.49 The dial indicator is indispensable for degreeing crankshafts, measuring valve lift, piston deck clearance, crankshaft endplay and a hose of other critical measurements

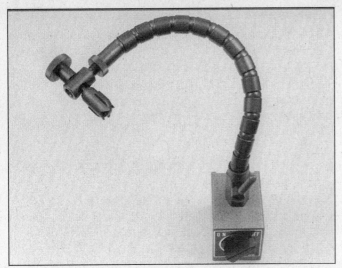

7.51 Get an adjustable, flexible fixture like this one, and a magnetic base, to ensure maximum versatility from your dial indicator

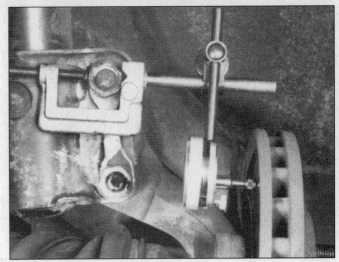

7.50 Measure the disc rotor runout with a dial indicator

these extensions together to reach into tight areas like pushrod holes.

Buy a dial indicator set that includes a flexible fixture and a magnetic stand **(see illustrations).** If the model you buy doesn't have a magnetic base, buy one separately. Make sure the magnet is plenty strong. If a weak magnet comes loose and the dial indicator takes a tumble on a concrete floor, you can kiss it good-bye. Make sure the arm that attaches the dial indicator to the flexible fixture is sturdy and the locking clamps are easy to operate.

Depth indicator

Some dial indicators are designed to measure depth **(see illustration).** They have a removable base that straddles a hole. This setup is indispensable for measuring deck height when the piston is below the block surface. To measure the deck height of pistons that protrude above the deck, you'll also need a U–shaped bridge for your dial indicator. The bridge is also useful for checking the flatness of a block or a cylinder head.

7.52 The dial indicator can be set-up quickly and easily when the flexible fixture and magnetic base are used

7.53 This dial indicator is designed to measure depth, such as deck height when the piston is below the block surface - with a U-shaped bridge (the base seen here is removable), you can measure the deck height of pistons that protrude above the deck (U-shaped bridges are also useful for checking the flatness of a block or cylinder head)

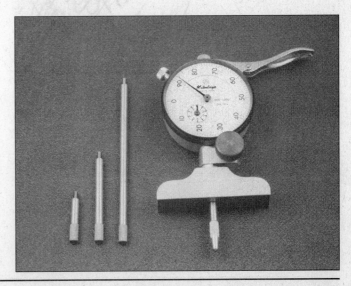

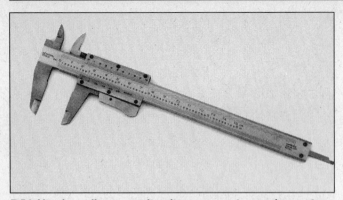

7.54 Vernier calipers aren't quite as accurate as micrometers, but they're handy for quick measurements and relatively inexpensive, and because they've got jaws that can measure internal and external dimensions, they're versatile

Calipers

Vernier calipers

Vernier calipers **(see illustration)** aren't quite as accurate as a micrometer, but they're handy for quick measurements and they're relatively inexpensive. Most calipers have inside and outside jaws, so you can measure the inside diameter of a hole, or the outside diameter of a part.

Better quality calipers have a dust shield over the geared rack that turns the dial to prevent small metal particles from jamming the mechanism. Make sure there's no play in the moveable jaw. To check, put a thin piece of metal between the jaws and measure its thickness with the metal close to the rack, then out near the tips of the jaws. Compare your two measurements. If they vary by more than 0.001 inch, look at another caliper - the jaw mechanism is deflecting.

Dial calipers

If your eyes are going bad, or already are bad, vernier calipers can be difficult to read. Dial calipers **(see illustrations)** are a better choice. Dial calipers combine the measuring capabilities of micrometers with the convenience of dial indicators. Because they're much easier to read quickly than vernier calipers, they're ideal for taking quick measurements when absolute accuracy isn't necessary. Like conventional vernier calipers, they have both inside and outside jaws which allow you to quickly determine the diameter of a hole or a part. Get a six inch dial caliper, graduated in 0.001-inch increments.

Digital calipers

The latest electronic digital calipers **(see illustration)** have a digital LCD display that can indicate either inch and metric dimensions with the touch of a button. This beautiful precision instrument uses battery power to operate a microchip. If you can afford one of these, it's the hot setup.

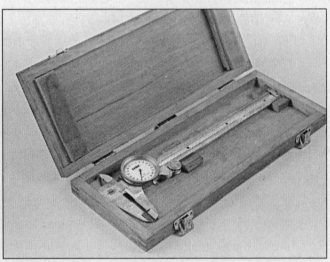

7.55 Dial calipers are a lot easier to read than conventional vernier calipers, particularly if your eyesight isn't as good as it used to be!

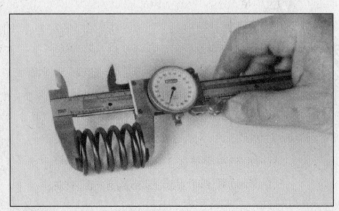

7.56 Dial calipers can be used to measure the free length of each valve spring

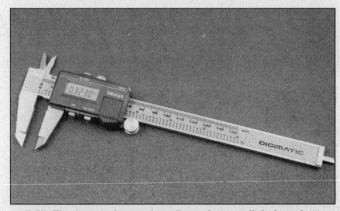

7.57 The latest electronic calipers have a digital readout that is even easier to read than a dial caliper - another advantage of digital calipers is that they have a small microchip that allows them to convert instantaneously from inch to metric dimensions

How to read a vernier caliper

On the lower half of the main beam, each inch is divided into ten numbered increments, or tenths (0.100 inch, 0.200 inch, etc.). Each tenth is divided into four increments of 0.025 inch each. The vernier scale has 25 increments, each representing a thousandth (0.001) of an inch **(see illustration)**.

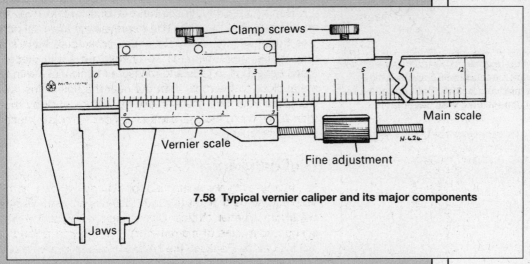

Clamp screws

Main scale

Vernier scale

Fine adjustment

Jaws

7.58 Typical vernier caliper and its major components

First read the number of inches, then read the number of tenths. Add to this 0.025 inch for each additional graduation. Using the English vernier scale, determine which graduation of the vernier lines up exactly with a graduation on the main beam. This vernier graduation is the number of thousandths which is to be added to the previous readings.

For example, let's say:

   1) The number of inches is zero, or 0.000 inch;

   2) The number of tenths is 4, or 0.400 inch;

   3) The number of 0.025's is 2, or 0.050 inch; and

   4) The vernier graduation which lines up with a graduation on the main beam is 15, or 0.015 inch.

   5) Add them up: 0.000

                         0.400

                         0.050

                         0.015

   6) And you get: 0.46-inch

That's all there is to it!

Inside micrometers

Cylinder bores, main bearing bores, connecting rod big ends, valve guides - automotive engines have a lot of holes that must be measured accurately within a thousandth of an inch. Inside micrometers **(see illustration)** are used for these jobs. You read an inside micrometer the same way you read an outside micrometer. But it takes more skill to get an accurate reading.

To measure the diameter of a hole accurately, you must find the widest part of the hole. This involves expanding the micrometer while rocking it from side to side and moving it up and down. Once the micrometer is adjusted properly,

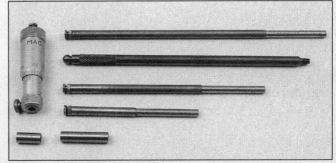

7.59 Inside micrometers are handy for measuring holes with thousandth-of-an-inch accuracy

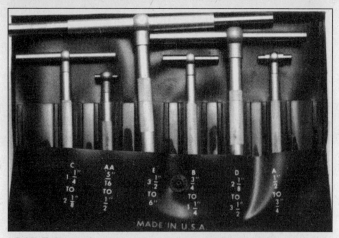

7.60 Telescoping snap gauges are used to measure smaller holes - simply insert them into a hole, turn the knurled handle to release their spring-loaded probes out to the wall, turn the handle to lock the probes into position, pull out the gauge and measure the length from the tip of one probe to the tip of the other probe with a micrometer

you should be able to pull it through the hole with a slight drag. If the micrometer feels loose or binds as you pull it through, you're not getting an accurate reading.

Fully collapsed, inside micrometers can measure holes as small as one inch in diameter. Extensions or spacers are added for measuring larger holes.

Telescoping snap gauges **(see illustration)** are used to measure smaller holes. Simply insert them into a hole and turn the knurled handle to release their spring-loaded probes, which expand out to the walls of the hole, turn the handle the other way and lock the probes into position, then pull the gauge out. After the gauge is removed from the hole, measure its width with an outside micrometer **(see illustrations)**.

7.61 To use a telescoping gauge, first set the gauge to the inside diameter of the bore . . .

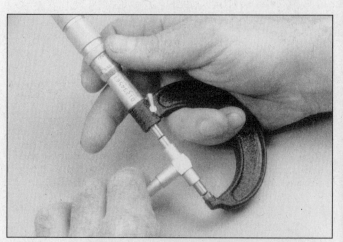

7.62 . . . then measure the gauge with a micrometer to arrive at the inside dimension of the bore

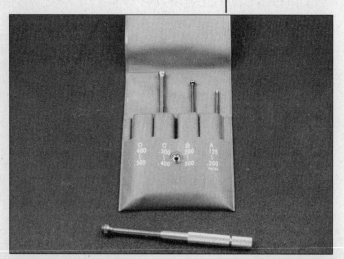

7.63 To measure really small holes, such as valve guides, you need a set of small hole gauges - to use them, simply stick them into the hole, turn the knurled handle until the expanding flanges are contacting the walls of the hole, pull out the gauge and measure the width of the gauge at the flanges with a micrometer

For measuring really small holes, such as valve guides, you'll need a set of small hole gauges **(see illustration)**. They work the same way as telescoping snap gauges, but instead of spring-loaded probes, they have expanding flanges on the end that can be screwed in and out by a threaded handle.

Dial bore gauge

The dial bore gauge **(see illustration)** is more accurate and easier to use – but more expensive – than an inside micrometer for checking the roundness of the cylinders, and the bearing bores in main bearing saddles and connecting rods. Using various extensions, most dial bore gauges have a range of just over 1 inch in diameter to 6 inches or more. Unlike outside micrometers with interchangeable anvils, the accuracy of bore gauges with interchangeable extensions is reliable. Bore gauges accurate to 0.0001 inch are available, but they're very expensive and hard to find. Most bore gauges are graduated in 0.0005 inch increments. If you use them properly, this accuracy level is more than adequate.

Brake gauge

Brake gauges are used to measure the wear limits of a brake disc or brake drum. The rotor gauge is similar to a micrometer. In fact, a micrometer with pointed anvils can be used **(see illustration)**. Brake drum wear limit gauges **(see illustration)** fit inside the drum and are expanded to measure the inside diameter of the drum before machining. The pointed anvils of both are necessary to allow precise measurement of the scores.

7.64 The dial bore gauge is more accurate and easier to use than an inside micrometer or telescoping snap gauges, but it's expensive - using various extensions, most dial gauges have a arrange of measurement from just over one inch to six inches or more

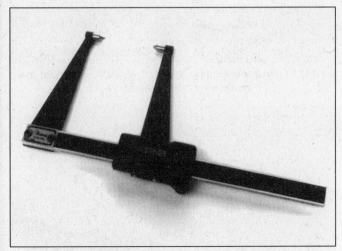

7.65 This brake rotor gauge features a digital display and self-calibrating pointed anvils to measure all rotors - it can also be used to accurately measure ball-joint wear

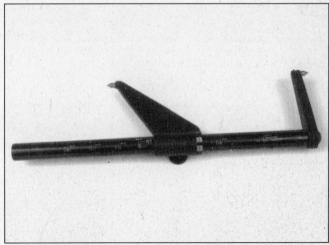

7.66 The brake drum wear limit gauge is a rugged, mechanical brake drum gauge that will measure all brake drums

Notes

8 Body and paint tools; working facilities

1 Tools and equipment

In addition to the tools normally found in any mechanic's toolbox, such as sockets, ratchets, open and box-end wrenches, screwdrivers, pliers, etc. **(see illustration)**, there are many tools specifically designed for body work that will be needed to properly repair distorted metal parts, apply and work fillers and sand and grind body panels in preparation for welding or painting. They range from simple cast-iron dollies to sophisticated (and expensive) hydraulic unibody/frame straighteners.

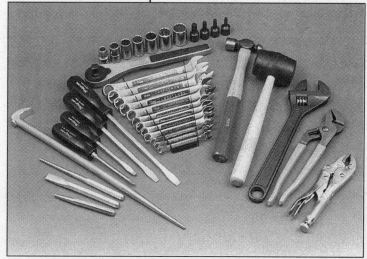

8.1 Many of the tools used for mechanical auto repairs are also needed for body work - wrenches, sockets, ratchets, screwdrivers and pliers should all be available

8.2 Body hammers are needed to align and shape sheet metal panels. They have a wide, almost flat, smooth surface on one end (which is normally round, but may be square) that ranges from about 3/4-inch to 1-1/2 inches in diameter. The edges are rounded to prevent the formation of sharp dents if the sheet metal is struck with the hammer held at a slight angle - if the edges on the hammers you have are sharp, round them over with progressively finer grades of wet-or-dry sandpaper. The opposite end of the hammer head is usually pointed or tapered and is used to flatten bumps and high spots.

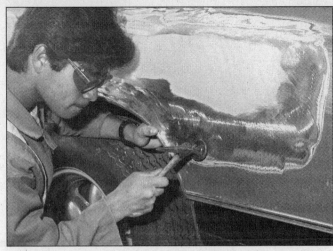

8.3 Here a body hammer is being used to reshape a portion of a rear quarter panel

8.4 Dollies are used to back up the wide, flat end of the body hammer when shaping panels . . .

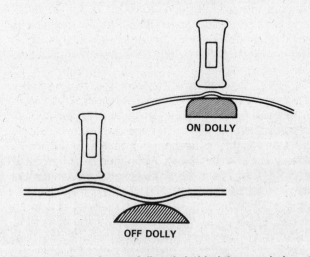

8.5 . . . and can be used directly behind the area being struck by the hammer, or off to one side - as the hammer strikes the sheet metal, the dolly is bumped off and then returns, shaping the panel from the back side in the process

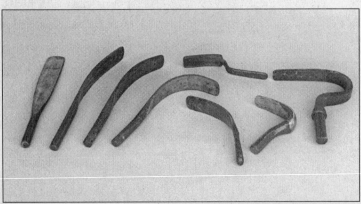

8.6 Body spoons are used just like dollies, but they'll reach into tight spots where dollies can't fit. Since they come in many shapes and sizes, it's easy to find one that matches the shape of the panel.

The two basic tools needed for body work are the body hammer and the dolly (see illustrations). In general, the hammer is used to stress (and shape) the metal, while the dolly keeps it from moving too far. There are dozens of different hammer and dolly designs, each with a different shape to handle a different type of dent or curvature in a metal body panel, but only four or five of each are really necessary for most body work (see illustrations)

One other basic tool belongs in any beginning bodyman's tool box - the body spoon (see illustration). A spoon is basically another form of dolly, designed with a handle so you can reach areas you can't reach with a conventional dolly. Spoons can also be used as a large surface hammer to knock out dents (see illustration).

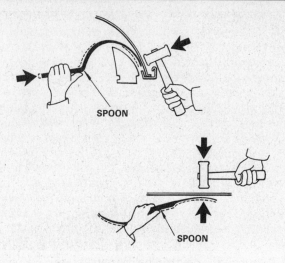

8.7 Body spoons in use

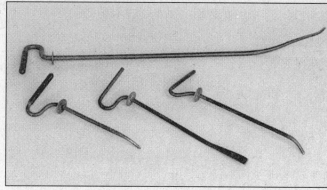

8.8 Pry tools are used to pry body panels back into shape. They're preferable to dent pullers if the distorted area is within reach and there's something to pry against. They can be inserted through drain holes and small openings in the back sides of panels.

Pry bars specially designed for body repair are available in several sizes **(see illustration)**. They're made to be inserted through holes along the edge of a panel (such as door drain holes) to pry the panel back into shape from the back side.

The dent puller is often the first tool used when you begin straightening a damaged area **(see illustration)**. Most dent pullers are a slide hammer design and the better ones have replaceable tips so you can use screws or L-shaped hooks to attach the slide hammer to the metal to be straightened **(see illustrations)**. Just remember when using a slide hammer that all those holes you make to attach the slide hammer to the sheet metal will have to be filled later.

A more sophisticated type of dent puller is also available. It uses metal pins spot welded to the sheet metal to pull on and doesn't require holes to be drilled in the body. This type of tool is generally used only by professional body shops, since you would have to do a lot of body work to justify its cost, but it's capable of doing a much cleaner job of

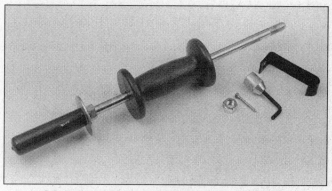

8.9 Inexpensive slide hammer dent pullers with interchangeable tips are widely available at hardware and auto parts stores

8.10 Special hook attachments are often used with slide hammer pullers to straighten body parts - here the hook is used to grip the edge of the fender opening so it can be pulled back into shape

8.11 A slide hammer dent puller is essential for pulling panels back into place before reshaping them

pulling out sheet metal than the screw tip slide hammer dent puller.

One other type of dent puller which can sometimes be used to straighten body panels is the suction cup puller. They're primarily used where the metal hasn't been creased or stretched, such as when a door panel has just been pushed in. The suction cup type dent puller can, in this case, often pull the panel out again, leaving only minor sheet metal damage to be repaired. They're also useful for holding the glass when removing and installing windows.

Once the sheet metal is straightened, the two most often used tools for body work are the metal file and the sureform or "cheese grater" file. The metal file is used to clean, shape and surface metal panels. It usually consists of two pieces - the curved tooth file itself and the handle it's attached to. The handle (or holder) is usually adjustable, so the file can be curved to match the metal surface being worked (it's because of this feature that it's sometimes called a flexible file) **(see illustration)**. The sureform file is not used to work metal, but to shape plastic body filler material. It's a very open tooth design to allow the cut-off filler material to escape, with hundreds of small, very sharp teeth that quickly work the plastic material before it completely hardens **(see illustrations)**.

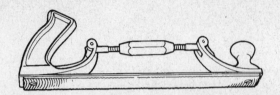

8.12 The flexible file can be adjusted to conform to the general shape of curved body sections and is used to shape and form metal particularly

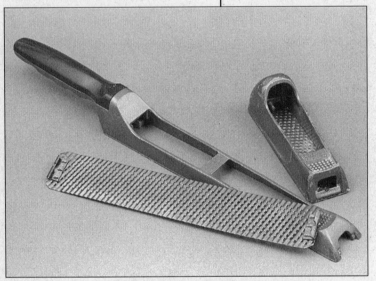

8.13 Sureform tools come in several sizes, have replaceable blades . . .

8.14 . . . and are excellent for rough shaping of body filler because they cut quickly and don't clog

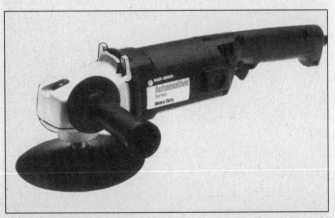

8.15 Electric sanders, polishers and grinders are available from many manufacturers - be sure to buy a heavy-duty model

Air or electric sanders are an absolute must for doing body work **(see illustration)**. Several types are available, including disc sanders, double action (DA) sanders, orbital action sanders, straight line sanders and belt sanders. Air disc sanders are used for light duty jobs such as paint removal **(see illustrations)**. They're light and compact and produce low rpm and high torque, so there's little heat produced **(see illustration)**. Double action sanders have a dual-rotation feature that prevents scratches from forming **(see illustration)**. They're used primarily for rough sanding of metal and plastic fillers. Orbital action sanders have a large, flat sanding pad that makes them useful for removing small surface imperfections **(see illustration)**. They're usually used for rough and medium sanding of plastic fillers **(see illustration)**. The straight line sander is excellent for removing paint or working down a large plastic filled sur-

8.16 The air disc sander is ideal for light work . . .

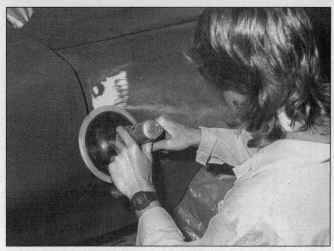

8.17 . . . like feathering out paint and body filler

8.18 They're also useful for buffing, since their low speed makes it difficult to burn the paint

8.19 The dual action sander is used for rapid shaping of body filler, as well as fine finishing work, and leaves a swirl-free finish

8.20 The orbital sander is great for quick removal of body fillers on both vertical and horizontal surfaces

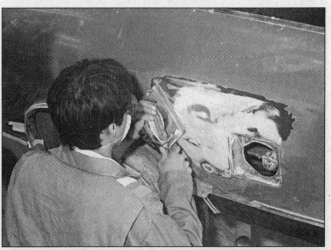

8.21 Since it has a large sanding pad, the orbital sander is very useful on large flat surfaces

8.22 The straight line air sander has an unusually long pad so it can bridge filled areas . . .

8.23 . . . and is particularly well suited for rapid sanding of body filler on long flat surfaces

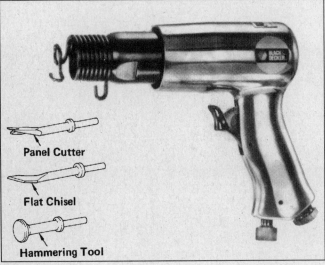

Panel Cutter

Flat Chisel

Hammering Tool

8.24 Air hammers accept many different types of chisels, are quite inexpensive . . .

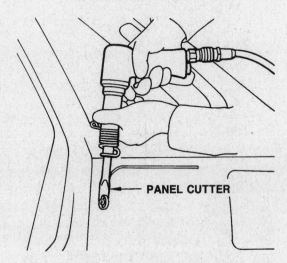

PANEL CUTTER

8.25 . . . and are very useful for cutting out sheet metal sections such as this quarter panel

face, but it leaves definite scratch marks which will later have to be sanded out before painting **(see illustrations)**. Recently, air powered belt sanders that are priced within the reach of any do-it-yourselfer have become available. They can be used in narrow or deep recesses that can't be reached with a disc sander and are very useful for removing paint from welds.

An air hammer with a selection of chisel heads is a required tool for any body repairs requiring panel replacement **(see illustration)**. It's almost impossible to remove a panel with a cutting torch without either warping the surrounding panels or setting fire to flammable components, such as headliners, door trim panels, etc. The air chisel can be used to make clean cuts and, if care is taken, cuts that will have a minimum of stretched metal along the edges, making the welding on of a new panel easier **(see illustration)**. See Chapter 4 for more information on power tools. Electric and air powered panel saws are also available. They work very well for cutting out door pillars, rocker panels and other structural components.

Grinders come in two types- air and electric - each with advantages and disadvantages **(see illustration)**. The air grinders are usually much lighter and are generally more powerful, making them easier to use on big jobs such as large

8.26 Electric grinders come in many different sizes - one of the most useful types is this compact design that also can be used for sanding simply by substituting a sanding disc for the grinding wheel

8.27 A wire brush mounted in an electric drill can be used for rust removal prior to the application of body filler or primer

panels or grinding down welds. However, they generally can't be used for light sanding or buffing, simply because they turn too fast. Electric grinders, on the other hand, can often be used for buffing and polishing as well as grinding. However, electric grinders must be used with caution, since some of them are too powerful (and turn too fast) to use for either sanding or buffing on painted surfaces.

One of the most indispensable tools around is the common electric drill **(see illustration)**. One with a 3/8-inch capacity chuck should be sufficient for most body repair jobs. Collect several different types of wire brushes to use in the drill and make sure you have a complete set of sharp bits (for drilling metal, not wood).

Keep in mind that air tools also require a power source - in this case a compressor **(see illustration)**. If you plan on spraying primer or paint, a compressor will be needed anyway, so buy one that has a large enough output to keep up with the demands of a spray gun and any air tools you'll be using. Don't buy a compressor that's too small for the job. You'll also need hoses and quick disconnect fittings to adapt the various air powered sanders, grinders and spray guns used for body work.

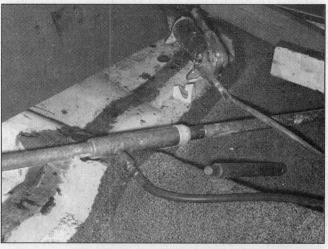

8.28 Buy a compressor that can handle the demands of your largest air tool and maintain it diligently!

If you intend to do any major straightening of automotive structures, a selection of hydraulic body jacks is an absolute must **(see illustration)**. Hydraulic power supplied through a body jack is often the only way sufficient force can be applied to a component to get it straight again. This is especially true of the roof and door pillars. Body jacks can also be used to a limited extent for frame straightening and, of course, are very useful for straightening bent unibody components.

If damage is minimal, pulling and pushing structural components back into place can be accomplished with such commonly available tools as bottle jacks, a comealong (a hand operated cable winch) and chains **(see illustrations)**. The main thing to keep in mind when attempting to remedy structural damage, even minimal damage, is that

8.29 Body jacks are used to push structural members back into shape prior to finishing work

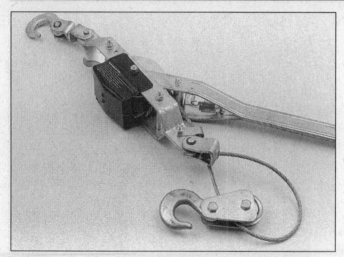

8.30 A 'come along' can be used to pull body parts into position, but make sure the car is securely anchored (don't attach the cable to a building and don't exceed the rated capability of the winch)

8.31 Commonly available, inexpensive bottle jacks can be used in conjunction with wood blocks and timbers to push body parts back into place

pulling and pushing on auto body parts can be very unsafe. If a jack slips or a chain comes off, things can happen very quickly and injury can occur. Always wear eye protection and leather work gloves. Most importantly - think about what you are doing before applying any force with a jack or winch!

If you're going to get involved in major body repair procedures, welding and cutting equipment is an absolute must. The most common and familiar type of welding equipment is the oxy-acetylene set - also known as a gas welder - which can be used for flame cutting, welding steel and brazing. It consists of two tanks, or cylinders (one containing oxygen and one containing acetylene), a regulator for each tank, hoses, torches and tips for different applications, eye protection, a spark lighter to ignite the gases and usually a hand truck for storage and movement of the gas cylinders. Compact, relatively inexpensive oxy-acetylene outfits are available from several sources - they should be adequate for the types of welding associated with body repairs (see illustrations).

Several types of electric arc welding machines are also suited for use in body repair procedures. They include the conventional arc welder (both AC and DC versions are available), MIG and TIG welders, which are arc welders that use inert gases to shield the

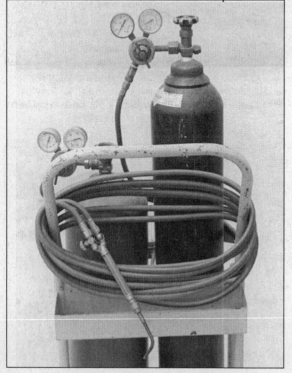

8.32 A typical oxy-acetylene welding outfit

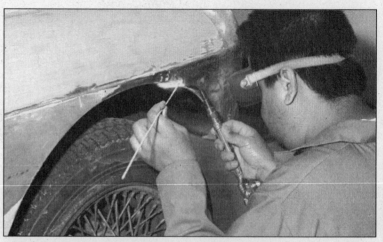

8.33 Gas welding is used to attach sheet metal panels and patches, not for welding structural members

weld (which produces a superior weld joint) and electric arc spot welders.

Gas welding is used for attaching relatively thin gauge sheet metal parts such as door skins, quarter panels, rocker panels, etc. and for welding in small patches used to repair rusted out areas. If the repair requires welding of heavy gauge steel, such as frame members and body reinforcements, arc welding, preferably MIG or TIG, is better than gas welding. Since it operates at low voltage and current, MIG welding equipment can also be used for welding thin panels without fear of warping them **(see illustrations)**. Although TIG welders can be used on a wide range of materials, they haven't enjoyed widespread acceptance in the auto body repair field. Electric arc spot welding is used mainly in the factory production of welded sheet metal parts. Although it's widely used in professional body shops, it really isn't a necessary piece of equipment for the do-it-yourselfer. However, special cutters (spot drills and hole saws) that can be used with an electric drill are available for cutting out spot welds when removing components **(see illustration)**. They're very useful because they prevent damage to and distortion of surrounding panels.

Some of the most useful tools you can have, especially when welding of sheet metal panels is being done, are Vise-Grip clamping pliers **(see illustrations)**. They are available in several configurations for clamping and holding sheet metal during body repairs. They're quickly and infinitely adjustable and can be attached and removed with one hand.

Not to be overlooked when discussing tools required for sheet metal work are the various types of snips needed to cut and fabricate sheet metal patches. Commonly known as "tin snips," the best ones for the job are actually "compound leverage snips" (although they're also labeled "aviation snips"). You'll need a set of three - one type will cut in a straight line, another cuts curves to the left and the other set cuts curves to the right **(see illustration)**.

For those on a limited budget, pop rivets can be used to fasten body panels and sheet metal patches in place as a sub-

8.34 A typical MIG welder

8.35 MIG welders are capable of handling virtually all welding jobs associated with body repairs - they're comparatively easy to use, produce a superior weld joint and won't warp the sheet metal

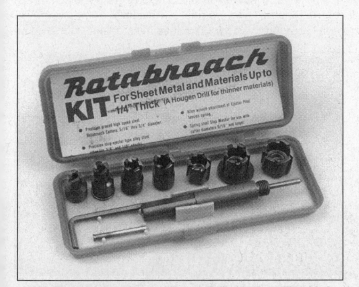

8.36 When mounted in an electric drill, a tool set like this is great for drilling out spot welds to remove panels

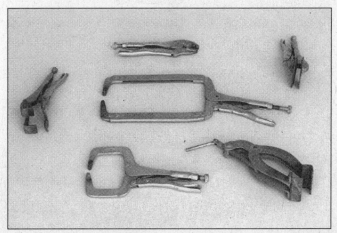

8.37 Vise-grip clamping tools, which come in a wide variety of shapes and sizes, . . .

8.38 . . . are indispensable when attaching body panels

8.39 Compound leverage snips are great for cutting sheet metal (they come in straight, left and right-hand cut versions)

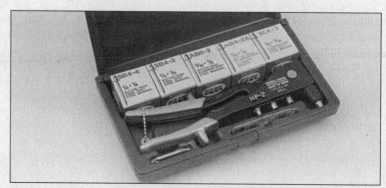

8.40 Pop rivets, which require a special installation tool, can be used for fastening body panels in place

8.41 A good shop vac is one of the most valuable pieces of equipment you can have around, particularly if you intend to do any painting and need to control the dust produced by sanding

8.42 Have a dry chemical fire extinguisher handy and know how to use it!

stitute for welding (see illustration). However, keep in mind that the rivet heads should be recessed to avoid having to use excess amounts of body filler to hide them. Buy a good quality pop rivet tool and steel rivets if this method is used.

One very helpful piece of equipment to have on hand is a vacuum cleaner (see illustration). Don't steal your wife's Hoover - use an industrial type shop vac to keep dust and debris under control. If you keep the car and the work area clean, the final results, especially if you are doing the painting, will be much better.

Safety equipment - perhaps the most important items needed - is usually overlooked during any discussion of tools. Since safety is actually a matter of simple common sense:

a) Be sure to purchase and use a good quality dust mask when sanding;
b) If painting is done, use a respirator for keeping paint out of your lungs;
c) When grinding and sanding, wear a face shield or safety goggles, not just safety glasses;
d) When grinding on metal for extended periods, wear ear plugs (you'll be glad you did!);
e) Never do any type of welding without adequate face and eye protection (arc welding is especially harmful to the eyes);
f) Buy a fire extinguisher that can be used on flammable liquid fueled fires and keep it handy at all times (see illustration)!

Additional important safety related information can be found in Chapter 1.

2 Working facilities

Body and paint shops usually have large, elaborate facilities (at least the good ones do), with areas specifically set apart and designed for body work, frame straightening, masking, paint spraying, paint drying and storage of tools, equipment and materials. They're also equipped with elaborate dust control systems and they have plenty of fluorescent lights and air outlets strategically placed around the shop.

Obviously, the typical do-it-yourselfer isn't going to have the luxury of working in such a facility. He's lucky if one side of the garage can be taken over for working on his car. And what about painting? Well, that's almost always done outside on a calm day or in a cramped, poorly lit garage. Actually, it's not as bad as it sounds - very good results (nearly as good as what a professional can do) can be achieved if you plan ahead and work carefully.

If you do your own vehicle maintenance, then you probably have a reasonably large area already available to work in, probably in a garage. If so, it can be used for body work as well, but be forewarned - body work is very messy! If possible, move all your mechanic's tools and equipment out and store them in a separate place. If that isn't possible, get some large plastic sheets to cover tools, workbenches and storage shelves (painter's drop cloths are widely available, very inexpensive and work very well). Keeping things covered will save you from having to do a massive clean-up job afterwards.

If you plan to do any painting, even if it's just the application of primer, you'll need to wet down the floor of the garage before doing any spraying (this minimizes airborne dust that inevitably will end up embedded in the paint), so move everything off the floor, onto shelving or to another location, before starting any work on the body. Moving things out of the way will not only keep them from getting wet, but will also make it much easier to work around the car.

Unless the garage has several fluorescent lights overhead, it's a very good idea to make a portable light unit out of a four foot fluorescent fixture (the type commonly available at hardware and home stores) to provide adequate light when spray painting. You can move the light around as you paint different sections of the car - just be sure to protect the light tubes with a stiff plastic cover or wire mesh shield.

Because of its messy nature, doing body work outside is a very good idea, as long as the weather cooperates. Just make sure there's a large enough concrete or asphalt surface to work on and don't use too many long extension cords to plug in tools and other equipment. If painting is done outside, it's still a good idea to wet down the area around the vehicle and wait for a day that's dead calm, overcast and slightly humid. Even under the best conditions, there's absolutely no way to guarantee good results when painting outside - the wind can come up suddenly, trees and birds can drop things on the car, bugs can fly into the wet paint and dust is unavoidable.

Be aware that many of the materials used for body repair and painting are very dangerous - they shouldn't be inhaled and they are definitely a fire hazard, so some type of storage area, preferably a metal cabinet, will be needed, regardless of the size of the job you're doing. Read through the Safety first! Section in Chapter 1 immediately before starting work. And have a fire extinguisher on hand at all times!

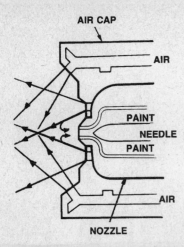

8.43 External mix spray gun air cap details - the air and paint passages must be kept clean!

Spray guns

GRAVITY FEED TYPE

SUCTION FEED TYPE

PRESSURE FEED TYPE

8.44 Spray guns commonly used for automotive painting come in three basic types - gravity feed, suction feed and pressure feed

3 Painting equipment

There's no way you can do a decent job of painting a car unless you thoroughly understand the operation of the paint spraying equipment you'll be using.

Spray guns

The paint spray gun is a device that uses air pressure to atomize a sprayable material, in this case, paint. For automotive refinishing, two types of paint guns are common. One has the gun (mixer) and the paint container (cup) integral, the other has the container separated from the gun by an extra hose. The two types are further divided into bleeder and nonbleeder, external and internal mix, and pressure, gravity or suction feed guns **(see illustrations)**.

The bleeder type gun is the most common and is designed without an air valve. The air passes through the gun at all times, which keeps the air pressure from building up in the hose. There are no air pressure control devices involved, so the gun is used with small low-pressure compressors. More suitable to automotive painting is the nonbleeder design which has an air valve to shut off the air as the trigger is released. Such a gun can control both the air and paint flow by trigger manipulation.

The internal mixing spray gun mixes the air and paint inside the cap, but this design also is not well suited to automotive work. Better yet is the external mix gun, which mixes and atomizes the air and paint just outside the cap. A suction feed gun uses the force of a stream of compressed air to cause a vacuum, which causes the paint to push out of the container. The fluid tip extends slightly beyond the air cap on this design. If the fluid tip is flush with the air cap, chances are the gun is a pressure feed type where the paint is forced to the gun by air pressure in the container attached to the spray gun.

The air cap is located at the extreme tip of the paint gun, with a knurled face so it can be gripped and removed by hand. Such a cap may have one to four orifices for air which is directed into the paint stream to atomize the mixture. As a rule, the average shop gun will have two orifices, but the more orifices available the better. Heavy materials will atomize better with multiple orifice caps.

A small removable nozzle is held in the gun body by the air cap. This is the fluid tip which meters and controls the flow of paint into the air stream. The fluid tip is a seat for the fluid needle valve, which controls the flow of material from the cup. These tips are available in a wide range of nozzle sizes. The larger the nozzle size, the larger the amount of paint that can be sprayed. The needle and fluid tip come in matched pairs, ranging up to 0.086-inch, but for average use something in the 0.036 to 0.045-inch range is best.

Because of the way a suction feed gun is made, it tends to apply an uneven layer on anything but vertical surfaces. This is because paint in a tipped container will flow over the vent in the cup cover. The only partial solution is to unplug the vent periodically and keep it toward the rear of the cup. The same air flow that atomizes and sprays the paint creates a siphon. If very large areas are being painted, where the fluid adjustment is wide open for maximum pattern, the atomization pressure can get as high as 35 to 40 pounds, which means the pressure required to operate the siphon is greater than that required to atomize the paint. The pressure feed gun eliminates most of the disadvantages of the suction feed gun, but it requires more skill because it applies a greater volume of paint in less time.

It is absolutely imperative to keep all spray painting equipment as clean as possible - that means cleaning the gun after each and every use. If the gun isn't cleaned, the paint will dry in those difficult to clean nozzles. When cleaning a suction feed gun, loosen the cup and hold the gun handle over it with the siphon tube inside the container. Unscrew the air cap several turns, then cover the cap with a rag and pull the trigger. Air pressure will be diverted through the fluid passages and will force any paint in the gun back into the cup.

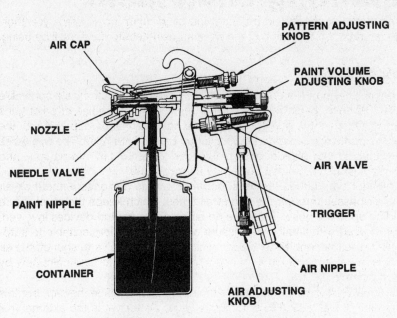

8.45 Suction feed spray gun components

Labels on figure 8.45:
- AIR CAP
- PATTERN ADJUSTING KNOB
- PAINT VOLUME ADJUSTING KNOB
- NOZZLE
- AIR VALVE
- NEEDLE VALVE
- TRIGGER
- PAINT NIPPLE
- AIR NIPPLE
- CONTAINER
- AIR ADJUSTING KNOB

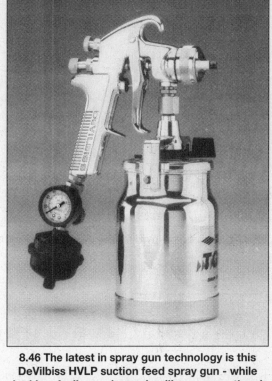

8.46 The latest in spray gun technology is this DeVilbiss HVLP suction feed spray gun - while looking, feeling and spraying like a conventional gun, it provides all the advantages of High Volume Low Pressure

Empty the cup and clean it thoroughly with thinner; then pour a small amount of thinner into it. Spray the thinner through the gun to flush the fluid passages. It's a good idea to keep a small can of thinner ready for gun cleaning. Either wipe the gun housing with a rag and thinner or use a bristle brush (the preferred method).

The air cap should be removed and cleaned by soaking it in clean thinner. Dry the cap with compressed air. If the small holes are plugged, soak the cap longer, then open the holes with a toothpick or broomstraw. DO NOT use a metal object as it may enlarge the orifice.

Never soak the entire spray gun in solvent, as this allows sludge and dirt to collect in the air passages or removes lubricants necessary for smooth gun operation. The lubricant points include the fluid needle valve packing, air valve packing and trigger bearing screw. The fluid needle valve can be lightly coated with petroleum jelly. Never use a caustic alkaline solution to clean a spray gun, as it will corrode the aluminum and die-cast parts. It takes only minutes to clean a gun shortly after use, but sometimes the cleaning requires hours if the gun has been left uncleaned for a long period of time.

8.47 Increasing in popularity, this DeVilbiss Gravity Feed Spray gun is designed to produce excellent results with a variety of refinishing materials

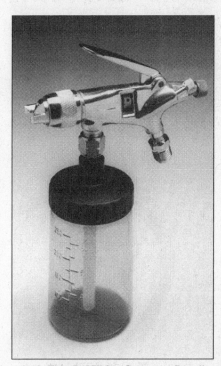

8.48 This DeVilbiss Compact Detail Spray Gun is used when delicate control is required for touch-up, detailing, edging and other types of precision painting

Air compressors

Air compressors are normally classified as single or two stage. The single stage unit has a single cylinder and will produce about 100 psi. A two stage unit has twin cylinders of unequal size with an intercooler between the cylinders and will pump well over 100 psi. In the two stage design, air is compressed first in the large cylinder, then it's compressed further by the small cylinder before being fed into the high pressure storage tank **(see illustration)**.

The size compressor needed will depend entirely upon what the job calls for. A do-it-yourselfer working at home can usually do very well with a single stage compressor that will hold at least 60 psi while the gun is being operated. A paint gun requires on the average 8.5 cubic feet per minute of air.

Seldom included with a new compressor is a regulator, which is used to maintain a close check on the air supply to paint guns. The regulator also prevents oil, water and dirt from entering the air lines. The regulator has numerous filter elements to trap foreign materials and a drain in the sump to release oil and moisture. Gauges on the regulator show exactly how much pressure is available and how much is being used.

It's important to use the correct type and size air hose as well **(see illustration)**. There are two types of hoses available: One type for air and one for paint. Air hose is normally red. Hose for paint is black or brown. Hose size is normally 5/16-inch inside diameter for suction feed guns.

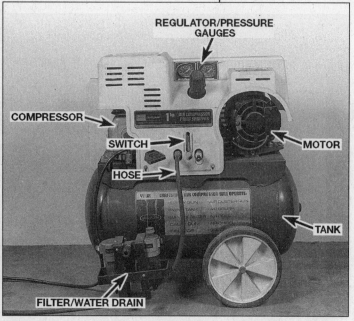

8.49 Typical air compressor components

8.50 Spray gun or air tool performance is many times blamed on the equipment while the real culprit is the lack of the required air pressure (psi) or volume (cfm) necessary to operate the equipment properly; one of the most overlooked areas of air line pressure drop is the quick disconnect hose connections - DeVilbiss hose connections are designed to have extremely low pressure drop and to allow the passage of air to the spray gun or air tool with little or no effect on performance

Respirators

Another very important piece of equipment needed when applying paint with a spray outfit is a respirator, which filters out fumes, dust and dirt that would otherwise enter your lungs **(see illustration)**. You can't overstate the importance of a respirator, so buy a good one and use it correctly. Never mix or spray primer or paint, especially in an enclosed area, without one!

8.51 A good respirator is absolutely essential when spraying paint (note that some paints - acrylic urethane and polyurethane to be specific - often require SPECIAL RESPIRATORS - be sure to read the paint can label carefully and follow all instructions)

Notes

Glossary of automotive tools

Adjustable wrench - Any of various types of wrenches which have adjustable jaws. They are often referred to colloquially as "Crescent wrenches," which is one of the most popular brand names in adjustable wrenches.

Air compressor -A power machine used to compress air to greater than atmospheric pressure; usually includes a storage tank.

Allen wrench - L-shaped hexagonal bars of steel which are used on set screws with hexagonal recesses in the screwheads.

Ammeter - A meter which measures the current flowing through an electric circuit.

Ball peen hammer - Hammer whose head has a flat portion at one end for hammering and a ball-shaped portion at the other which is used primarily for rivet work.

Battery pliers - Pliers which are designed to spread battery cable clamps for easier cleaning.

Battery post and cable cleaning tool - Generally a cylindrical wire-brush device which is designed for cleaning battery posts and cable ends.

Bench grinder - A high-speed revolving circular electric grinder, usually mounted on a bench. It normally has a grinding wheel at both ends and is used for sharpening a variety of tools as well as grinding down metal. The grinding wheels are removable and may be replaced by a variety of wire-brush and buffing wheels.

Block tester - Tests for cracked blocks or cylinder heads and leaking head gaskets by detecting combustion gases in the coolant.

Body spoon - Large, flat "spoon" shaped tools used to hammer out dents from the auto body.

Bondo - Very popular retail brand of plastic body filler.

Brake adjusting spoon - Use one of these specially shaped tools rather than a standard screwdriver for star adjustment wheels on drum brakes.

Brake bleeder wrench - Specialized wrench, somewhat L-shaped, designed specifically to tighten and loosen bleeder screws on hydraulic brake systems.

Brake cylinder hone - An abrasive device similar in appearance and function to an engine cylinder hone, but on a smaller scale. It is used to abrade brake wheel cylinders during the rebuilding process.

Brake gauge - Measuring gauge used to measure the thickness of a brake disc or the inside diameter of a brake drum for the purpose of determining the serviceability of the component.

Brake spring pliers - Pliers-type tool which helps remove or replace hydraulic or mechanical brake springs.

Breaker bar - Any kind of unusually long socket handle or handle extension used to provide extra leverage to a wrench while attempting to remove stubborn or frozen bolts.

C-clamp - A metal clamp whose design resembles the letter "C."

Calibrated spark tester - Tester providing visual confirmation that each spark plug circuit is operational, or not.

Cape chisel - A chisel with a narrow cutting edge used primarily for cutting keyways and narrow grooves.

Center punch - A punch with a tapered, pointed tip used with a hammer to score a surface so that a drill bit may take a steady bite and not slide around during initial drilling.

"Cheese grater" file -A body file that is used to shape and surface plastic body filler. Gets its name from its cheese grater-like cutting teeth.

Clutch-plate alignment tool - A metal, hard rubber or plastic tool which fits into the splines of a clutch plate and used to align the clutch plate while installing the clutch assembly.

Clutch tip screwdriver - A screwdriver with a fluted end designed to engage a corresponding screw head.

Code scanner - Allows you to "read" the diagnostic trouble code emitted by your vehicle's computer (assuming your vehicle is computer-equipped).

Cold chisel - Used for cutting metal, cutting heads from rivets, to split rusted nuts, and to chip metal. A heavy-duty chisel.

Combination box and open end wrench - A wrench with open jaws at one end and boxed jaws at the other.

Compression gauge - A pressure gauge consisting of a dial readout, a hose, and a fitting, designed to test a cylinder's compression pressure.

Computer scan tool A hand-held microprocessor that interfaces with the vehicles's on-board computer, and the actual operating conditions of the engine management system are displayed on the scan tool's digital display.

Cooling system pressure tester - A tester used to pressurize the cooling system for the purpose of finding leaks in the system. Adapters are also available to check the pressure rating of the radiator cap.

Cotter pin puller - Pronged tool whose tip is specially adapted for slipping into the eyes of cotter pins for easy removal.

Crowfoot wrench - An open end or flare-nut wrench which has, instead of a handle, a square drive opening for use with a ratchet handle.

Cylinder hone - An device used to abrade cylinder bores prior to the installation of new pistons and/or piston rings.

Cylinder leak-down tester -A piece of test equipment which indicates the rate at which pressure leaks from the combustion chamber, past the piston rings, valves or the head gasket.

Deep socket - A socket with a deeper than normal well used for irregular bolts or bolt-like objects such as spark plugs and sending units.

Dent puller - Dent pullers, as their name implies, are used in body repair work. Most dent pullers are a slide hammer design and the better ones have replaceable tips so you can use screws or L-shaped hooks to attach the slide hammer to the metal to be straightened.

Dial bore gauge - The dial bore gauge is more accurate and easier to use than an inside micrometer for checking the roundness of the cylinders, and the bearing bores in main bearing saddles and connecting rods.

Dial Calipers - Calipers whose measurement readings is done by an attached dial rather than the typical vernier scale.

Dial indicator - A precision tool designed to measure movements in thousandths of an inch.

Die - A thread-cutting tool designed to cut external threads on bolts and studs.

Distributor offset wrench - A specially designed box-end wrench whose unique shape allows easy access to distributor hold-down bolts.

Dolly - Curved metal stock used to back-up the blows from a hammer when shaping body panels.

Dremel tools - Dremel is a brand name for a small, extremely high-rpm motor with various attachments for drilling, cutting, sanding and polishing smaller areas or objects.

Automotive Tools Manual

Drift punch - Bar stock with no taper, used to drive rivets, bolts, etc. from holes.

Dwell/tach meter - An electronic device which measures the number of degrees of distibutor rotation in which the ignition contact breaker points are closed (the dwell) and the angular velocity (or rpm) of a running engine.

Dynamometer - An instrument used for measuring the horsepower output of automobile engines.

Engine hoist - Engine hoists are hydraulic crane devices designed to lift engines from their bays for exchange, repair or overhaul work.

Engine hanger - An engine hanger is a device used to hold the engine securely from above when the engine mounts or transmission are to be removed. Most commonly used on front wheel drive vehicles.

Engine stand - An engine stand is used to mount the engine block at a comfortable work height after the engine has been removed from the vehicle.

E-Z out - Brand name for one particular type of screw extractor.

Feeler gauge - A device consisting of a series of graduated metal blades of known thicknesses used to measure minute air gaps of various components such as ignition points, spark plugs, piston ring gaps, valve clearances etc.

Files - Hardened steel tools used for removing small amounts of metal in a controlled fashion.

Flare-nut wrench - An end wrench used to remove flared tubing fittings.

Flexplate wrench - A flexplate wrench grips the starter ring gear teeth and can be used to rotate the flexplate or flywheel.

Floor jack - A heavy duty hydraulic jack which may be wheeled around on the floor.

Fuel pressure gauge - A pressure gauge with special fittings and or adapters for measuring fuel-system pressure.

Galvanometer - Device which measures the direction and amount of electrical current.

Gapping tool - A graduated measuring device which may be used for both measuring and setting proper spark plug electrode air gaps.

Gear puller - A device used to loosen gears from shafts when they are wedged too tight to remove by hand.

Grease gun - A levered grease dispenser whose nozzle is attached to appropriate chassis lubrication access points.

Hacksaw - A hacksaw consists of a handle and frame supporting a flexible steel blade under tension and are intended for cutting metal.

Hole saw - A cylindrical saw driven by a drill motor which can cut holes in wood, metal or other material.

Hose clamp pliers - Specialized pliers whose jaw tips are designed to fit into the circular openings of wire hose clamps for easy removal.

Hydraulic lifter removal tool - A special tool used to grip the hydrauic lifters, allowing removal of lifters that are stuck in their bores.

Ignition wrenches - Miniature open-end wrenches designed for work on small fasteners found in ignition and electrical systems.

Impact driver - A driver used to free very stubborn fasteners by converting a hammer blow on the end of its handle into a sharp twisting movement.

Internal pipe wrench - Wedging type of toothed device which slides into a pipe and braces itself against the pipe's interior walls as it is turned by a wrench. In this way, a pipe may be unscrewed from areas where it cannot be gripped on the outside by a regular pipe wrench.

Jack stands - Triangular or tripod shaped support stands designed to bear the heavy load of an automobile raised from the ground.

Lineman's pliers - Pliers with both toothed jaws and cutter heads for snipping wire.

Magnetic retrieving tool - A cylindrical, jointed hand tool with a built-in magnet at its tip designed to retrieve metallic objects (bolts, nuts, washers, screws, etc.) which have been dropped and are in difficult places to reach.

Mechanic's creeper - A shallow wheeled platform upon which a mechanic lies while working underneath a car to enable him to slide in, out, and around the vehicle with ease.

Micrometer - A micrometer is designed for linear measurement of 0.001 inch or closer. There are generally two types of micrometer: inside and outside. The inside micrometer is used for measurement of two parallel surfaces, while the outside micrometer measures the outside diameter of cylindrical forms.

Multimeter - A multipurpose electrical measuring device which can function as an ohmmeter, ammeter and voltmeter.

Needle nose pliers - Pliers with a finely tapered nose for close, delicate work.

Offset screwdriver - A screwdriver that, instead of having a straight-line design, is L-shaped. This allows for the removal or installation of screws in low overhead areas and also provides far greater leverage.

Ohmmeter - An electronic meter which measures the resistance of electronic circuits.

Oil pressure gauge - A dial type test gauge for measuring the pressure of the lubrication system.

Automotive Tools Manual

Oil filter wrench - An O-shaped metal strap wrench which fits around engine oil filters to enhance leverage when installing or removing filters.

Open end wrench - A wrench whose jaws are set at an angle and which grasps a nut on only two flats or sides.

Oscilloscope - An electrical testing device which shows a pattern wave form on a viewing screen.

Paint spray gun - The paint spray gun is a device that uses air pressure to atomize a sprayable material, in this case, paint.

Phillips head screwdriver - A type of screwhead having a cross instead of a slot for a corresponding type of screwdriver.

Pin punch - Similar to a drift punch, but with a smaller diameter driving shank. Used to drive small pins, bolts, etc.

Pipe wrench - A heavy- duty adjustable wrench which tends to lock itself around a pipe as it is pulled in a direction away from the top jaw. Pipe wrenches often come with extremely long handles for extra leverage in breaking free rusty, corroded old pipes and therefore must be used with care in more delicate automotive applications.

Pneumatic tools - These are the air-pressure driven tools.

Point file - A small, flat abrasive tool which is used for filing the surfaces of ignition points which have become pitted or corroded through wear. Filing points is not a recommended procedure, however, because it is best just to replace worn points.

Ratchet - A socket handle with a reversible "ratcheting" action.

Reamer - Machine tool used to finish a bored hole to a smooth surface or an exact diameter.

Remote starter switch - A switch, when installed in the starter circuit, energizes the starter when closed. It can be used any time remote operation of the starter is desired.

Respirator - A breathing apparatus worn over the face which filters out fumes, dust and dirt that would otherwise enter your lungs.

Ridge reamer - A tool which removes the top ring ridge of worn cylinders so that the pistons may be removed.

Ring compressor - An adjustable strap which, when tightened over a piston and rings, allows easy installation into the cylinder.

Ring groove cleaner - A tool which fits into the ring grooves of a piston after the rings have been removed. When rotated around the piston, the ring groove cleaner scrapes off carbon and other deposits so that newly installed rings may seat properly.

Rubber mallet - A hard rubber mallet is used for hammering objects which may otherwise be damaged by pounding with a regular metal hammer.

Scissors jack - A mechanical (non-hydraulic) car jack with metal bands that "scissor" as the jack is operated.

Scratch awl - A tool similar to an ice pick, but with a hardened tip.

Screw extractor - A hardened metal bit resembling a drill which is inserted into broken studs, bolts or screws in an attempt to remove them.

Screwdriver socket - A screwdriver bit which is attached to a ratchet.

Scribe - A pointed tool used for scoring metal surfaces.

Sheet metal snips - Scissors-like tool which is used for cutting sheet metal.

Small hole gauge - Small hole gauges work the same way as telescoping snap gauges, but, instead of spring-loaded probes, they have expanding flanges on the end that can be screwed in and out by a threaded handle.

Snap gauge - Snap gauges are used to measure holes too small for an inside micrometer. Consisting of spring-loaded probes, which expand out to the walls of the hole. After the gauge is removed from the hole, measure its width with an outside micrometer.

Socket - Cylindrical tool with one end that fits around the nut or bolt and the other end accepting a drive handle.

Socket drive adapter - There are four main socket drives useful for automotive work: 1/4", 3/8", 1/2", and 3/4." A socket drive adapter enables the use of sockets with ratchets of differing drive sizes.

Socket extension - Placed between the socket and drive handle to extend the reach of the socket.

Socket flex handle - A long, fixed, socket drive handle providing greater leverage than a normal ratchet handle, and, in addition, the angle of the handle in relation to the nut can be varied.

Socket sliding T-handle - This type of handle makes it possible to slide the handle back and forth without detaching it from the nut.

Socket speed handle - A short-leverage handle, designed much like an auger hand drill, which enables quick removal or installation of nuts or bolts.

Socket universal joint - A joint fitting between a ratchet and socket which allows for free rotation of the ratchet angle in relation to the socket.

Soldering iron - A heating element which, when brought into contact with solder, creates hot, liquid solder which may then be used as needed for bonding metals or electrical connections.

Spanner wrench - Spanner wrenches are used to tighten and loosen round nuts which have notches cut into the outer edge.

Spinner handle - A screwdriver-like handle, whose shaft accepts sockets or bits.

Standard screwdriver - Refers to a straight-slot screwdriver.

Stethoscope - Listening device similar to the one a doctor uses, except that it's equipped with a noise attenuator to dampen the harsh sounds of the engine.

Stud wrench - A wedging-type wrench inserted over studs to remove or install them.

Tap - A thread-cutting tool designed to cut internal threads into which bolts or studs are inserted.

Test light - An automotive circuit tester consisting of a light bulb, a test probe and a wire lead with a ground clip used to check for voltage in a circuit while power is connected to the circuit.

Thread gauge - A gauge designed to measure the thread size of screws, bolts and studs.

Timing light - A stroboscopic light which, when attached to the number one spark plug of an engine and aimed at a rotating "timing mark" on an engine pulley, allows a mechanic to rotate the distributor in the direction needed to set the proper timing.

Tire iron - A crowbar-like tool with a wrench at one end and a flat end at the other; used for prying off hubcaps and removing and installing wheel lug nuts.

Tire pressure gauge - An air pressure measuring tool whose scale reads in pounds per square inch. It is inserted into a tire's valve stem to take a reading.

Torque angle meter - The torque angle meter is needed to tighten critical fasteners on modern vehicles which specify the torque-angle method of tightening.

Torque wrench - A wrench with an indicator to measure applied force.

Tube bender - The tube bender is necessary to form tubing into tight bends without kinking the tubing.

Tube cutter - A clamp-like device with a sharp tapered roller used for cutting metal tubing.

Tube flaring tool - A tool used to form flared fittings at tubing ends.

Twist drills - Twist drills (or drill bits, as they're usually called) consist of a round shank with two cutting edges used to create holes in a variety of material. Spiral flutes are formed into the upper two-thirds to clear the waste produced while drilling.

Vacuum gauge - A measuring device which, when used to measure engine vacuum at various points, is used for diagnostic purposes.

Valve spring compressor - A tool for depressing valve springs to allow for the installation or removal of engine valves.

Vernier calipers - A measuring device that can measure internal and external dimensions to within one-thousandths of an inch.

Vise grip pliers - Adjustable pliers with toothed, locking jaws.

Voltmeter - Meter which measures the voltage potential of an electric circuit.

Wire stripper/crimping tool - Pliers-like tool capable of cutting wire, stripping the ends of insulation and crimping non-soldering type electrical terminals connectors to the wire.

Notes

Listing of tool manufacturers

Actron Manufacturing Co.
9999 Walford Ave.
Cleveland, OH 44102
216-651-9200
Test equipment

Alden Corp.
Munson Rd.
Wolcott, CT 06716
800-832-5336
Power extractor

Alltest, Inc.
1420 N. Meacham Rd.
Schaumburg, IL 60173
800-255-8378
Test equipment

Associated Equipment Corp.
5043 Farlin Ave.
St. Louis, MO 63115
800-949-1472
Battery chargers, booster cables

Astro Pneumatic Tool Co.
4455 E. Sheila St.
Los Angeles, CA 90023
800-221-9705
Power tools

Black and Decker
701 E. Joppa Rd.
Towson, MD 21286
410-716-7000
Electric power tools

Blackhawk Hand Tools
14117 Industrial park Blvd.
Covington, GA 30209
404-787-3800
Hand tools

Campbell Hausfeld
100 Production Dr.
Harrison, OH 45030
800-543-8622
Air compressors

Automotive Tools Manual

Central Tools, Inc.
456 Wellington Ave.
Cranston, RI 02919
800-866-5287
Presicion measuring tools

Chicago Pneumatic Tool Co.
2210 Bleecker St.
Utica, NY 13501
800-367-2442
Power tools

Classic Tool Design, Inc.
31 walnut St.
New Windsor, NY 12553
914-562-8596
Air-conditioning service tools

Clayton Brake Cleaning
Equipment
490 Oberlin Ave. South
Lakewood, NJ 08701
800-248-8650
Brake washer

Coilhose Pneumatics
200 Clay Ave.
Middlesex, NJ 08846
908-752-5000
Air hose and fittings

Coleman Cable Systems
2500 Commonwealth Ave.
North Chicago, IL 60064
800-338-8755
Booster cables, work lights

Coopertools
3535 Glenwood Ave.
Raleigh, NC 27622
919-781-7200
Hand tools

Designer's Edge
11730 NE 12th St.
Bellevue, WA 98005
206-637-9601
Work lights

Devilbiss Spray Booth
Products
1724 Indianwood Cir. Suite G
Maumee, OH 43537
800-445-3988
Paint spray guns

Double Duty Container Co.
3526 South 1470 West
St. George, UT 84770
801-634-1735
Oil change container

ESCO
15450 Flight Path Dr. Suite 2
Brooksville, FL 34609
800-352-9852
Wheel stud rethreaders, torque sticks

Eastwood Co.
580 Lancaster Ave.
Malvern, PA 19355
800-345-1178
Auto Restoration Tools

Easypower Corp.
4006 West Beldon Ave.
Chicago, IL 60639
800-327-9769
Flex-a-wrench, drivers and bits

Eklind Tool Co.
2255 W. Logan Blvd.
Chicago, IL 60647
800-373-1140
Hex and Torx key sets

John Fluke Mfg. Co., Inc.
P.O. Box 9090
Everett, WA 98206
800-443-5853
Test equipment

Fred V. Fowler Co.
66 Rowe St.
Newton, MA 02166
800-788-2353
**Precision Measuring
equipment**

GSI Industries, Inc.
12813 Riley St.
Holland, MI 49424
616-399-4633
Test equipment

Ingersoll-Rand Co.
Allen and Martinsville Roads
Liberty Corner, NJ 07938
908-647-6007
Power tools

International Tool boxes
506 W. 5th Ave.
Naperville, IL 60563
800-348-5854
Tool boxes

K-D Tools
805 Estelle Dr.
Lancaster, PA 17604
800-866-5753
Hand tools, specialty tools

K-Tool International
31111 Wixom Rd.
Wixon, MI 48393
313-669-5000
Hand tools, specialty tools

Kent-Moore Tools
29784 Little Mack
Roseville, MI 48066
800-345-2233
GM specialty tools

KEN-Tool
768 E. North St.
Akron, OH 44305
216-535-7177
Tire tools

Walter Kidde
1394 S. Third St.
Mebane, NC 27302
800-654-9677
Fire Extinguishers

Latshaw Tools
11020 Ambassador Dr. Suite 500
Kansas City, MO 64153
800-833-3125
**Ratcheting and fixed shaft
screwdrivers**

Lisle Corp.
807 E. main
Clarinda, IA 51632
712-542-5101
Specialty tools

MAC Tools
South Fayette St.
Washington Court house, OH
43160
800-622-8665
Hand and power tools

Mastercool, Inc.
285 Franklin Ave.
Rockaway, NJ 07866
201-625-8383
Air-conditioning service tools

MATCO Tools
4403 Allen Rd.
Stow, OH 44224
800-321-8227
Hand and power tools

Mechanics Time Savers, Inc.
414 Grand Prairie Rd.
Grand Prairie, TX 75051
800-824-1834
Magnetic tool holders

Micro Processor Systems, Inc.
6405 19 Mile Rd.
Sterling Heights, MI 48314
800-242-6774
Test equipment, analyzers

Miller Special Tools
12842 Farmington Rd.
Livonia, MI 48150
313-522-6717
Chrysler special tools

Mityvac/Neward Ent., Inc.
9251 Archibald Ave.
Rancho Cucamonga, CA 91730
800-648-9822
**Vacuum pump,
pressure test kit**

OTC Division/SPX Corp.
655 Eisenhower Dr.
Owatonna, MN 55060
507-455-7000
Test equipment

Posi Lock Puller, Inc.
Box 246
Coopertown, ND 58425
800-533-5761
Pullers

Pro Motorcar Products, Inc.
22025 US 19 North
Clearwater, FL 34625
800-323-1090
Paint thickness gauge

Pro Products
P.O. Box 84
Palitine, IL 6078
800-358-5394
Body patch, cheater bar

Products Research, Inc.
1550A Fullerton Ave.
Addison, IL 60101
800-525-0093
Test Equipment

R&B Inc./Motormite
3400 E. Walnut St.
Colmar, PA 18915
215-997-1800
Specialty tools

RIMAC Tools
69 Armour Pl.
Dumont, NJ 07628
800-932-0513
Hand tools

Rinda Technologies
5112 N. Elston Ave.
Chicago, IL 60630
312-736-6633
Diacom diagnostic software

Rotary Lift
2700 Lanier Dr.
Madison, IN 47250
800-445-5438
Service lift

Rotunda Tools
P.O. Box 1000
Plymouth, MI 48170
800-762-6181
Ford special tools

SK Hand Tool Corp.
3535 W. 47th St.
Chicago, IL 60632
312-523-1300
Hand tools

Schumacher Electric Corp.
7474 N. Rodgers Ave.
Chicago, IL 60626
312-973-1600
Battery chargers, arc welders

Sears Power and Hand Tools
20 Presidential Dr.
Roselle, IL 60172
800-377-7414
Hand and power tools

Sheffield Research
257 Harbour Ave.
North Vancouver, BC V7J2E8
604-983-2830
Test equipment

Shinn Fu Co. of America, Inc.
10939 N. Pamona Ave.
Kansas City, MO 64153
816-891-6390
Hydraulic Jacks

Shure Mfg. Corp.
1601 S. Hanley Rd.
St. Louis, MO 63144
800-227-4873
Workbenches

Snap-On Tools
2801 80th St.
Kenosha, WI 53141
800-759-8877
Hand and power tools

Sunex International
P.O. Box 4215
Greenville, SC 29608
800-833-7869
Power tools, specialty tools

Thexton Mfg. Co. Inc.
7685 Parklawn Ave.
Minneapolis, MN 55435
800-328-6277
Test equipment, specialty tools

Thorsen Tool Co.
1801 Morgan St.
Rockford, Il 61102
800-435-2931
Hand and power tools

Tracer Products
956 Brush hollow Rd.
Westbury, NY 11590
800-641-1133
Leak detection kits

Tru-cut Automotive
75 Elm St.
Salem, OH 44460
800-634-7267
Ramps, jack stands, creepers

Vacula Automotive Products
212 Ambrogio Dr.
Gurnee, IL 60031
800-633-8267
Brake bleeders

Vermont American Tool Co.
P.O. Box 340
Lincolnton, NC 28093
800-742-3869
Hand tools

Index

Automotive Tools Manual

HAYNES AUTOMOTIVE MANUALS

NOTE: *New manuals are added to this list on a periodic basis. If you do not see a listing for your vehicle, consult your local Haynes dealer for the latest product information.*

ACURA
*1776 **Integra & Legend** all models '86 thru '90

AMC
      Jeep CJ - see *JEEP (412)*
694 **Mid-size models,** Concord, Hornet, Gremlin & Spirit '70 thru '83
934 **(Renault) Alliance & Encore** all models '83 thru '87

AUDI
615 **4000** all models '80 thru '87
428 **5000** all models '77 thru '83
1117 **5000** all models '84 thru '88

AUSTIN
      Healey Sprite - see *MG Midget Roadster (265)*

BMW
*2020 **3/5 Series** not including diesel or all-wheel drive models '82 thru '92
276 **320i** all 4 cyl models '75 thru '83
632 **528i & 530i** all models '75 thru '80
240 **1500 thru 2002** all models except Turbo '59 thru '77
348 **2500, 2800, 3.0 & Bavaria** all models '69 thru '76

BUICK
      Century (front wheel drive) - see *GENERAL MOTORS (829)*
*1627 **Buick, Oldsmobile & Pontiac Full-size (Front wheel drive)** all models '85 thru '93
      Buick Electra, LeSabre and Park Avenue; **Oldsmobile** Delta 88 Royale, Ninety Eight and Regency; **Pontiac** Bonneville
1551 **Buick Oldsmobile & Pontiac Full-size (Rear wheel drive)**
      Buick Estate '70 thru '90, Electra'70 thru '84, LeSabre '70 thru '85, Limited '74 thru '79 **Oldsmobile** Custom Cruiser '70 thru '90, Delta 88 '70 thru '85,Ninety-eight '70 thru '84 **Pontiac** Bonneville '70 thru '81, Catalina '70 thru '81, Grandville '70 thru '75, Parisienne '83 thru '86
627 **Mid-size Regal & Century** all rear-drive models with V6, V8 and Turbo '74 thru '87
      Regal - see *GENERAL MOTORS (1671)*
      Skyhawk - see *GENERAL MOTORS (766)*
552 **Skylark** all X-car models '80 thru '85
      Skylark '86 on - see *GENERAL MOTORS (1420)*
      Somerset - see *GENERAL MOTORS (1420)*

CADILLAC
*751 **Cadillac Rear Wheel Drive** all gasoline models '70 thru '92
      Cimarron - see *GENERAL MOTORS (766)*

CAPRI
296 **2000 MK I Coupe** all models '71 thru '75
      Mercury Capri - see *FORD Mustang (654)*

CHEVROLET
*1477 **Astro & GMC Safari Mini-vans** '85 thru '93
554 **Camaro V8** all models '70 thru '81
866 **Camaro** all models '82 thru '92
      Cavalier - see *GENERAL MOTORS (766)*
      Celebrity - see *GENERAL MOTORS (829)*
625 **Chevelle, Malibu & El Camino** all V6 & V8 models '69 thru '87
449 **Chevette & Pontiac T1000** '76 thru '87
550 **Citation** all models '80 thru '85

*1628 **Corsica/Beretta** all models '87 thru '92
274 **Corvette** all V8 models '68 thru '82
*1336 **Corvette** all models '84 thru '91
1762 **Chevrolet Engine Overhaul Manual**
704 **Full-size Sedans** Caprice, Impala, Biscayne, Bel Air & Wagons '69 thru '90
      Lumina - see *GENERAL MOTORS (1671)*
      Lumina APV - see *GENERAL MOTORS (2035)*
319 **Luv Pick-up** all 2WD & 4WD '72 thru '82
626 **Monte Carlo** all models '70 thru '88
241 **Nova** all V8 models '69 thru '79
*1642 **Nova and Geo Prizm** all front wheel drive models, '85 thru '92
420 **Pick-ups '67 thru '87** - Chevrolet & GMC, all V8 & in-line 6 cyl, 2WD & 4WD '67 thru '87; Suburbans, Blazers & Jimmys '67 thru '91
*1664 **Pick-ups '88 thru '93** - Chevrolet & GMC, all full-size (C and K) models, '88 thru '93
*831 **S-10 & GMC S-15 Pick-ups** all models '82 thru '92
*1727 **Sprint & Geo Metro** '85 thru '91
*345 **Vans - Chevrolet & GMC,** V8 & in-line 6 cylinder models '68 thru '92

CHRYSLER
*2058 **Full-size Front-Wheel Drive** '88 thru '93
      K-Cars - see *DODGE Aries (723)*
      Laser - see *DODGE Daytona (1140)*
*1337 **Chrysler & Plymouth Mid-size** front wheel drive '82 thru '93

DATSUN
402 **200SX** all models '77 thru '79
647 **200SX** all models '80 thru '83
228 **B - 210** all models '73 thru '78
525 **210** all models '78 thru '82
206 **240Z, 260Z & 280Z** Coupe '70 thru '78
563 **280ZX** Coupe & 2+2 '79 thru '83
      300ZX - see *NISSAN (1137)*
679 **310** all models '78 thru '82
123 **510 & PL521 Pick-up** '68 thru '73
430 **510** all models '78 thru '81
372 **610** all models '72 thru '76
277 **620 Series Pick-up** all models '73 thru '79
      720 Series Pick-up - see *NISSAN (771)*
376 **810/Maxima** all gasoline models, '77 thru '84
368 **F10** all models '76 thru '79
      Pulsar - see *NISSAN (876)*
      Sentra - see *NISSAN (982)*
      Stanza - see *NISSAN (981)*

DODGE
      400 & 600 - see *CHRYSLER Mid-size (1337)*
*723 **Aries & Plymouth Reliant** '81 thru '89
*1231 **Caravan & Plymouth Voyager Mini-Vans** all models '84 thru '93
699 **Challenger & Plymouth Saporro** all models '78 thru '83
      Challenger '67-'76 - see *DODGE Dart (234)*
236 **Colt** all models '71 thru '77
610 **Colt & Plymouth Champ (front wheel drive)** all models '78 thru '87
*1668 **Dakota Pick-ups** all models '87 thru '93
234 **Dart, Challenger/Plymouth Barracuda & Valiant** 6 cyl models '67 thru '76
*1140 **Daytona & Chrysler Laser** '84 thru '89
*545 **Omni & Plymouth Horizon** '78 thru '90
*912 **Pick-ups** all full-size models '74 thru '91
*556 **Ram 50/D50 Pick-ups & Raider and Plymouth Arrow Pick-ups** '79 thru '93
*1726 **Shadow & Plymouth Sundance** '87 thru '93
*1779 **Spirit & Plymouth Acclaim** '89 thru '92
*349 **Vans - Dodge & Plymouth** V8 & 6 cyl models '71 thru '91

EAGLE
      Talon - see *Mitsubishi Eclipse (2097)*

FIAT
094 **124 Sport Coupe & Spider** '68 thru '78
273 **X1/9** all models '74 thru '80

FORD
*1476 **Aerostar Mini-vans** all models '86 thru '92
788 **Bronco and Pick-ups** '73 thru '79
*880 **Bronco and Pick-ups** '80 thru '91
268 **Courier Pick-up** all models '72 thru '82
1763 **Ford Engine Overhaul Manual**
789 **Escort/Mercury Lynx** all models '81 thru '90
*2046 **Escort/Mercury Tracer** '91 thru '93
*2021 **Explorer & Mazda Navajo** '91 thru '92
560 **Fairmont & Mercury Zephyr** '78 thru '83
334 **Fiesta** all models '77 thru '80
754 **Ford & Mercury Full-size,** Ford LTD & Mercury Marquis ('75 thru '82); Ford Custom 500,Country Squire, Crown Victoria & Mercury Colony Park ('75 thru '87); Ford LTD Crown Victoria & Mercury Gran Marquis ('83 thru '87)
359 **Granada & Mercury Monarch** all in-line, 6 cyl & V8 models '75 thru '80
773 **Ford & Mercury Mid-size,** Ford Thunderbird & Mercury Cougar ('75 thru '82); Ford LTD & Mercury Marquis ('83 thru '86); Ford Torino,Gran Torino, Elite, Ranchero pick-up, LTD II, Mercury Montego, Comet, XR-7 & Lincoln Versailles ('75 thru '86)
*654 **Mustang & Mercury Capri** all models including Turbo. Mustang, '79 thru '92; Capri, '79 thru '86
357 **Mustang V8** all models '64-1/2 thru '73
231 **Mustang II** 4 cyl, V6 & V8 models '74 thru '78
649 **Pinto & Mercury Bobcat** '75 thru '80
1670 **Probe** all models '89 thru '92
*1026 **Ranger/Bronco II** gasoline models '83 thru '93
*1421 **Taurus & Mercury Sable** '86 thru '92
*1418 **Tempo & Mercury Topaz** all gasoline models '84 thru '93
1338 **Thunderbird/Mercury Cougar** '83 thru '88
*1725 **Thunderbird/Mercury Cougar** '89 and '90
*344 **Vans** all V8 Econoline models '69 thru '91

GENERAL MOTORS
*829 **Buick Century, Chevrolet Celebrity, Oldsmobile Cutlass Ciera & Pontiac 6000** all models '82 thru '93
*766 **Buick Skyhawk, Cadillac Cimarron, Chevrolet Cavalier, Oldsmobile Firenza & Pontiac J-2000 & Sunbird** all models '82 thru '92
1420 **Buick Skylark & Somerset, Oldsmobile Calais & Pontiac Grand Am** all models '85 thru '91
*1671 **Buick Regal, Chevrolet Lumina, Oldsmobile Cutlass Supreme & Pontiac Grand Prix** all front wheel drive models '88 thru '90
*2035 **Chevrolet Lumina APV, Oldsmobile Silhouette & Pontiac Trans Sport** all models '90 thru '92

GEO
      Metro - see *CHEVROLET Sprint (1727)*
      Prizm - see *CHEVROLET Nova (1642)*
*2039 **Storm** all models '90 thru '93
      Tracker - see *SUZUKI Samurai (1626)*

GMC
      Safari - see *CHEVROLET ASTRO (1477)*
      Vans & Pick-ups - see *CHEVROLET (420, 831, 345, 1664)*

(Continued on other side)

Haynes North America, Inc., 861 Lawrence Drive, Newbury Park, CA 91320 • (805) 498-6703

HAYNES AUTOMOTIVE MANUALS

NOTE: New manuals are added to this list on a periodic basis. If you do not see a listing for your vehicle, consult your local Haynes dealer for the latest product information.

HONDA

351	**Accord CVCC** all models '76 thru '83
1221	**Accord** all models '84 thru '89
2067	**Accord** all models '90 thru '93
160	**Civic 1200** all models '73 thru '79
633	**Civic 1300 & 1500 CVCC** '80 thru '83
297	**Civic 1500 CVCC** all models '75 thru '79
1227	**Civic** all models '84 thru '91
*601	**Prelude CVCC** all models '79 thru '89

HYUNDAI

*1552	**Excel** all models '86 thru '93

ISUZU

*1641	**Trooper & Pick-up,** all gasoline models Pick-up, '81 thru '93; Trooper, '84 thru '91

JAGUAR

*242	**XJ6** all 6 cyl models '68 thru '86
*478	**XJ12 & XJS** all 12 cyl models '72 thru '85

JEEP

*1553	**Cherokee, Comanche & Wagoneer Limited** all models '84 thru '93
412	**CJ** all models '49 thru '86
*1777	**Wrangler** all models '87 thru '92

LADA

*413	**1200, 1300. 1500 & 1600** all models including Riva '74 thru '91

MAZDA

648	**626** Sedan & Coupe (rear wheel drive) all models '79 thru '82
*1082	**626 & MX-6** (front wheel drive) all models '83 thru '91
267	**B Series Pick-ups** '72 thru '93
370	**GLC Hatchback** (rear wheel drive) all models '77 thru '83
757	**GLC** (front wheel drive) '81 thru '85
*2047	**MPV** all models '89 thru '93
460	**RX-7** all models '79 thru '85
*1419	**RX-7** all models '86 thru '91

MERCEDES-BENZ

*1643	**190 Series** all four-cylinder gasoline models, '84 thru '88
346	**230, 250 & 280** Sedan, Coupe & Roadster all 6 cyl sohc models '68 thru '72
983	**280 123 Series** gasoline models '77 thru '81
698	**350 & 450** Sedan, Coupe & Roadster all models '71 thru '80
697	**Diesel 123 Series** 200D, 220D, 240D, 240TD, 300D, 300CD, 300TD, 4- & 5-cyl incl. Turbo '76 thru '85

MERCURY

See FORD Listing

MG

111	**MGB** Roadster & GT Coupe all models '62 thru '80
265	**MG Midget & Austin Healey Sprite** Roadster '58 thru '80

MITSUBISHI

*1669	**Cordia, Tredia, Galant, Precis & Mirage** '83 thru '93
*2022	**Pick-up & Montero** '83 thru '93
*2097	**Eclipse, Eagle Talon & Plymouth Laser** '90 thru '94

MORRIS

074	**(Austin) Marina 1.8** all models '71 thru '78
024	**Minor 1000** sedan & wagon '56 thru '71

NISSAN

1137	**300ZX** all models including Turbo '84 thru '89
*1341	**Maxima** all models '85 thru '91
*771	**Pick-ups/Pathfinder** gas models '80 thru '93
876	**Pulsar** all models '83 thru '86
*982	**Sentra** all models '82 thru '90
*981	**Stanza** all models '82 thru '90

OLDSMOBILE

	Bravada - see CHEVROLET S-10 (831)
	Calais - see GENERAL MOTORS (1420)
	Custom Cruiser - see BUICK Full-size RWD (1551)
*658	**Cutlass** all standard gasoline V6 & V8 models '74 thru '88
	Cutlass Ciera - see GENERAL MOTORS (829)
	Cutlass Supreme - see GM (1671)
	Delta 88 - see BUICK Full-size RWD (1551)
	Delta 88 Brougham - see BUICK Full-size FWD (1551), RWD (1627)
	Delta 88 Royale - see BUICK Full-size RWD (1551)
	Firenza - see GENERAL MOTORS (766)
	Ninety-eight Regency - see BUICK Full-size RWD (1551), FWD (1627)
	Ninety-eight Regency Brougham - see BUICK Full-size RWD (1551)
	Omega - see PONTIAC Phoenix (551)
	Silhouette - see GENERAL MOTORS (2035)

PEUGEOT

663	**504** all diesel models '74 thru '83

PLYMOUTH

Laser - see MITSUBISHI Eclipse (2097)
For other PLYMOUTH titles, see DODGE listing.

PONTIAC

	T1000 - see CHEVROLET Chevette (449)
	J-2000 - see GENERAL MOTORS (766)
	6000 - see GENERAL MOTORS (829)
	Bonneville - see Buick Full-size FWD (1627), RWD (1551)
	Bonneville Brougham - see Buick Full-size (1551)
	Catalina - see Buick Full-size (1551)
1232	**Fiero** all models '84 thru '88
555	**Firebird** V8 models except Turbo '70 thru '81
867	**Firebird** all models '82 thru '92
	Full-size Rear Wheel Drive - see BUICK Oldsmobile, Pontiac Full-size RWD (1551)
	Full-size Front Wheel Drive - see BUICK Oldsmobile, Pontiac Full-size FWD (1627)
	Grand Am - see GENERAL MOTORS (1420)
	Grand Prix - see GENERAL MOTORS (1671)
	Grandville - see BUICK Full-size (1551)
	Parisienne - see BUICK Full-size (1551)
551	**Phoenix & Oldsmobile Omega** all X-car models '80 thru '84
	Sunbird - see GENERAL MOTORS (766)
	Trans Sport - see GENERAL MOTORS (2035)

PORSCHE

*264	**911** all Coupe & Targa models except Turbo & Carrera 4 '65 thru '89
239	**914** all 4 cyl models '69 thru '76
397	**924** all models including Turbo '76 thru '82
*1027	**944** all models including Turbo '83 thru '89

RENAULT

141	**5 Le Car** all models '76 thru '83
079	**8 & 10** 58.4 cu in engines '62 thru '72
097	**12** Saloon & Estate 1289 cc engine '70 thru '80
768	**15 & 17** all models '73 thru '79
081	**16** 89.7 cu in & 95.5 cu in engines '65 thru '72
	Alliance & Encore - see AMC (934)

SAAB

247	**99** all models including Turbo '69 thru '80
*980	**900** all models including Turbo '79 thru '88

SUBARU

237	**1100, 1300, 1400 & 1600** '71 thru '79
*681	**1600 & 1800** 2WD & 4WD '80 thru '89

SUZUKI

*1626	**Samurai/Sidekick and Geo Tracker** all models '86 thru '93

TOYOTA

1023	**Camry** all models '83 thru '91
150	**Carina** Sedan all models '71 thru '74
935	**Celica Rear Wheel Drive** '71 thru '85
*2038	**Celica Front Wheel Drive** '86 thru '92
1139	**Celica Supra** all models '79 thru '92
361	**Corolla** all models '75 thru '79
961	**Corolla** all rear wheel drive models '80 thru '87
*1025	**Corolla** all front wheel drive models '84 thru '92
636	**Corolla Tercel** all models '80 thru '82
360	**Corona** all models '74 thru '82
532	**Cressida** all models '78 thru '82
313	**Land Cruiser** all models '68 thru '82
200	**MK II** all 6 cyl models '72 thru '76
*1339	**MR2** all models '85 thru '87
304	**Pick-up** all models '69 thru '78
*656	**Pick-up** all models '79 thru '92
*2048	**Previa** all models '91 thru '93

TRIUMPH

112	**GT6 & Vitesse** all models '62 thru '74
113	**Spitfire** all models '62 thru '81
322	**TR7** all models '75 thru '81

VW

159	**Beetle & Karmann Ghia** all models '54 thru '79
238	**Dasher** all gasoline models '74 thru '81
*884	**Rabbit, Jetta, Scirocco, & Pick-up** gas models '74 thru '91 & Convertible '80 thru '92
451	**Rabbit, Jetta & Pick-up** all diesel models '77 thru '84
082	**Transporter 1600** all models '68 thru '79
226	**Transporter 1700, 1800 & 2000** all models '72 thru '79
084	**Type 3 1500 & 1600** all models '63 thru '73
1029	**Vanagon** all air-cooled models '80 thru '83

VOLVO

203	**120, 130 Series & 1800 Sports** '61 thru '73
129	**140 Series** all models '66 thru '74
*270	**240 Series** all models '74 thru '90
400	**260 Series** all models '75 thru '82
*1550	**740 & 760 Series** all models '82 thru '88

SPECIAL MANUALS

1479	**Automotive Body Repair & Painting Manual**
1654	**Automotive Electrical Manual**
1667	**Automotive Emissions Control Manual**
1480	**Automotive Heating & Air Conditioning Manual**
1762	**Chevrolet Engine Overhaul Manual**
1736	**GM and Ford Diesel Engine Repair Manual**
1763	**Ford Engine Overhaul Manual**
482	**Fuel Injection Manual**
2069	**Holley Carburetor Manual**
1666	**Small Engine Repair Manual**
299	**SU Carburetors** thru '88
393	**Weber Carburetors** thru '79
300	**Zenith/Stromberg CD Carburetors** thru '76

* *Listings shown with an asterisk (*) indicate model coverage as of this printing. These titles will be periodically updated to include later model years - consult your Haynes dealer for more information.*

Over 100 Haynes motorcycle manuals also available

5-94

Haynes North America, Inc., 861 Lawrence Drive, Newbury Park, CA 91320 • (805) 498-6703

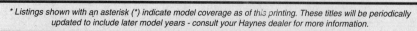

586216